# Building an Intelligent Enterprise with SAP Business AI

SAP BTP Business AI Foundation and the Future of Business Applications

Avijit Dhar

apress®

***Building an Intelligent Enterprise with SAP Business AI: SAP BTP Business AI Foundation and the Future of Business Applications***

Avijit Dhar
Kolkata, West Bengal, India

ISBN-13 (pbk): 979-8-8688-1979-7  ISBN-13 (electronic): 979-8-8688-1980-3
https://doi.org/10.1007/979-8-8688-1980-3

Copyright © 2026 by Avijit Dhar

This work is subject to copyright. All rights are reserved by the Publisher, whether the whole or part of the material is concerned, specifically the rights of translation, reprinting, reuse of illustrations, recitation, broadcasting, reproduction on microfilms or in any other physical way, and transmission or information storage and retrieval, electronic adaptation, computer software, or by similar or dissimilar methodology now known or hereafter developed.

Trademarked names, logos, and images may appear in this book. Rather than use a trademark symbol with every occurrence of a trademarked name, logo, or image we use the names, logos, and images only in an editorial fashion and to the benefit of the trademark owner, with no intention of infringement of the trademark.

The use in this publication of trade names, trademarks, service marks, and similar terms, even if they are not identified as such, is not to be taken as an expression of opinion as to whether or not they are subject to proprietary rights.

While the advice and information in this book are believed to be true and accurate at the date of publication, neither the authors nor the editors nor the publisher can accept any legal responsibility for any errors or omissions that may be made. The publisher makes no warranty, express or implied, with respect to the material contained herein.

Managing Director, Apress Media LLC: Welmoed Spahr
Acquisitions Editor: Aditee Mirashi
Development Editor: James Markham
Editorial Assistant: Gryffin Winkller
Copy Editor: Kezia Endsley

Cover designed by eStudioCalamar

Distributed to the book trade worldwide by Springer Science+Business Media New York, 1 New York Plaza, Suite 4600, New York, NY 10004-1562, USA. Phone 1-800-SPRINGER, fax (201) 348-4505, e-mail orders-ny@springer-sbm.com, or visit www.springeronline.com. Apress Media, LLC is a California LLC and the sole member (owner) is Springer Science + Business Media Finance Inc (SSBM Finance Inc). SSBM Finance Inc is a **Delaware** corporation.

For information on translations, please e-mail booktranslations@springernature.com; for reprint, paperback, or audio rights, please e-mail bookpermissions@springernature.com.

Apress titles may be purchased in bulk for academic, corporate, or promotional use. eBook versions and licenses are also available for most titles. For more information, reference our Print and eBook Bulk Sales web page at http://www.apress.com/bulk-sales.

Any source code or other supplementary material referenced by the author in this book is available to readers on GitHub. For more detailed information, please visit https://www.apress.com/gp/services/source-code.

If disposing of this product, please recycle the paper

*I lovingly dedicate this book to my lovely daughter and son, Avni and Anvit and my wife Laboni, for their unconditional sacrifise and support, made this book possible. There were many weekends when Avni and Anvit would ask "Daddy are you still writing your book? When will you play with us?"- a reminder of precious moments that they gave up, so that I can finish my journey"*

*I also want to dedicate this book to my dear father whom we sadly lost while I was still writing. And lastly, to my mother, whose prayers, love, and blessings have always been our greatest source of courage.*

# Table of Contents

**About the Author** .................................................................................................. ix

**About the Technical Reviewer** ............................................................................ xi

**Acknowledgments** ............................................................................................ xiii

**Chapter 1: Introduction to Artificial Intelligence** .............................................. 1

    Artificial Intelligence (AI) .................................................................................................. 1

        The History of Artificial Intelligence ............................................................................. 2

        Types of AI ................................................................................................................... 3

    Machine Learning ............................................................................................................... 4

        Types of Machine Learning ......................................................................................... 5

    Deep Learning .................................................................................................................... 9

        Types of Deep Learning ............................................................................................. 10

        Neural Networks ........................................................................................................ 12

    Conclusion ....................................................................................................................... 18

**Chapter 2: Fundamentals of Generative AI** ...................................................... 21

    Generative AI ................................................................................................................... 21

        The Evolution of Generative AI .................................................................................. 23

        The Roles of Neural Networks ................................................................................... 25

        Components of GenAI ............................................................................................... 28

        The GenAI Technology Stack .................................................................................... 32

        GenAI Model Types ................................................................................................... 38

        Benefits of GenAI ...................................................................................................... 43

        Limitations of GenAI ................................................................................................. 45

    Conclusion ....................................................................................................................... 49

TABLE OF CONTENTS

## Chapter 3: Transformer Architecture and Large Language Models ........................ 51
The Transformer Architecture .................................................................................... 51
The Transformer vs. RNN vs. CNN ............................................................................. 54
Key Components of the Transformer Architecture ................................................... 58
    Tokenization ............................................................................................................ 59
    Embedding .............................................................................................................. 59
    Positional Encoding ............................................................................................... 61
    Attention ................................................................................................................. 63
    Multi-Attention ....................................................................................................... 65
    Masked Multi-Head Attention ............................................................................... 66
    Feedforward Network (FFN) ................................................................................. 67
    Add & Norm Layer ................................................................................................. 68
    Encoder ................................................................................................................... 69
    Decoder ................................................................................................................... 70
Types of Transformers ................................................................................................. 71
    Encoder-Only Models ............................................................................................ 71
    Decoder-Only Transformer Models ..................................................................... 73
    Encoder-Decoder Transformer Models ............................................................... 74
Benefits and Limitations of the Transformer Architecture ..................................... 75
    Benefits .................................................................................................................... 75
    Limitations .............................................................................................................. 77
Conclusion .................................................................................................................... 78

## Chapter 4: Large Language Models (LLMs) ............................................................. 79
Large Language Models ............................................................................................... 79
The Evolution of LLMs ................................................................................................. 81
The LLM Architecture .................................................................................................. 83
The LLM Development Process .................................................................................. 87
Why RAG? ...................................................................................................................... 91
The Key Components of RAG ...................................................................................... 92
    Embedding .............................................................................................................. 93

| Vector Databases | 94 |
| Similarity Searches | 95 |
| How RAG Works | 96 |
| Conclusion | 99 |

## Chapter 5: Introduction to SAP Business AI Foundation .................. 101

| SAP Business AI | 101 |
| SAP Joule | 103 |
| SAP AI Foundation | 104 |
| AI Services | 106 |
| SAP AI Core | 108 |
| SAP AI Launchpad | 111 |
| SAP AI Core Administration | 118 |
| The Generative AI Hub | 123 |
| The Model Library Section | 124 |
| The Chat Section | 125 |
| The Prompt Editor Section | 127 |
| The Orchestration Section | 129 |
| The Administration Section | 133 |
| Business Data and Context | 134 |
| Conclusion | 137 |

## Chapter 6: Building Custom AI Applications Using SAP Business AI Foundation ............................................................................. 139

| Use Case Identification | 139 |
| Choosing an LLM | 147 |
| Preparing an Estimation | 163 |
| Building the RAG-Based Solution | 178 |
| Conclusion | 198 |

## Chapter 7: Building AI Agents Using SAP Business AI Foundation .................. 199

| Introduction | 199 |
| What Are AI Agents? | 200 |

## TABLE OF CONTENTS

Key Components of AI Agents ............... 201
Agentic AI Use Cases ............... 204
Building AI Agents ............... 206
Supply Chain Industry Use Case ............... 208
    Building Steps ............... 209
Conclusion ............... 218

**Index** ............... **219**

# About the Author

**Avijit Dhar** works as a senior architect for IBM India. Avijit has more than 19 years of experience in leading the design and implementation of multiple large-scale implementations for various global clients. He is also currently involved in the growing IBM Business AI and Automation initiative. Avijit is a subject matter expert in emerging areas like SAP BTP, AI, ML, low-code/no-code, Agentic AI, intelligent automation, integration, and sustainability. Avijit has won several awards for his professional contribution and has authored multiple books from SAP Press on various topics.

# About the Technical Reviewer

**Laxmi Vanam** is a data and analytics professional with 16+ years of experience driving AI-powered modernization, data strategy, and self-service BI initiatives across finance, insurance, and technology sectors. She specializes in bridging business needs with technical execution, leveraging expertise in data architecture, cloud analytics, and applied machine learning. As a Apress reviewer, she brings a deep appreciation for clarity, precision, and real-world relevance in technical writing."

# Acknowledgments

*I would like to express my heartfelt thanks to my IBM team members—Muthu, Akula Madhavi, and Rutuja Patil—for their unwavering support and invaluable contributions in preparing the PoC solution for this book.*

# CHAPTER 1

# Introduction to Artificial Intelligence

In today's rapidly evolving world of Generative AI, we are experiencing groundbreaking innovations, especially in the area of natural language processing (NLP). This chapter delves into the history of artificial intelligence, machine learning, deep learning, and neural networks, covering their historical as well as technical aspects and explaining how each component is part of the foundation of today's Generative AI. This knowledge will ease your understanding in subsequent chapters.

## Artificial Intelligence (AI)

Since its inception in 1950 and the introduction of the term "artificial intelligence" by John McCarthy at the Dartmouth Conference, this field has seen enormous transformation, especially over the last few decades. With an aim to make computer systems reason, learn, and solve problems, the essence of AI revolves around crafting algorithms and frameworks capable of processing vast datasets, discerning patterns, making decisions, and even imitating humans. Harnessing AI technology empowers machines to execute tasks with enhanced efficiency, precision, and scalability across various sectors, including healthcare, finance, transportation, and entertainment.

In today's world, a plethora of systems fall into the category of AI. They utilize the concept of a "neural net" to simulate the human brain's architecture. However, the human brain cannot be imitated nor is it always advantageous to mimic neurobiological information processing.

CHAPTER 1   INTRODUCTION TO ARTIFICIAL INTELLIGENCE

# The History of Artificial Intelligence

The field of AI has undergone a tremendous transformation journey since its origin due to a horse named Hans in the early 20th century. According to Wikipedia, Hans was purportedly the world's smartest horse: he could solve math problems, understand the calendar, tell time, and even spell out words and sentences. A detailed study later revealed that Hans was not performing arithmetic or understanding questions, but was instead incredibly good at picking up unconscious cues from the questioner. While Hans is not directly a part of AI history, the phenomena surrounding the legend mirrors important themes in AI. The case of Hans highlights the need for careful design in AI systems to avoid misinterpreting signals—a challenge still relevant in modern AI development.

The introduction of cybernetics in late 1940 by Norbert Weiner laid the AI foundation for viewing machines not just as inert tools but as entities capable of emulating processes observed in living organisms. In 1943, scientists Walter Pitts and Warren McCulloch researched artificial neural networks, hinting at machines replicating the brain's neural activities. This ultimately set the stage for future technologies. Then came 1951, when Marvin Minsky, being inspired by the work of Pitts and McCulloch, composed the first neural network machine called SNARC. This wasn't just an academic curiosity but a step toward machines with cognitive abilities.

Significant advancements in hardware made neural network simulation a reality. This led to remarkable progress and the 1970s brought forth a deeper understanding that made it apparent that AI applications, such as vision or natural language processing, required vast amounts of information. The 1980s experienced a significant increase in investment in AI around the globe, including the in UK and United States, leading to renewed interest in neural networks.

In 1997, IBM's Deep Blue AI competed in a chess game against world champion Garry Kasparov and won, surprising a lot of critics. During the 2000s and 2010s, significant advancements in deep learning and natural language processing sparked a renewed fascination with AI, giving rise to a fresh wave of AI startups and applications. From 2010 to the present day, AI has seen remarkable progress, becoming deeply integrated into our daily lives. As AI advances, so do the discussions around its ethical dimensions and possible risks. Finding a harmonious balance between progress and responsible implementation is the key to guaranteeing that AI serves the greater good of humanity.

# Types of AI

According to Arend Hintze, former professor of integrative biology, computer science, and engineering at Michigan State University, AI is classified primarily into four categories—reactive machines, limited memory, theory of mind, and self-representation:

- **Reactive AI:** This category of AI is the most basic and an initial manifestation of AI characterized by extremely limited memory capacity. Reactive AI works solely at the present moment and does not consider historical data, which means it cannot learn from past interactions. It delivers predictions based on incoming input. Reactive AI is used in some aspects of self-driving cars, such as immediate obstacle avoidance, although modern systems often integrate limited memory for enhanced performance.

- **Limited Memory:** In contrast to reactive AI, this category of AI leverages a temporary memory that aids in decision-making based on learning from past actions. Limited memory AI is driven by historical and observational data along with pre-programmed information to facilitate predictions and complex classification tasks. Autonomous vehicles are an example of limited memory, because they use recent data from memory to navigate and respond to traffic movements.

- **Theory of Mind:** This third category of AI represents an innovative stage that delves into the realm of human thoughts and emotions, focusing on individuals whose mental states are influenced by various factors. The key to this concept is its potential to enhance understanding of the entities it interacts with, and this advancement is crucial for interpreting human emotions, sentiments, and thoughts. These are emotionally intelligent robots capable of mimicking human-like conversations and making decisions akin to humans by studying and comprehending human behavior and moods.

- **Self-Aware AI:** This kind of AI is a speculative, theoretical concept at this point. This category also represents the ultimate goal of AI research, aiming to create AI systems that are autonomous, capable of self-representation, and can achieve a level of self-awareness comparable to the human brain. Unlike the previous category, self-aware AI possess the ability to not only understand but also experience emotions, needs, desires, and beliefs. The prospect of self-aware AI also carries a potential threat, as it could lead to humanity being overtaken by technology, with these AI systems overwriting human intelligence and acting independently. But on the positive side, there's also the possibility of collaboration between humans and self-aware AI, although the outcome remains unpredictable.

# Machine Learning

Machine learning (ML) is a branch of AI that gives computer systems the ability to learn from data and improve over time without human intervention. ML originates from the idea of making machines learn to program all by themselves instead of having to be manually programmed. With the traditional approach, in order to go through routes of logic to find answers, programmers had to manually create `if`, `elseif`, and `else` statements so the computer could reach the optimal answer; this became a burden when the answer was too complex. Such a burden then led to the idea that computers could learn this logic and deliver answers by assigning weights, values, or statements to logic flows to obtain similar or even better answers, all without being manually programmed. This approach could also better accommodate more complex programs.

Machines are guided by diverse machine learning models, constructed with a range of algorithms and fed quality data. The type of data at hand and the tasks needing automation are pivotal to selecting the right algorithm. Since its inception, the machine learning field has expanded significantly to encompass a plethora of techniques and algorithms. These include models like K-means clustering for data grouping, random forest regression for individual value prediction, and support vector machines for categorizing data points. However, the main advancement has been the democratization of machine learning, marked by numerous open-source packages and accessible datasets that enable virtually anyone, with or without a computer, to deploy machine learning solutions on datasets.

# Types of Machine Learning

Depending on the specific problem you're aiming to address and the data available to you, it's crucial to select an appropriate machine learning algorithm. Machine learning encompasses various learning types, including supervised, unsupervised, semi-supervised, and reinforcement learning. Each learning type is suited to a different context, enabling you to generate answers tailored to the specific nature of your objectives.

## Supervised Learning

Supervised learning is all about teaching machine learning algorithms using carefully labelled data, which helps them predict outputs based on this input. As depicted in Figure 1-1, supervised learning algorithms learn from labelled training data, where you provide pairs of inputs and their corresponding outputs. The primary goal is to teach the algorithm how to map input data to the correct output. During training, the algorithm adjusts its internal parameters to reduce the difference between its predicted outputs and the actual ones, thus improving its ability to make accurate predictions even on new, unseen data. It's all about providing meticulously labelled data so the algorithm can learn how to predict outcomes based on that information. The algorithm learns from this labelled training data, which provides pairs of input-output examples, essentially teaching the algorithm the relationship between input data and the correct output. As part of the training process, the algorithm fine-tunes its internal settings to minimize the gap between its predicted outputs and the actual ones. This process enhances the model's ability to generalize and make accurate predictions on new, unseen data instances.

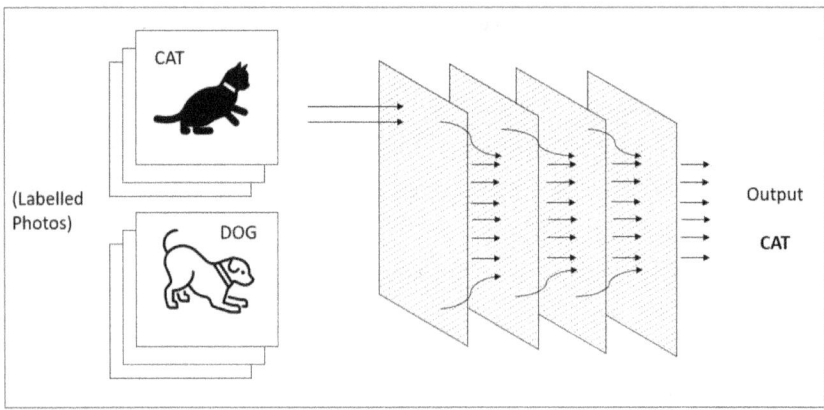

*Figure 1-1. Supervised learning*

## Semi-Supervised Learning

Semi-supervised learning, as depicted in Figure 1-2, is a type of machine learning that uses a combination of a small amount of labelled data and a large amount of unlabeled data to train models. This machine learning approach is basically a combination of supervised machine learning, which uses labelled training data, and unsupervised learning, which uses unlabeled training data. In other words, it is partially supervised and unsupervised and is especially crafted for scenarios where it's difficult to extract relevant features from data and the data volume is also high. For example, you can apply a semi-supervised learning algorithm to a dataset with millions of images, yet only a few thousand of those images are labelled.

To further illustrate by example, consider natural language processing where you have a large dataset of customer reviews for a product. Labelling each review manually can be time-consuming and expensive, so you only have a small subset of labelled reviews, and most of the dataset remains unlabeled. However, this limited labelled data may not capture the full complexity and diversity of the language used in customer reviews and the resultant model may not generalize well to any unseen data. In contrast, semi-supervised learning allows you to leverage the vast number of unlabeled reviews to improve the model's performance. By incorporating the unlabeled data, the model can learn additional patterns and structures in the reviews, which can ultimately help the model understand the sentiment expressed in the reviews and make more accurate predictions.

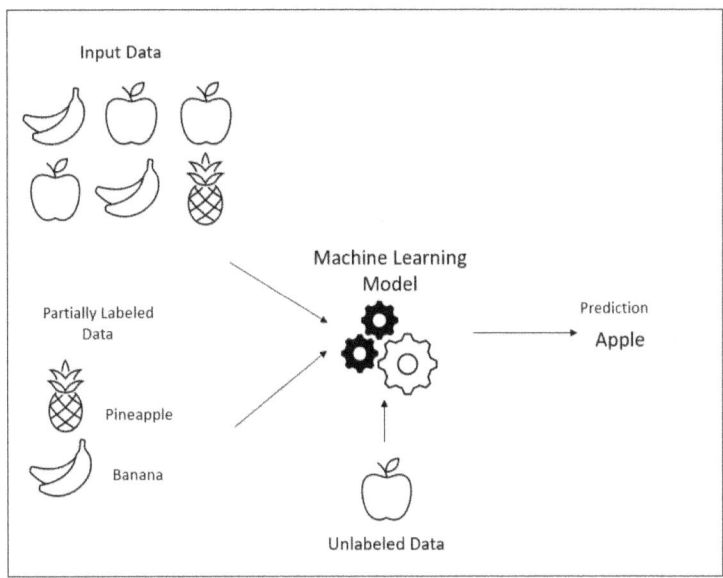

***Figure 1-2.*** *Semi-supervised learning*

## Unsupervised Learning

Unsupervised learning operates differently from supervised learning, as it doesn't guide or instruct the model and autonomously focuses toward uncovering hidden patterns and information that might not be immediately apparent to humans. In unsupervised learning, the model's primary task is to detect underlying patterns or relationships in the data without predefined labels and categorize data points based on these intrinsic structures. As demonstrated in Figure 1-3, in a collection of panda photos, an unsupervised learning system might learn to recognize features like black fur patches around the eyes, thick paws, and an identifiable head shape, thereby clustering similar images together based on these common traits. Unlike supervised learning, where there's a clear outcome or label variable, unsupervised learning operates in a more exploratory manner, searching for patterns across all data and variables. It's a type of machine learning where the computer is trained on raw, unlabeled data, allowing it to uncover hidden structures or groupings without the explicit guidance of labelled examples.

CHAPTER 1  INTRODUCTION TO ARTIFICIAL INTELLIGENCE

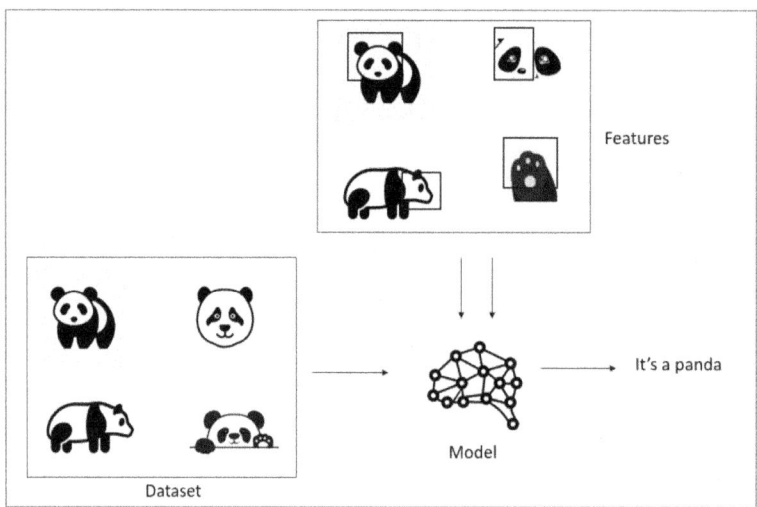

***Figure 1-3.*** *Unsupervised learning*

The ultimate goal of the algorithm is to recognize hidden patterns within the dataset and classify the data points depending on the same recognized patterns. The ability to discover similarities and differences in information makes unsupervised learning ideal for exploratory data analysis, cross-selling strategies, customer segmentation, and image and pattern recognition.

## Reinforcement Learning

This type of machine learning is all about how a machine learning system should act in an environment to maximize a specific outcome. Humans train the system with a positive or negative reward (essentially a numerical value) when it delivers a correct or incorrect output. Reinforcement learning is different from supervised learning in that it does not rely on labelled data to learn. Rather, the agent must explore its environment and apply a learning process, *called trial and error* learning, whereby an agent takes actions in an environment and receives rewards or penalties. Based on the feedback, the agent keeps updating its policy, leading to better rewards. The agent uses a value function to estimate the expected cumulative reward from each state or state-action pair, which is used to guide its decision making.

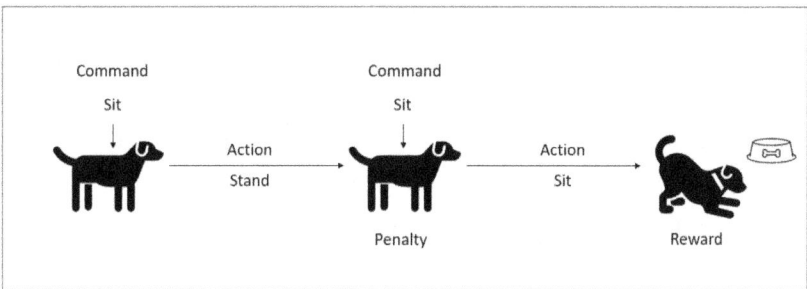

***Figure 1-4.*** *Reinforcement learning*

As depicted in Figure 1-4, say that you are trying to train your dog Charlie, starting with the action to sit. During the course of training, when Charlie fails to sit and does not follows the sitting instruction, he is punished, and he eventually learns from that punishment. Likewise, when he does happen to sit after being told to do so, he receives a reward. After many training sessions, Charlie becomes fully trained. When you tell Charlie to sit, he obeys and is rewarded. The objective is to determine actions that maximize a defined cumulative reward. In contrast to supervised and unsupervised learning, in the case of RL, no data is needed in advance. Rather, the learning agent (Charlie in this case) learns the optimal policy on the fly based on interactions with the environment and the feedback it receives.

# Deep Learning

Deep learning, an advanced form of artificial intelligence, has surged in popularity over recent years due to the availability of vast datasets and increased computational capabilities. It serves as the foundational technology for numerous everyday applications, such as online language translation and automated facial recognition on social media platforms. Traditional machine learning algorithms have addressed many challenges that rule-based systems struggled with, especially while handling unstructured data types like images, videos, audio files, and freeform text, but they are onerous to create. For example, in the field of medical science, developing a breast cancer prediction model using traditional machine learning techniques would necessitate the coordination between numerous domain experts, software developers, mathematicians, and researchers. These teams would need to engage in extensive feature engineering, leading to a painstaking process that involved programming computers to recognize established patterns in x-ray and MRI scans. Subsequently, machine learning algorithms would be applied to these engineered features, and it might take several years to build the system.

Deep learning algorithms tackle challenges through deep neural networks, a software architecture inspired by the human brain (although distinct from biological neurons). These neural networks consist of layers of variables that adjust to the data they're trained on, enabling tasks like image classification and speech-to-text conversion. While the concepts and mathematics behind deep learning and neural networks date back to 1943, their widespread recognition and utilization only emerged in the early 2000s and gained momentum after 2010. Previously, data was limited, hindering the performance of traditional ML algorithms like SVM and logistic regression. However, the past decade has witnessed a monumental increase in digitization and electronic device usage, leading to vast data collection and storage. Coupled with significant algorithmic advancements and robust computational power, deep learning algorithms can provide results that are far more than the traditional ML algorithms could provide.

# Types of Deep Learning

With their wide spectrum of capabilities, especially in the area of decoding patterns and predictions, deep learning models can be classified into two categories—generative and discriminative models.

## Discriminative Models

Discriminative models, sometimes called conditional models, are designed to distinguish between various classes or outcomes based on the given data. The main goal is to identify the decision boundary that separates these classes. These models focus on estimating the conditional probability $P(y|x)$, where $y$ represents the class label and $x$ stands for the input features. Essentially, discriminative models predict the likelihood of a particular class based on known features. Unlike some models that generate new data points, discriminative models stick to making predictions about the data they've already seen. They excel at handling unusual data points, like outliers, making them particularly effective when the data doesn't follow typical patterns. Discriminative models are designed to map input variables directly to output labels without needing to model the underlying data distribution. Their strength lies in effectively distinguishing between different classes or categories using the provided input features. Essentially, discriminative models are a type of AI model built to identify and separate data classes. For example, discriminative models power spam email filters by classifying emails as spam or not spam based on features like word frequency and sender information.

A well-known example of a discriminative model is email spam filtering. In this scenario, models like logistic regression or support vector machines are trained to distinguish between spam and non-spam emails. These models rely on various features to make accurate predictions. For instance, they may analyze word frequencies to identify terms that frequently appear in spam messages. They also consider sender information to differentiate trusted contacts from unfamiliar senders. Additionally, the model examines the email's structure, such as the presence of links or specific formatting patterns, to enhance its classification accuracy.

## Generative Models

Generative models are a type of machine learning algorithm designed to create new, original outputs based on the data they've been trained on. These models have diverse applications, ranging from generating artwork and music to developing new products and enhancing medical treatments. To achieve this, a generative model must first understand the data's underlying distribution and then use that understanding to classify data points effectively. For instance, if a generative model is trained on images of cats and dogs, it learns the unique features that define each class. This knowledge allows the model to perform multiple tasks—it can classify images by comparing features, similar to how discriminative models work, or generate entirely new images resembling the training data. Generative models rely on joint probability distributions to create new data points. By understanding how data points are embedded within a given space, these models can generate realistic and accurate outputs.

To achieve this, generative models leverage Bayes Theorem to determine conditional probabilities. The reason these models emphasize joint probability is that it accounts for all variable dependencies, unlike conditional probability, which only considers one. While generative models do calculate conditional probabilities, this step helps them grasp how data is embedded in the probability space. Essentially, they aim to simulate the combined probability distribution of input features (x) and their corresponding labels (y) to create new data points.

To highlight the difference between generative and discriminative models, consider an example involving hotel customer reviews. Imagine you have a dataset filled with positive and negative reviews. By analyzing this data, a discriminative model can be trained to predict whether a review is positive or negative. It achieves this by identifying key words, phrases, and sentiments that commonly appear in each type of review, assigning greater importance to these features to improve prediction accuracy. On the other hand, a generative model would focus on learning the overall distribution of words and sentiments within the reviews. Instead of simply classifying existing reviews, it can generate new, realistic reviews that mirror the style and content of the original dataset. This ability to create synthetic reviews is valuable for tasks like data augmentation, image and speech synthesis, and language translation. Furthermore, generative models can be used to craft personalized responses to customer feedback, improving the overall user experience.

## Neural Networks

A neural network is a network of neurons inspired by the human brain, where all the nodes (neurons) are connected to each other through weights to form a complex network. Being inspired by human brain network, the term "neural" in the neural network is nothing but an identical representation. In essence, a neural network is a simplified model of our brain's powerful functionality. It operates by utilizing neurons interconnected through weighted connections where the connections are represented by weights, which play a pivotal role in the neural network's functioning. By adjusting these weights to specific numerical values, the network can process diverse inputs and produce desired outputs. Similar to our brain, a neural network is just a way to process data; it can learn from experience and adapt its behavior. Neural networks can recognize patterns, make predictions, and even learn from their mistakes, just as the human brain does. By mimicking the brain's structure and functionality, neural networks can perform tasks such as image recognition, natural language processing, and data analysis with remarkable accuracy and efficiency.

CHAPTER 1   INTRODUCTION TO ARTIFICIAL INTELLIGENCE

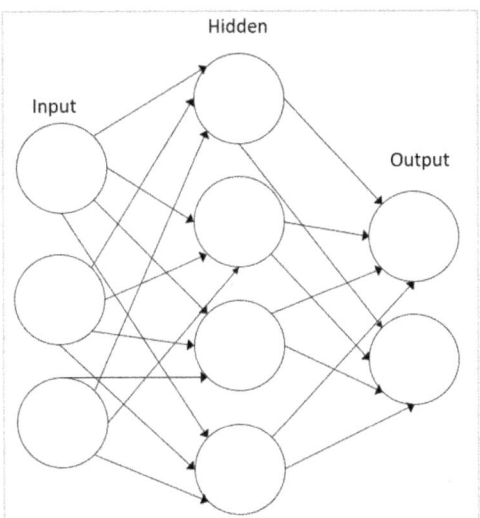

***Figure 1-5.*** *A neural network*

Neural networks, as depicted in Figure 1-5, consist of several key components that work together to process and analyze data. Understanding these components is crucial for comprehending how neural networks function. Carefully configuring these components can lead to neural networks that excel at various applications:

- **Neurons:** Neurons are the fundamental units of a neural network. They are capable of receiving inputs, performing computations, and producing outputs. After receiving the input, the neuron multiplies them by the corresponding weights and passes them through an activation function to calculate an output. Neurons are interconnected through layers, forming the foundation of the neural network.

- **Activation function:** Activation functions determine the output of a neuron based on its inputs and adds non-linearity to the neural network required for learning and modeling complex relationships in the data. Common activation functions include the Sigmoid function, the hyperbolic tangent function, and the rectified linear unit (ReLU) function.

- **Weights:** Weights and biases are essential parameters in a neural network. Each neuron has associated weights that determine the strength of connections between neurons in different layers. During the course of training, weights are adjusted to optimize the network's performance. Biases are additional parameters that are added to the weighted sum of inputs to introduce flexibility into the network's decision-making process.

- **Layers:** Layers inside neural networks organized them into different levels of abstraction and perform specific computations. As shown in Figure 1-5, there are three main types of layers—input layers, hidden layers, and output layers. The depth and arrangement of layers in a neural network impact its ability to learn complex patterns and make accurate predictions. Data moving through the layers ultimately makes the network better at recognizing more intricate patterns and complex data.

- **Bias:** Biases are additional parameters being added to the weighted sum of inputs to introduce flexibility into the network's decision-making process. Imagine you're thinking about various possible situations while trying to make a decision. Sometimes it's difficult to cover all possible combinations, factors, and parameters in your imaginations and you may miss some of the critical ones. In terms of neural net, these unforeseen or non-observable factors are represented as bias. Each neuron that is not part of the input layer has a bias linked to it and the bias also carries a weight. Baises ultimately help the network recognize more complex patterns and deliver better predictions.

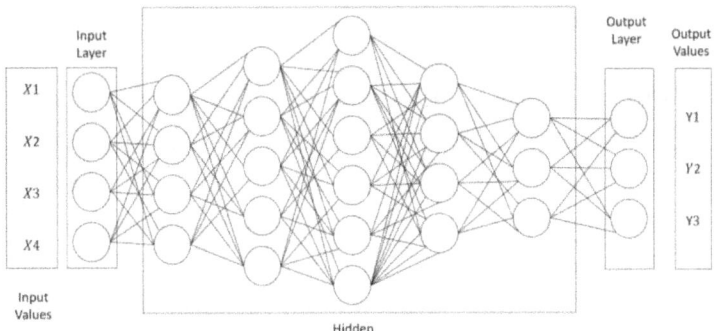

***Figure 1-6.*** *How a neural network works*

As shown in Figure 1-6, this list breaks down how neural networks function in practical scenarios:

- **Input layer:** This is the starting layer of the neural network. It accepts input signals (values) and forwards them to the next layer without performing any computations. The input layer doesn't have weights or biases associated with it. In the network shown in Figure 1-6, there are four input signals: x1, x2, x3, and x4.

- **Hidden layers:** These layers consist of neurons (nodes) that apply various transformations to the input data. Each hidden layer is made up of multiple neurons stacked vertically for representation. In the example network, there are five hidden layers. The first hidden layer contains four neurons, the second has five, the third has six, the fourth has four, and the fifth has three. The final hidden layer sends its output to the next layer. Since every neuron in one layer connects to every neuron in the next layer, these hidden layers are fully connected.

- **Output layer:** This is the final layer of the network, receiving input from the last hidden layer. The output layer provides the desired number of values in the required range. In this particular network, the output layer contains three neurons, which generate outputs y1, y2, and y3.

CHAPTER 1   INTRODUCTION TO ARTIFICIAL INTELLIGENCE

# The History of Neural Networks

While machine learning has only gained widespread attention in the past decade, its roots trace back to the 1940s. This section looks at the contribution of pioneering scientists in building today's endless possibilities in the fields of AI, deep learning, and related fields and how they evolved over the time. The concept of artificial neurons traces its origins to the 1940s when Warren McCulloch, a neuroscientist, and Walter Pitts, a logician, developed the first artificial neuron to demonstrate how basic units could emulate logical functions by mimicking biological neurons. Being inspired by this development, Frank Rosenblatt, a research psychologist at Cornell Aeronautical Laboratory, introduced the concept of a *perceptron,* leading to a single layer of neurons capable of classifying images comprised of a few hundred pixels. This laid the foundation for modern-day neural networks.

Following this, in 1957, Frank Rosenblatt demonstrated how to train neurons by using datasets. The perceptron's design was much like that of the modern neural net. Paul Werbos introduced *backpropagation* as an optimization method for neural networks in his 1974 PhD thesis. However, during the initial neural network winter, his groundbreaking work went largely unnoticed by the research community. It wasn't until 1986, when Rumelhart and others popularized backpropagation as a key training technique for neural networks. This advancement armed researchers with a powerful tool, enabling the widespread application of neural networks across various domains. One notable application emerged in 1989, when Yann LeCun proposed a technique using neural networks to recognize handwritten digits. This model was remarkably successful, leading to its implementation in processing around 10 to 20% of all handwritten checks in the United States. However, this success was accompanied by a new challenge—training neural networks became slow and unstable, presenting a significant hurdle for further advancements. Today, neural networks stand as a crucial and potent element of AI. However, for several dreadful decades, they remained ahead of their era. Despite the existence of backpropagation in the 1980s, it wasn't until 2006 that researchers were able to leverage it effectively for training deep networks. Also, further emergence of affordable GPUs offerings and rapid computing capabilities—alongside Internet availability and large datasets for training—propelled deep networks into the future and made them the driving force behind numerous groundbreaking technologies that have become integral to our daily routines.

## Types of Neural Networks

The architecture of a neural network defines its design and structure, which can vary depending on the intended task. Different neural network architectures offer distinct features and capabilities that are tailored to specific use cases. Some of the most common and popular architectures include *feedforward networks, convolutional networks,* and *recurrent networks.* These diverse architectures cater to various problems and challenges, with their own set of strengths and weaknesses. Selecting the best one for the job hinges on factors such as the nature of your data inputs, the desired model outputs, and any computational complexity constraints. Some architectures exhibit flexibility and adaptability during training, while others maintain more rigid frameworks.

### Feedforward Neural Networks (FNNs)

A feedforward neural network is structured as an artificial neural network where nodes are organized without forming cycles. Within this network, perceptrons are arranged in layers: an input layer receives input, an output layer generates output, and any intermediate layers are termed hidden layers due to their isolation from external inputs or outputs. Each perceptron in one layer is linked to every node in the subsequent layer, forming complete connectivity throughout the network. Notably, there are no connections between nodes within the same layer, ensuring a lack of back-loops within the feedforward design. To refine prediction accuracy and minimize errors, the backpropagation algorithm is commonly utilized to adjust weight values within this network configuration. At the heart of the feedforward network lies the basic building block, the neuron. The feedforward network organizes sets of neurons into layers, including an input layer, a hidden layer(s), and an output layer. Neurons in the same layer do not communicate among themselves and instead solely interact with neurons in adjacent layers.

### Convolutional Neural Networks (CNNs)

Convolutional neural networks (CNN) are all the rage in the deep learning community, especially in image and video processing. CNNs often include pooling layers to reduce spatial dimensions, improving computational efficiency and reducing overfitting in tasks like image recognition. At a high level, CNNs consist of an input layer, one or more hidden layers, and an output layer. The input layer receives the raw data, which in the case of image recognition tasks is typically a two-dimensional array of pixel values. The hidden layers are composed of a series of interconnected neurons, which perform a series of mathematical operations on the input data to extract useful features. The output layer produces the predicted result based on the extracted features. In a convolutional layer, the input data is processed using a set of filters, or kernels, which are designed to detect specific patterns or features in the data. As the input data is passed through the convolutional layer, the filters slide across the data, performing a dot product between the filter weights and the input data at each location. This results in a set of output maps, one for each filter, which highlight the locations where the detected pattern is present in the input data. As the network learns, the weights of the filters in the convolutional layers are updated, allowing the network to improve its performance of the task at hand. CNNs are particularly well-suited for image recognition tasks such as object recognition, image classification, and facial recognition.

## Recurrent Neural Networks (RNNs)

In a feedforward neural network, the information only moves in one direction—from the input layer, through the hidden layers, to the output layer. In contrast, RNN cycles information through a loop and, as part of decision-making process, it considers the current input and what it has learned from the inputs it received. This type of neural network is suitable when you need to access previous information in current iterations. For example, when predicting the next word in a sentence, you first need to know the previous words. In this context, the challenge with neural networks is their slow computational speed and inability to remember info from a long time ago. RNNs can remember their input due to an internal memory, making them perfect for learning problems involving sequential data like time series, speeches, text, financial data, audios, videos, weather information, and much more. These deep learning algorithms are commonly used for ordinal or temporal problems, such as language translation, natural language processing, speech recognition, and image captioning. They are incorporated into popular applications such as Siri, voice search, and Google Translate.

# Conclusion

Starting with the concept of AI, this chapter navigated through the history of AI and explained how it all started with the introduction of cybernetics, which began to shape the early foundations of AI. It did this by introducing an innovative lens through which machines were viewed—not just as inert tools but as entities capable of emulating intricate processes observed in living organisms. This was followed by looking at different types of AI—reactive, limited memory, self-aware, and theory-of-mind. Next, the chapter discussed the concept of machine learning and covered its various types—supervised, unsupervised, reinforcement, and semi-supervised. This was followed by a comprehensive discussion of deep learning and its advantages. Neural networks are the nucleus of deep learning, and they were explained in depth, including the history and types of neural networks—feedforward neural networks, recurrent neural networks and convolutional neural networks. As an extended topic, the chapter also covered deep learning model types, including discriminative and generative models, followed by various potential applications of deep learning across the industry. Understanding these core concepts in the fields of AI, ML, and deep learning lays the foundation for the advanced concepts covered in the following chapters.

# CHAPTER 2

# Fundamentals of Generative AI

This chapter introduces the concept of Generative AI (GenAI), starting with a basic overview. It takes you through the story of GenAI's evolution followed by an explanation of the role of neural networks. In the later part of the chapter, you learn how Generative AI works, potential use cases and limitations, and in-depth description of topics like synthetic data. It also covers Generative AI's learning methods and topics like ethics, bias, and deepfakes.

## Generative AI

This ever-evolving era of technological revolutions, advancements, and breakthroughs in the field of AI has led to generating new content, such as text, images, audio, and video in a fraction of a second. This is done by learning from existing data and using that knowledge to generate new output that is similar to the data it was trained on. This capability is known as Generative AI (GenAI).

Where traditional programming must give AI explicit instructions, Generative AI uses machine learning (ML) to mine vast amounts of human-generated data. It then recognizes patterns and performs activities like generating, summarizing, and making inferences based on those patterns. For example, if a Generative AI model is prompted to provide a cover for a gothic novel, it will respond with an illustration that is moody. On being asked to write an email denying an employee a raise, the model will respond with a note that is professional. All of this occurs even though no programmer has instructed the AI model about what tone would be appropriate in the given context.

Generative AI can do this because it has learned the patterns of human language and behavior. Generative AI models, trained on diverse datasets, learn contextual patterns (e.g., moody tones for gothic novels or professional language for emails) through

CHAPTER 2   FUNDAMENTALS OF GENERATIVE AI

statistical modeling of text and image data. One of the key advantages of GenAI is its ability to learn from data without explicit instructions, which allows GenAI to be more creative and flexible than traditional programming. The adoption of GenAI—driven by models like IBM Watson.X, OpenAI's Generative Pre-Trained Transformer (GPT), Google Bard, Amazon Bedrock, and Adobe's Firefly—is increasing at a groundbreaking pace and rapidly democratizing the technology in business and society.

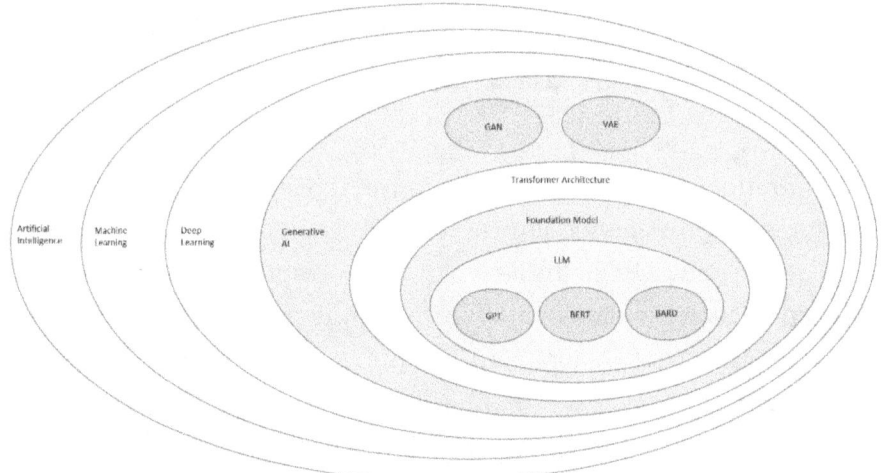

***Figure 2-1.*** *Introduction to Generative AI*

As shown in Figure 2-1, AI is an expansive domain that includes a range of methods and strategies aimed at building machines capable of sensing their surroundings and carrying out tasks autonomously. On the other hand, machine learning is a subset of AI that allows computers to learn and improve their performance of a task without being explicitly programmed. ML does this using algorithms that can identify patterns and make predictions based on data. ML can be divided into three categories: supervised learning, unsupervised learning, and reinforcement learning. Supervised learning algorithms learn to make predictions based on labelled data; unsupervised learning algorithms learn from unlabeled data to identify patterns or groupings; and reinforcement learning algorithms learn to make decisions based on rewards and punishments.

Deep learning is a crucial branch of machine learning, built on the foundation of artificial neural networks. These networks are inspired by the architecture of the human brain and composed of multiple layers to automatically extract hierarchical features from raw data, enabling complex pattern recognition. The term "deep" refers to the presence of several layers—input, output, and multiple hidden layers—each transforming the data in a way that helps the following layer perform specific predictive tasks. Generative AI refers to systems capable of producing entirely new content—such as text, music, or images—rather than simply analyzing or categorizing existing data, as seen in traditional machine learning. Today's advanced large language models (LLMs) are a prime example of Generative AI, capable of generating original text by identifying and learning from patterns in vast datasets. To achieve this, Generative AI often leverages methods like generative adversarial networks (GANs) and variational autoencoders (VAEs), which are designed to synthesize new data by learning from previously seen examples.

## The Evolution of Generative AI

The concept of Generative AI was introduced in chatbots in 1960. While AI has been around for quite a long time, the power of content creation, understanding speech and text, and extracting insights were not possible before 2014, when GANs were introduced as a type of machine learning algorithm that could create credibly authentic images, videos, and audio of real people. First-generation Generative AI algorithms were developed in the 1950s and 1960s and these algorithms were based on Markov chains, which are a type of probabilistic model that can be used to generate sequences of events. According to Wikipedia, the Markov chain or Markov process is a stochastic model describing a sequence of possible events in which the probability of each event depends only on the state attained in the previous event. Markov chains were used to generate text, music, and other types of content. According to the theguardian.com, the Eliza chatbot created by Joseph Weizenbaum in the 1960s was one of the earliest examples of Generative AI. In this context, it is important to mention that these early implementations used a rules-based approach had a limited vocabulary, lack of context, and heavy reliance on patterns, along with many other shortcomings. These chatbots were also difficult to customize and extend.

Neural networks, which are a type of machine learning model that can learn from data and generate outputs that are similar to the data it was trained on, were first applied to Generative AI tasks in the 1980s. During the 2000s, deep learning techniques were developed. They apply neural networks with multiple layers, which enabled Generative AI models to learn from massive datasets and generate more realistic and complex outputs.

CHAPTER 2   FUNDAMENTALS OF GENERATIVE AI

The first decade of the 2000s saw a rapid advancement in machine learning techniques for analysis and prediction. This was driven by the increasing availability of massive amounts of data, which could be used to train these techniques. Machine learning algorithms were able to analyze this data to deliver conclusions and learn from the results, which led to significant improvements in the field of analysis and prediction. This advancement acted as motivation to use machine learning to analyze data, find patterns, generate insights, make predictions, and automate tasks at a pace and scale impossible earlier. In the 2010s, there were many advancements in AI's perception capabilities in the field of machine learning, enabling computer vision to classify and detect objects, as well as voice recognition, which responded to users in a natural way through AI-based digital assistant. This also led to the development of new applications, such as self-driving cars, facial recognition software, and augmented reality. Ian Goodfellow, Yoshua Bengio, and Aaron Courville, in their paper "Generative Adversarial Nets," introduced GANs in 2014. GANs are a type of machine learning model that can be used to generate new data that is similar to existing data. They do this by training two neural networks against each other in a zero-sum game.

Fueled by rapid advancements in the scale and performance of deep learning models, the 2020s are poised to center on the mastery of language. OpenAI's GPT-3 model signaled a major leap forward in language-based AI, ushering in a new era of applications with transformative potential for businesses. Since language underpins nearly every aspect of an organization—from communication and internal knowledge to daily operations—models like GPT-3 are set to have a profound impact. This breakthrough journey in AI can be traced back to August 2017, when the landmark paper, "Attention Is All You Need," was published by Ashish Vaswani et al. The paper introduced the transformer architecture, a neural network design highly effective for natural language processing. Transformers excel at capturing long-range relationships between words in a sequence, making them particularly powerful for tasks like translation, summarization, and question answering.

So far, you have read how the concept of Generative AI evolved over the time to reach to its current form. The next section explains the immense significance of neural networks in establishing the core foundation of Generative AI and its associated concepts.

# The Roles of Neural Networks

Neural networks play a key role in Generative AI. They learn the patterns of data and generate new data that follows similar patterns, and this ultimately helps Generative AI models create realistic images, text, and other forms of content. What lies ahead requires an understanding of the breakthroughs that have enabled the rise of Generative AI, which were decades in the making. Generative AI is defined as applications typically built using foundation models and these underlying foundation models contain expansive artificial neural networks inspired by the billions of neurons in the human brain. Neural networks were first developed in the 1950s and 1960s, but they were limited by a lack of computational power and small datasets. It was not until the mid-2000s, with the advent of big data and improvements in computer hardware, that neural networks became practical for generating content. Before we get into more detail, it's important to understand what a neural network is. A *neural network* is a type of machine learning model that is inspired by the human brain and made up of a collection of interconnected nodes, called *neurons*. As shown in Figure 2-2, the neurons have a cell body, multiple receptors called *dendrites*, and one transmitter unit called the *axon*. Neurons receive nerve impulses from surrounding neurons through the dendrites, process these collected impulses, and then pass the resulting impulse to the neighboring neurons through the axon. The exchange of nerve impulses from one neuron to another take place through synapses, which act as connectors between axons of the sender neurons and dendrites of the receiver neurons. Neurologists have discovered that the brain learns through this complex network of neurons, by adjusting the strength of synoptic connections under repeated stimulation by the same impulse.

Each neuron receives input from other neurons and outputs a signal that is passed to other neurons. The whole network learns by adjusting the weights of the connections between neurons and performing a task, such as recognizing images or translating languages. Today, neural networks are the core foundation of many AI and machine learning applications. In contrast to traditional AI approaches, which require humans to explicitly define the rules that the computer should follow, neural networks work by finding patterns in datasets.

CHAPTER 2  FUNDAMENTALS OF GENERATIVE AI

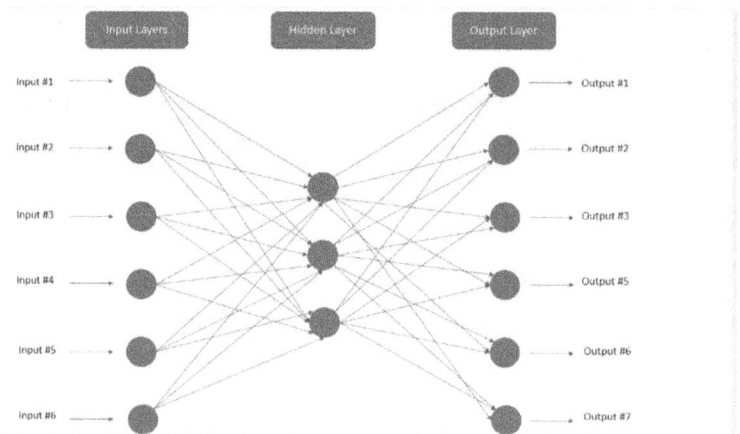

***Figure 2-2.*** *Neural network layers*

The neural network image shown in Figure 2-2 has three layers of neurons. The beginning layer is the input layer; it receives the input data. The second layer comes is the hidden layer, and it performs the calculations. The third layer is the output layer, which basically outputs the results of the calculations. The weights of the connections between neurons in a neural network are adjusted using a process called *backpropagation*. The backpropagation process works by calculating the error in the output of the network and then adjusting the weights of the connections to reduce that error. This process is repeated many times, until the network learns to perform the task at a desired level of accuracy. In the context of Generative AI, neural networks are used to learn the patterns and relationships in a dataset; the target dataset can be anything from images to text to music. Once the neural network has learned these patterns, it can generate new content that is similar to the content in the dataset. The math behind Generative AI is based on probability theory and statistics. The neural network is trained on a dataset of existing content, and the goal of the training is to learn the probability distribution of that content. Once the neural network has learned the probability distribution, it can be used to generate new content by sampling from the distribution.

CHAPTER 2  FUNDAMENTALS OF GENERATIVE AI

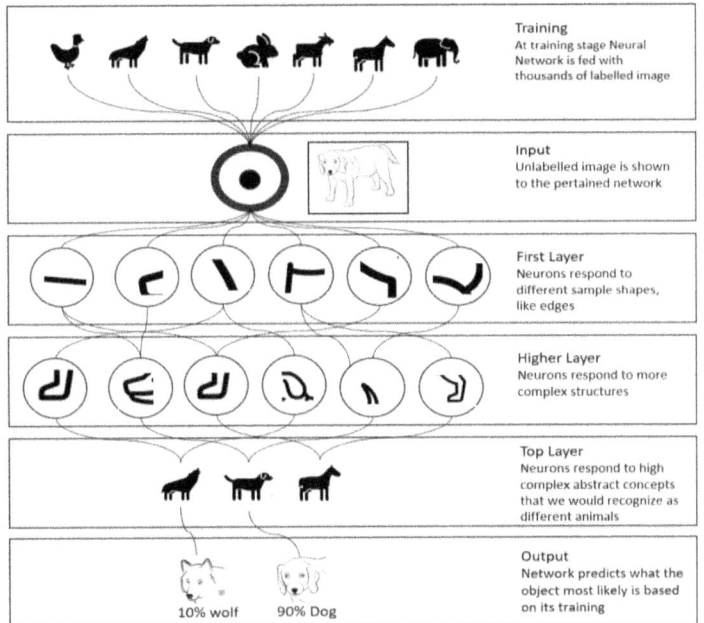

***Figure 2-3.*** *Neural network use case*

For example, as shown in Figure 2-3, a neural network could be trained on a dataset of dog images, where the neural network would learn the patterns of dogs in the images, such as the shape of their bodies, the color of their fur, and the size of their eyes. Once the neural network has learned these patterns, it could be used to generate new images of dogs. The first image might be a jumble of pixels that does not look like a dog. It would compare the random image to the patterns it has learned and if the random image does not match the patterns, the neural network would make changes to the image. This process would continue to make changes to the image until it finds a match to the patterns it has learned. The image would not be perfect, but it would be similar to the dogs in the dataset. This is a classic example of how neural networks can be leveraged in Generative AI to generate text, audio, and video.

Neural networks are the key driving force behind GenAI. This helps in a number of ways:

- Makes it possible to generate more realistic and creative content based on the capability to learn patterns in existing content, and then use those patterns to generate new content that is similar. This capability of neural networks make Generative AI generate realistic images, text, music, and other forms of content.

27

- Enables neural networks to be trained on a variety of different datasets, including text, images, and audio and used to generate content from a wider variety of sources. For example, a neural network could be trained on a dataset of text and images of dogs and then used to generate new images of dogs.

- Makes it possible for Generative AI to generate content more quickly and efficiently, including generating content on demand, which can be useful for a variety of applications.

Overall, neural networks are a powerful tool for Generative AI, making it possible to generate more realistic, creative, and diverse content quickly and efficiently. This is leading to new and exciting applications for Generative AI in a variety of fields, including art, entertainment, and education. However, neural networks can also be biased. This is because neural networks are trained on data that is created by humans. If the data is biased, the neural network will be biased as well.

## Components of GenAI

Generative AI is a form of AI that utilizes extensive trained data models to generate new content such as text, images, audio, and videos. Prominent applications in this domain include ChatGPT, which is a language model service trained on vast amounts of data, and models like DALL-E and Midjourney, which focus on generating images. For a Generative AI model to operate and generate the output, underlying elements must work in an integrated manner. A wide spectrum of underlying elements including data, foundation of knowledge, models, natural language processing, neural networks, vector data, latent space, and several other components. These components function by acquiring knowledge of the combined probability distribution of the input data and their associated labels or target variables. These labels or target variables denote the intended outcomes that the generative model aims to comprehend and forecast. The joint probability distribution adeptly encapsulates the statistical interconnection between the input data and their respective labels. Following the training of a generative model on a dataset, it not only grasps the inherent distribution of input data and labels but also establishes this acquired knowledge as a probabilistic model of the training dataset. Subsequently, the generative model employs this learned distribution to produce novel data samples through the process of sampling. This list explains each of these key components in detail:

- **Data:** In any Generative AI project, collecting and preparing relevant, diverse, and high-quality data that will be used to train the model is the first step. The final outcome of the project depends on the quality of the data. Based on the type and size of the data, you may need to adopt different tools and methods to clean, label, augment, or transform the data. Various methods, like web scraping, annotation, or other image processing techniques can be handy in this context. The size of the dataset affects both the accuracy and training time of the model, especially with larger datasets. It may also take additional computational resources and longer training times, leading to more robust and accurate outcomes from the target Generative AI models.

- **Probability distribution:** To understand generative models better, you need to understand probability distributions, as they play a vital role by enabling the framework to model uncertainty and randomness. Generative models aim to approximate by applying a probability distribution of the data they're given. The most common probability distributions is the Gaussian distribution, also known as normal distribution or as a bell curve in statistics. Generative AI aims to create models that can generate new, realistic samples that resemble a given dataset. They take advantage of probability distributions to capture inherent uncertainty in real-world data and generate diverse and realistic samples.

- **Natural language processing (NLP):** As one of the initial expressions of AI, NLP has undergone substantial transformation over the years. Despite its early origins, the enhancement of NLP systems spanned several decades, with most remarkable progress attributed to the deployment of advanced deep learning models. NLP holds significance across various applications, exercising deep impacts across diverse industries, especially in the customer support segment providing classification, sentiment analysis, and finger-tip digital assistants such as Siri and Alexa. This played an extensive role in enhancing their operational efficiency. The architecture of NLP can be split into two main categories—natural language understanding (NLU) and natural language generation (NLG). NLU basically forms the crux of a computer's ability to comprehend human language by employing complex algorithms to decode sentence structures, context, intent, and entities, facilitating human-computer communication. Natural language generation, on the other hand, is essentially the culmination of the NLP process, wherein the interpreted content is generated. Generative AI has introduced an era of transformation for both NLU and NLG oriented tasks by reshaping the way machines interact with and produce human language. These models have proven to be pivotal in comprehending and generating natural language, owing to their remarkable capabilities in processing and generating text with a depth of understanding and fluency that was once considered beyond the reach of machines.

- **Foundation model:** Generative AI models are categorized based on their output types, such as language models, image models, and video models. However, the current trend is the development of multi-modal models, capable of concurrently learning from images and text along with their performance and capabilities evolving rapidly. Multi-modal models are being treated as the cornerstone of Generative AI, and they are also emerging as foundational models, a concept that originated from researchers at Stanford University and outlined in the paper titled "Opportunities and Risks of Foundation Models." Being geared toward tasks involving human creativity and reasoning, foundation models undergo training with extensive datasets encompassing text, images, audio, structured data, 3D signals, and more. The term "foundation model" signifies a fundamental shift in the AI paradigm, underscoring their pivotal role in the AI landscape, especially in the context of LLMs, where unsupervised learning with vast amounts of data is employed to train them. Post-training, the model is distributed and can be fine-tuned or undergo in-context learning for downstream tasks tailored to user requirements. Foundation models exhibit versatility in handling diverse data types, enabling them to process input in any format, without being confined to a single output type.

- **Large language models:** LLMs in the context of Generative AI serve as foundational models for NLP and NLG tasks. To manage the intricate and interconnected nature of language, these models are first pre-trained on massive datasets, then refined through fine-tuning and advanced strategies such as in-context learning, as well as zero-shot, one-shot, and few-shot learning. Importantly, the effectiveness of LLMs is heavily shaped by the quality of the data used during pre-training. Compared to smaller language models, LLMs have a higher demand for high-quality data for pre-training. The model's capacity relies heavily on the collection of training corpora and the methods used for pre-training. LLMs, such as OpenAI's GPT series and Google's BERT, have gained significant attention in the field of Generative AI.

- **Prompt engineering:** In the context of Generative AI, the quality of the generated content depends greatly on how well the prompts (questions or requests) are crafted and conveyed. This is why prompt engineering, which involves finding combinations of prompt input values from LLM, plays a crucial role. Prompt engineering is important because it seeks to improve the quality of answers without the need for extensive parameter updates through large-scale data or fine-tuning processes. One effective approach to enhance answer quality is by providing example answer instances when prompting questions. This method helps the model generate responses that are similar to the provided examples, thereby improving response quality. This is achieved without necessarily relying on massive data or fine-tuning procedures for parameter updates. Using examples within prompt instructions can be categorized into three types—zero-shot, where no examples are included; one-shot, where a single example is provided; and few-shot, where two or more examples are included. Providing a variety of examples in the prompt tends to yield better responses. For example, a zero-shot prompt might be "Write a poem about autumn", while a few-shot prompt could include "Write a poem about autumn like these examples: [poem1], [poem2]".

- **Parameters:** In the ever-advancing landscape of Generative AI models, you will frequently encounter expressions such as "3 billion parameters," "7 billion parameters," or even "70 billion parameters." But what significance do these parameters hold and what kind of role do they play? In the context of Generative AI, a parameter serves as a value dictating the behavior of a machine learning model. Generative AI models, rooted in mathematical algorithms, are crafted to discern patterns within data and subsequently formulate predictions based on that acquired knowledge. Parameters, on the other hand, guide them to process the data and shape the predictions it generates. For instance, in a text generation model, parameters can be used to shape the style, tone, and substance of the generated content. Tweaking these parameters allows users to steer the model's output, enabling them to create text that aligns with particular goals or requirements. In a broader sense, the magnitude of a model's parameters correlates with its accuracy and potency. A model endowed with more parameters can assimilate a broader spectrum of relationships and patterns in the data, thereby enhancing its overall performance and predictive accuracy. However, having too many parameters can force the model to become overfit and can lead to poor performance on test data. This can limit the model's ability to make accurate predictions.

Now that you have a pretty good understanding of the key components of Generative AI, the next section focuses on the Generative AI tech stack, which serves as the bedrock for making well-informed decisions.

## The GenAI Technology Stack

To get a comprehensive understanding of Generative AI, it is essential to understand the essential elements, frameworks, and technologies that the Generative AI landscape contains. Understanding Generative AI's integral components helps users make well-informed decisions and is instrumental in selecting the best tools and technologies throughout the various stages of Generative AI development. Generative AI's technology stack consists of several essential layers, starting with the application layer and continuing to the safety layer. These layers work together to drive innovation. The first layer, called the Application Layer, includes user-facing apps and third-party APIs that can seamlessly integrate Generative AI models. They enrich user interactions and enhance products, followed by layers associated with synthetic data, labelling, fine-tune, databases, and frameworks. Next is the Model Layer, which contains proprietary APIs and open-source checkpoints. This provides the computational power behind AI-driven solutions driven by robust hosting solutions for effective deployment. Next comes the Infrastructure Layer, which effectively manages the complex training and inference workloads essential for Generative AI models. It ensures scalability and optimal performance.

- **Computer hardware:** The beginning layers of the Generative AI technology stack is its computational or resource layer accommodating the underlying computer hardware specifically designed to handle the computational demands of AI workloads. Inside it, you have graphics processing units (GPUs), which play a critical role in fueling deep learning models by accelerating the training and inference processes. GPUs excel at handling parallel processing tasks, which makes them a perfect fit for training Generative AI models that require intensive computational power. In addition to GPUs, other hardware designed specifically for AI—like Google's Tensor Processing Units (TPUs)—also support model training and deployment. Specialized processors like GPUs (Graphics Processing Units) and TPUs (Tensor Processing Units) enable faster experimentation and fulfill the computations required for AI training and inference. They significantly accelerate the time required for data processing and model training. The Infrastructure Layer is often hidden from view but is critical to providing the foundational support for Generative AI.

- **Foundation models/LLMs:** Computational layers are immediately followed by the layers for foundation models and LLMs, trained on large amounts of data and capturing patterns and contextual understanding. They form the core layer of the Generative AI technology stack. This can be treated as the point for enterprises to build on and customize according to their specific business requirements. The foundational model can either be proprietary or sourced from open-source repositories, and model hubs. It can further be classified into general or specialized models, which are fine-tuned for specific purposes and trained on specific content. For instance, GPT-3, DALL-E-2, Whisper, and Stable Diffusion are designed to be user-friendly and replicate human-like thinking. They can handle a wide range of outputs, including text, images,

CHAPTER 2    FUNDAMENTALS OF GENERATIVE AI

voice, and games. These models have the potential to automate tasks across various industries and improve productivity, making precise predictions, especially in areas like healthcare, where vast amount of data analysis is critical to perform diagnoses. On the other hand, hyperlocal models are specialized models that are trained and tailored for domain-specific needs and deliver accuracy and specificity in their output. For instance, some AI models are tailored to analyze product images from e-commerce sites to understand the shades of effective product photography, considering factors like lighting, composition, and product placement. In the field of art and creativity this kind of model can even generate lyrics tailored to specific genres or artists, capturing the stylistic variation of each.

- **Framework:** The next layer in the stack is the application frameworks. They form the cornerstone of the stack and accommodate seamless integration of AI models with different data sources, empowering developers to prototype and launch applications quickly using Generative AI models. A frontrunner in this niche space is LangChain, started with an open-source framework and specifically designed to streamline application development using LLMs by chaining together various components to create chatbots, Generative Question-Answering (GQA), and summarization. LangChain provides a collection of abstractions, each representing a different module that is necessary for building complex LLM applications and common ways of doing more complex sequences of LLM calls to enable RAG, summarization, and so on. Other key players, like Fixie AI, Microsoft's Semantic Kernel, and Google Cloud's Vertex AI, help developers create stack applications that establish connections between text-generating models like OpenAI's ChatGPT and enterprise-level data, systems, and workflows. The goal is to create customer support workflows, where agents can process customer tickets, automatically retrieve relevant purchase information, issue refunds if required, and generate draft replies to the customers.

- **Vector databases:** In the context of Generative AI, the database layer is all about data loaders and vector databases play a pivotal role to facilitate the ingestion of structured and unstructured data and efficient storage. They help with retrieval of data vectors in a manner that facilitates finding similar data. This is accomplished by representing each piece of data as a list of numbers, known as a vector, and each number in the vector corresponds to features or attributes of the data. For example, when working with images, the values within a vector may correspond to features like color, shape, and brightness. In vector databases, a process known as embedding is used to capture and store the semantic essence of data, enabling AI systems to understand content and retain information over time—an essential capability for tackling complex problems. Take an image of a motorcycle: it can be translated into a set of numerical values that describe traits such as size, wheel color, body color, and handle color. These numerical forms make storage and analysis more efficient and practical compared to relying solely on the image itself. Many companies have already introduced vector databases and embeddings. Some of the prominent players in this space are Pinecone, Chroma, and Weaviate. They have introduced open-source vector databases designed for large-scale machine-learning applications that focus on high-performance similarity search and are compatible with other model hubs, such as OpenAI and Hugging Face.

- **Fine-tuning:** One layer up is the layer of fine-tuning, encapsulating model fine-tuning related features, which are essential in the context of Generative AI to train a model on a specific task or dataset. With a fine-tuning process in place, any model's performance can be easily tuned to meet the unique requirements of a given task or dataset. While developers do try to build new applications on top of preexisting language models trained on massive datasets that can produce grammatically correct and fluent text, this approach may still lack precision in certain areas like medicine and law. This is where fine-tuning comes to the rescue. It acquires knowledge from domain-specific datasets and enhances its ability to generate relevant text. This fine-tuning process in Generative AI helps developers save substantial computational power.

- **Labelling:** Next layer up is data labelling, which is crucial for the success of Generative AI models. Data can take various forms, including images, text, and audio. Labels act as descriptions of the data. For example, an image of a bike can be labelled as "bike" or "bicycle". A very tedious aspect of machine learning is affixing a set of labels to make the machine learning model learn from the data. The algorithm's learning capabilities depend on the accuracy of the labels and inaccurate data can easily lead to inaccurate results. Data labelling remains a significant challenge across many industries due to several factors, including cost, intensive labor, and time for it. This has led to sourcing data from crowdsourcing platforms, especially when privacy and expertise constraints are minimal. For example, Snorkel AI originated as a research project at the Stanford AI Lab, aiming to tackle the data labelling bottleneck in AI. The company empowers subject matter experts to label data programmatically using a method called "weak supervision," rather than relying on time-consuming manual labelling. This approach keeps humans involved in the process while greatly enhancing the efficiency of labelling. This kind of automated labelling process can decrease the required months to hours or days, depending on the data complexity, and makes models easier to maintain in the long run.

- **Synthetic data:** Synthetic data, also known as artificially created data that mimics real data, offers several benefits and has many applications in the context of machine learning and AI. One primary use case for synthetic data arises when realistic training data is unavailable or cannot be utilized. Synthetic data accurately addresses this concern by generating artificial datasets which developers can leverage to develop and test AI models without compromising privacy. Synthetic data safeguards privacy. It's compliant with data regulations, such as GDPR, because it lacks personally identifiable information (PII) and HIPAA-related risks. Synthetic data enables scalable machine learning and AI applications by generating data for training and deployment. It also enhances diversity and minimizing biases by promoting fairness and inclusivity in the AI models. In the realm of synthetic data solutions, a number of companies offer dependable services. Notable players in this field include Gretel.ai, Tonic.ai, and Mostly.ai.

- **Model supervision/AI observability:** The next level in the technology stack, which is called AI observability, is all about monitoring, comprehending, and explaining the behavior of AI models. Basically, it ensures the accurate functioning of AI models by driving them to make unbiased, non-harmful decisions. Being a subset of AI observability, model supervision ensures that AI models are aligned with their intended purpose and are not making decisions that could be harmful or unethical. Continuous changes in the data distribution over time, which is known as *data drift,* can result in AI models becoming less accurate and producing more biased or unfair decisions. AI observability platforms also provide solutions to tackle challenges related to these issues.

- **Model safety:** At the top of the stack is the model safety layer. It addresses one of the major concerns of Generative AI—generating biased outputs based on the biases present in the training data. According to some recent instances, an AI-driven resume screening tool has demonstrated bias toward candidates with specific naming patterns and lacrosse experience, revealing biases in the dataset. Enterprise like Amazon faced a similar challenge when their AI resume screening tool exhibited an intrinsic bias toward male candidates due to the training data predominantly consisting of male employees. Malicious use of AI to create deepfakes is another area of concern, especially when it involves the dissemination of misinformation through believable yet fabricated images, videos, or text. To prevent such misuse, techniques like bias detection and mitigation are crucial in identifying biases in the model's output. Implementing measures such as training data diversity, fairness techniques, and user feedback mechanisms can play a vital role in refining AI models.

- **Machine learning operations (MLOps):** Beyond all these mentioned layers, the MLOps layer takes center stage, integrating tools, technologies, and workflows to optimize, train, and enhance Generative AI models. Its primary role is efficient management of the model development lifecycle, covering aspects like tooling, model versioning, experimentation, and training. Various forms of MLOps solutions, each equipped with different tools and functionalities, can be leveraged to further refine models and create focused, differentiated capabilities tailored to the specific needs and functions of the business. MLOps was a part of the traditional ML landscape. However, in the realm of Generative AI, also known as LLMOps, the complexity increases, primarily due to the large scale and size of the involved models. LLMOps encompasses activities such as selecting a foundation model, adapting it to the use case, model evaluation, deployment, and monitoring. Adapting a foundation model is primarily achieved through prompt engineering or fine-tuning. Fine-tuning introduces additional complexities such as data labelling, model training, and deploying the model to production. The LLMOps space has seen the emergence of several tools. There are standalone solutions for experimentation, deployment, monitoring, observability, prompt engineering, governance, and more. Additionally, there are comprehensive tools that offer end-to-end LLMOps capabilities.

The tech stack plays a key role in shaping development choices by highlighting the most appropriate technologies and tools for each phase of Generative AI development. With this knowledge, developers can tailor their approach to maximize precision, scalability, and trustworthiness. The next section dives deep into the underlying models that form the foundation of Generative AI.

# GenAI Model Types

As mentioned, Generative AI uses techniques such as neural networks and deep learning algorithms to identify patterns in data and generate new outputs based on those patterns. The training phase of any generative model involves providing it with a massive dataset containing examples like images, text, audio, or videos. The model then studies these inputs to identify patterns and connections, allowing it to grasp the fundamental rules that shape the structure and meaning of the content. It generates new data by sampling from a probability distribution it has learned and continuously adjusting its parameters to maximize the probability of generating accurate output. For example, a generative model trained on an image dataset of bags could be used to create new images of bags by sampling from the learned distribution and then refining the output through a process called *inference*. Inference in Generative AI is the process of using a trained model to generate new data and can be achieved by sampling from a model's probability distribution, or by applying a search technique called beam search. As part of the inference process, the model adjusts its output to better match the desired output or correct any errors to ensure that the generated outcome becomes more realistic and aligns better with expectations. To understand how Generative AI works, it's critical to first understand how its underlying model works, so let's dive deep into some of the most popular deep learning techniques being used for Generative AI:

- **Generative adversarial networks (GANs):** GANs were introduced in the paper "Generative Adversarial Networks" by Ian Goodfellow, Yoshua Bengio, and Aaron Courville in 2014. You can refer to the original research paper for more details at https://arxiv.org/abs/1406.2661. A GAN is a type of Generative AI system that can be used to generate realistic images, text, data augmentations, music, and synthetic data. In the context of statistical models, *generative* refers to models that can create new data that is similar to the data they were trained on. As an example, generative models can generate new photos of animals similar to real animals, whereas a discriminative model could only distinguish a dog from a tiger.

- **Variational autoencoders (VAEs):** VAEs were proposed in 2013 by Kingma and Welling at Google. Qualcomm is a type of Generative AI system trained to learn a low-dimensional representation of a dataset and generate new data points that are similar to the original dataset, but with variations. An autoencoder is a type of neural network that learns to reconstruct its input data by first encoding the input data into a latent space and then decoding the latent space back into the original data. In contrast, VAEs are a type of autoencoder that learns a probabilistic latent space, which is not just a fixed representation of the input data, but rather a distribution over possible latent representations. The primary goal of a VAE is to generate a realistic image given a random vector that is generated from a pre-defined distribution. VAEs, being more complex than autoencoders, are useful in many aspects like synthetic data generation, where they can be leveraged to generate new data that is more realistic than the data that autoencoders can generate. VAEs can also be used for anomaly detection, data compression, realistic images creation, art synthesis, and semi-supervised learning, which are not possible with autoencoders.

- **Recurrent neural networks (RNNs):** RNNs, also known as sequence models, are specifically designed to model patterns in sequential data. RNNs stand out from many other deep learning models by their ability to account for the element of time, making them well-suited for identifying patterns and relationships across sequences. They were originally developed to overcome the shortcomings of traditional architectures like feedforward neural networks (FNNs) when dealing with sequential input. FNNs process each input separately through a series of hidden layers, without taking into account the order or context of other inputs. As a result, they struggle to manage sequences and fail to capture the dependencies between inputs effectively. For tasks like language modeling, machine translation, speech recognition, time series analysis, and many other applications that require sequential processing, the limitation of FNNs led to the rise of RNN. Where traditional neural networks view each observation as independent and cannot retain past or historical information due to their lack of memory, RNNs can store memory based on context; this is, they learn repeated patterns.

- **Autoregressive models:** Autoregressive models are statistical models that perform time series analysis, where determination of a variable's current value depends linearly on its own previous values. As the name implies, autoregressive means regression on self, which implies predicting future outcomes of a sequence from the previously observed outcomes of that sequence. Being inferred as a type of Generative AI system, these models can be leveraged to generate text from the learned patterns of language and generate new sentences that are grammatically correct and coherent. Additionally, autoregressive models can even be leveraged to forecast financial markets and climate studies due to their capability to interpret past data to predict future values. This helps analysts and researchers make more informed decisions and forecasts. Where many regression models use linear combinations of predictors to forecast a variable, autoregressive models in contrast use the past values of variables to determine future values.

- **Flow models:** Present deep learning models, exemplified by GANs and VAEs, demonstrate proficiency in image generation but struggle with notable challenges. GANs contend with issues of training instability and limitations in generating diverse images owing to their adversarial training approach. Concurrently, VAEs encounter challenges stemming from surrogate loss. Denoising diffusion modeling unfolds as a two-step process, encompassing forward and reverse diffusion steps. The forward diffusion process unfolds as a Markov chain of diffusion steps, systematically introducing random noise to the original data. In contrast, the reverse diffusion process undoes the diffusion steps, re-creating the original data from the introduced noise. A flow-based generative model employed in machine learning explicitly constructs a probability distribution through the utilization of normalizing flow. This statistical technique leverages the change-of-variable law of probabilities to convert a simple distribution into a more intricate one. This stands in contrast to various alternative generative modeling approaches, like VAEs and generative adversarial networks, which do not explicitly articulate the likelihood function.

- **Diffusion models:** A diffusion model represents a sophisticated deep neural network equipped with latent variables that can discern and understand the inherent structure of a given image by eliminating its blur, commonly referred to as *noise*. Once the network of the model undergoes training to comprehend the conceptual essence behind an image, it can generate novel variations of that image. For instance, by eliminating the noise from an image featuring a cat, the diffusion model effectively perceives a clear depiction of the cat, assimilates an understanding of its appearance, and applies this acquired knowledge to generate diverse variations of cat images. The versatile applications of diffusion models extend to denoising or sharpening images, thereby enhancing and refining visual content. Additionally, these models can manipulate facial expressions or generate images that project how a person's appearance might evolve over time, used in face-aging simulations. To witness the remarkable capabilities of these AI models in action, explore the Lexica search engine, where the prowess of diffusion models in generating innovative images becomes evident. The core concept underpinning diffusion models revolves around converting a straightforward and easily sampleable distribution into a more intricate data distribution that holds interest. This conversion process is achieved through a sequence of reversible operations.

- **Transformer models:** Since their debut in 2017, transformer models have dramatically reshaped the landscape of natural language processing. Before their arrival, the top-performing models were LSTMs and RNNs. The key reason that transformers surpass these earlier models is that LSTMs and RNNs process language strictly from left to right. Take, for instance, these phrases: *On the river bank* and *On the bank of the river*. Broadly speaking, transformers are built to capture the meaning of words based on their context within a sentence or text. They do this through a technique known as *self-attention,* which enables the model to determine how much focus to place on each word relative to the others in the sequence. Unlike traditional recurrent models that handle input step-by-step and lack a comprehensive view, transformers can assess the entire sentence at once. Of the many strengths the transformer models offer, one major benefit is their capacity to handle input sequences simultaneously, rather than step by step. This parallel processing gives them a significant speed advantage over RNNs in a variety of NLP applications. Moreover, transformers have demonstrated strong performance across numerous language tasks, such as building language models, classifying text, answering questions, and translating between languages. The transformer's encoder-decoder framework is commonly applied to tasks such as language translation, where the objective is to receive a sentence in one language and produce its equivalent in another. In this architecture, the encoder processes the input sentence and converts it into a fixed-length vector representation. This representation is then passed along to the decoder, which constructs the translated sentence. The decoder employs both self-attentions to analyze its own generated sequence and cross-attention to focus on the encoder's output while forming the translation.

After a comprehensive walkthrough of GenAI model types, the chapter now shifts focus to the benefits that organizations can enjoy from Generative AI and its technology stack.

# Benefits of GenAI

Generative AI's sudden popularity is driven by its clear benefits, including the following:

- Decisions in business are often akin to navigating a complex maze, and the ability to make informed, data-driven choices is paramount. Generative AI steps into this arena not as a replacement for decision-makers but as a formidable ally, offering insights derived from the synthesis of vast datasets. In traditional decision-making processes, the challenge lies in sifting through enormous amounts of data to extract meaningful patterns. Generative AI does this heavy lifting with finesse, providing decision-makers with synthesized information that is not only comprehensive but also presented in a digestible format.

- The integration of Generative AI in decision support systems is a paradigm shift. It's not about replacing human intuition but augmenting it with the analytical prowess of AI. The synergy between human expertise and machine-generated insights elevates decision-making to new heights. Generative AI's impact on corporate decision support goes beyond mere automation. It's about creating a symbiotic relationship where human decision-makers leverage AI as a strategic partner. As we navigate Generative AI's influence on decision-making, it's clear that this technology is not just a tool; it's a catalyst for informed, forward-thinking choices.

CHAPTER 2    FUNDAMENTALS OF GENERATIVE AI

- The heartbeat of any successful business is efficiency, and Generative AI emerges as a silent powerhouse in achieving just that. Gone are the days when automation was confined to repetitive, mundane tasks. Generative AI introduces a new era of creative automation. Imagine having a virtual assistant that not only handles routine administrative duties but also crafts engaging content for your marketing campaigns. This isn't just automation; it's creative collaboration with machines. Efficiency is the name of the game, and Generative AI is the player that elevates your team's productivity. By automating tasks that would traditionally consume valuable time, your workforce can redirect their energy toward strategic endeavors that demand human ingenuity.

- Generative AI optimizes your business workflows by identifying bottlenecks and automating repetitive elements. It's like having a virtual efficiency expert embedded in your processes, constantly fine-tuning for optimal performance. Generative AI doesn't just automate; it brings intelligence to the process. By leveraging generative models, businesses gain insights into their operations that go beyond traditional analytics. The integration of Generative AI isn't just a cost-saving measure; it's an investment in growth. As businesses embrace this technology, they position themselves for a future where efficiency isn't just a goal but a reality.

- The integration of Generative AI isn't just about automating tasks; it's about innovating marketing strategies. By analyzing consumer behavior, generative algorithms can suggest personalized content that speaks directly to your target audience. Content creation is at the core of marketing, and generative models are the new tools in the content creator's arsenal. The marriage of AI and creativity isn't a distant dream; it's happening now. Generative AI doesn't replace the creative process; it enhances and accelerates it. As we navigate the landscape of AI-powered innovation in marketing, it's clear that the traditional boundaries of creativity are expanding.

- Generative AI can deliver effectively even with minimal training data. In fact, some Generative AI models are specifically designed to work with small datasets. They can learn to extract patterns from data, even when the data is limited.

- Generative models are typically unsupervised; they do not need pre-labelled data. This makes Generative AI particularly useful, especially in applications where structured or organized data is not feasible.

- Generative AI models can be tuned to improve the quality of generated content by making it more realistic, creative, and diverse. This can be done by adjusting the parameters of the model to control the features of the generated content.

- With Generative AI, you can have diverse models that generate a wide variety of content, including different styles, genres, and topics. This is possible because the model has a wider range of data to draw from, which can help it come up with new and innovative ideas for different needs and interests.

- It can be used to create more realistic and diverse data based on learning from underlying patterns and distributions of real-world data and then use this knowledge to generate new data. This helps train machine learning models that need to be able to generalize to new data.

The list of benefits covered so far only capture a subset of benefits. Considering the nature of Generative AI, the possibilities and benefits are endless. The next section covers some of the challenges and limitations of Generative AI.

## Limitations of GenAI

"With great power comes great responsibility" is an adage attributed to Voltaire and popularized by Marvel's Spider-Man. It is very much applicable in the context of Generative AI, as it can give you superpowers. Since its release, many people across the industries, from marketers and developers to product designers, are discovering the ways in which Generative AI can help them do their jobs better. However, there are potential pitfalls, and organizations need to deal with these pitfalls when drafting a course of action for implementing Generative AI in meaningful and beneficial ways. Here are some of the prevalent limitations and ethical concerns surrounding Generative AI:

- **Hallucinations:** A *hallucination* describes a model output that is either nonsensical or outright false. Hallucinations are a serious concern for Generative AI models, as they can easily mislead users into believing that a hallucinated output is true or accurate. This can have serious consequences, such as spreading misinformation or making decisions based on false information. Hallucinations happen when the underlying model is trained on data that contains errors or biases. If the model is not given enough data to learn the underlying patterns of the real world or is asked to generate something that is outside of its training data, hallucinations can happen. For example, as part of drafting a contract process, the Generative AI was fine-tuned using contracts from the financial services industry. It may not have sufficient exposure to terms and concepts in healthcare law to draft contracts for that industry. In most cases, Generative AI's primary goal is to produce an output in response to a prompt. Even if it doesn't understand the prompt, it might craft a response based on insufficient training data, thereby leading to a faulty result. While Generative AI hallucinations are a concerning issue, there are ways to reduce their frequency and intensity. This is done using methods like quality training data without any bias, limiting the scope of the model's outputs to what it is trained on, using techniques to detect and remove hallucinations from the model's output, and more.

- **Legal risk:** The second most prevailing reason for concerns are legal issues, risk, and compliance. Especially for enterprise-oriented sustainable solutions, the legal implications of utilizing Generative AI remain uncertain. This is especially true when it comes to copyrighted AI-generated content. Whether the development of a model is a potential infringement of copyright or falls under the umbrella of a "transformative" use protected by U.S. copyright law still remains to be answered. Other risk factors such as reputational harm arising from incorrect output, emergence of new security vulnerabilities, and various other concerns further emphasize the complexities around the adoption of Generative AI.

- **Deepfakes:** Generative AI's creative aspect helps people generate real-life images and videos, which is a great boon to many industries. However, it can be a concern when deepfakes are maliciously created, which can be used to generate synthetic media that's difficult or impossible to distinguish from real media. This poses serious ethical implications. Deepfake detection uses AI models that are trained to identify artifacts in synthetic media, such as inconsistencies in lighting or unnatural facial movements. Deepfakes can easily spread misinformation, can be used to manipulate public opinion, or can even harass or defame individuals. One example of a deepfake video is a political figure saying or doing something that they did not actually say or do. This could easily manipulate public opinion and interfere with the democratic process.

- **Misuse:** In the educational sector, Generative AI can be misused to generate false or misleading information that is presented as fact. Additionally, it can be used to create material that is not only factually incorrect but also ideologically biased. For example, a student could use a Generative AI model to generate a research paper on a topic that they know nothing about. The paper would likely be full of inaccuracies and falsehoods, but the student could pass it off as their own work. A teacher could use a Generative AI model to create a test that is full of trick questions and misleading answers, and this could make it difficult for students to pass the test, even if they know the material. Mitigating the risk of misuse of Generative AI in the education sector can be managed by increasing awareness among students and teachers and monitoring Generative AI models for bias and misinformation.

- **Accuracy:** Generative AI models are trained on massive amounts of data, which can lead to inaccurate information if the data is outdated, biased, or simply incorrect. Additionally, Generative AI models cannot always keep up with new information, which can further contribute to inaccuracies. According to the TruthfulQA benchmark (Lin et al., 2021), generative models are truthful only 25 percent of the time, which means that there is a high risk of receiving inaccurate information when applying Generative AI products and tools. Mitigating this kind of risk requires an additional layer of validation, with fact checking methods and cross-referencing information, especially with enterprise use cases.

CHAPTER 2   FUNDAMENTALS OF GENERATIVE AI

- **Biased output:** One of the most prominent issues of Generative AI is bias, which can lead to unfair or discriminatory outcomes. Several factors can be the reason behind biased output. For example, if the optimization process was not carefully controlled, it may be more likely to find solutions that are biased toward certain groups of people. If the training data is mostly images of white people, the model is more likely to generate images of white people. It is important to be aware of the potential for bias in Generative AI models and take steps to mitigate this risk. This may include using a diverse training dataset, using a fair optimization process, and continuously monitoring the model for bias.

- **Prompt injection:** Prompt injection is a security attack that targets the underlying LLMs. It involves embedding malicious code or instructions, which are given in the form of a prompt to the LLM inside Generative AI. The LLM then executes those instructions, which can result in generating harmful or misleading output. For example, an attacker could inject the following prompt into an LLM: Write a poem that contains the following words: "bomb", "explosion", and "kill." The LLM would then generate a poem that contains these words, which could be used to create propaganda or to threaten someone. There are certain ways to mitigate the risk associated with prompt injection, including secure prompt generation, continuous monitoring of the LLM output for signs of malicious content, and training the LLM on data that is free of malicious content. Secure prompts avoid ambiguous instructions. For example, they use explicit constraints such as "generate a poem without violent themes" to prevent harmful outputs.

- **Disparate performance:** In the context of assessing the influence of Generative AI systems, the concept of disparate performance relates to AI systems exhibiting varied effectiveness across different subpopulations, resulting in unequal outcomes for those groups, especially when the underlying model is trained on a dataset that predominantly represents one demographic group. Disparities arise due to various reasons, including geographical biases in data collection, differences in digitization of content across the globe due to erratic Internet access levels, and the prioritization of certain languages or accents in infrastructure, among other factors. A substantial portion of the training data for generative models is sourced from the Internet, which also contributes to disparate performance.

## Conclusion

In this ever-evolving era of technological revolutions, Generative AI has revolutionized content creation and innovation by enabling machines to generate realistic images, text, music, and videos. Since its inception in 1960, Generative AI has become a powerful technology with the potential to disrupt nearly every industry, promising both competitive advantage and creative destruction. Generative AI, driven by neural networks and components like LLMs and transformers, is transforming industries. Generative AI is driven by several key components, including data, NLP, foundation models, prompt engineering, and LLMs. The underlying technology stack requires robust computing resources. This chapter also explained a set of potential Generative AI use cases, followed by limitations and various constraints related to the adoption of Generative AI. You were also introduced to some of the most popular Generative AI models. As we navigate the future, these Generative AI models will continue to shape creativity and drive innovation in unprecedented ways.

CHAPTER 3

# Transformer Architecture and Large Language Models

Since its inception in 2017, the Transformer architecture has taken the world of NLP processing by storm, surpassing various other models in the same space. This chapter introduces the Transformer architecture and explains its evolution. It also compares the transformer model to other models. You also learn about its key components, underlying foundation, use cases, and limitations. This is followed by a taxonomy of transformer-based models and a detailed deep dive into one of the most popular transformer-based models, which will help you better understand how it works behind the scenes.

## The Transformer Architecture

In natural language processing, sequence-to-sequence models are one of the most critical models dealing with language processing. An encoder reads and encodes the input sentence once and the decoder uses this embedding and produces an output. The human brain doesn't interpret or translate language in a strict, word-by-word sequence. Instead, it uses contextual clues and focuses on key words or phrases to derive meaning, rather than memorizing the entire sentence and reproducing it. A major breakthrough in natural language processing came in 2017 with the release of the paper "Attention Is All You Need" by Vaswani et al., which introduced the transformer model. This work highlighted how attention mechanisms alone, without relying on recurrent or convolutional structures, could deliver powerful results in language tasks.

## CHAPTER 3  TRANSFORMER ARCHITECTURE AND LARGE LANGUAGE MODELS

Developed by the Google Brain team, the Transformer architecture fundamentally changed how NLP models are built. It quickly emerged as a superior alternative to earlier models like Recurrent Neural Networks (RNNs) and Convolutional Neural Networks (CNNs), both of which had notable drawbacks such as limited ability to handle long-range dependencies and challenges in training parallelization. The Transformer's efficiency, scalability, and contextual understanding have made it the go-to architecture for modern NLP solutions.

The paper proposed a very novel approach to NLP tasks that relied solely on the Attention mechanism, which allows the model to weigh the importance of different words in a sentence when encoding it into a fixed-size vector representation. This was in contrast to previous NLP models, which relied on RNNs or CNNs to process sequences of words. The Transformer architecture is significant for the following reasons:

- **Basis for successive innovations:** Since its inception, the Transformer architecture became the foundation for many popular models like BERT, GPT, and T5, which have dominated NLP tasks ranging from translation to text generation.

- **AI at its best**: With the introduction of a powerful Attention mechanism, AI models can now generate more coherent and contextually relevant content, leading to enriched chatbots, improved search engines, and more reliable language translation tools.

- **Democratization of AI**: The emergence of pre-trained models, rooted in the Transformer architecture, signifies that businesses and developers lacking extensive resources can now tap into cutting-edge AI capabilities.

Transformers are designed to handle sequential data, and their self-attention mechanism weighs the importance of each part of the input data differently, which enables faster training and improved performance on various NLP tasks. Transformers require less computation to train and are a better fit for modern machine learning hardware, speeding up training by up to an order of magnitude. Beyond computational performance and higher accuracy, an interesting aspect of the Transformer architecture is to visualize which other parts of a sentence the network attends to when processing or translating a given word, thus providing insight into how information travels through the network.

CHAPTER 3    TRANSFORMER ARCHITECTURE AND LARGE LANGUAGE MODELS

Neural networks handle language by converting individual words—or sometimes even fragments of words—into vector representations of either fixed or variable length. These vectors are then combined with information from surrounding words to help the model interpret the meaning of each word within its specific context. For example, consider the sentence: "I arrived at the bank after crossing the river." Here, the word "bank" has a meaning that depends entirely on the surrounding context. When using a RNN to understand this sentence, the model reads each word in sequence between "bank" and "river" in order to determine that "bank" most likely refers to the side of a river. As more steps are needed to reach this understanding, it becomes increasingly difficult for the RNN to correctly learn and make such context-based decisions.

CNNs are much less sequential in compared to RNNs, but in CNN architectures like ByteNet or ConvS2S, the number of steps required to gather information from distant parts of the sentence increase with growing distance. Unlike traditional sequential models, Transformers carry out a fixed number of operations—determined empirically—using a self-attention mechanism at each step. This approach enables them to capture relationships between all words in a sentence simultaneously, regardless of how far apart the words are. Revisit the sentence, "I arrived at the bank after crossing the river." Instead of processing this sentence word by word, transformers can instantly focus on the word "river" and use that information to interpret "bank" correctly in a single step. This is possible because the Transformer recalculates the representation of "bank" by evaluating its relationship with every other word in the sentence. It assigns attention scores to each word, indicating how much influence each one should have on the updated meaning of "bank." In this case, the word "river" could receive a high attention score when computing a new representation for "bank".

Before diving deep into further details about the Transformer architecture, the following sections looks at history behind the rise of the Transformer architecture in the field of natural language processing.

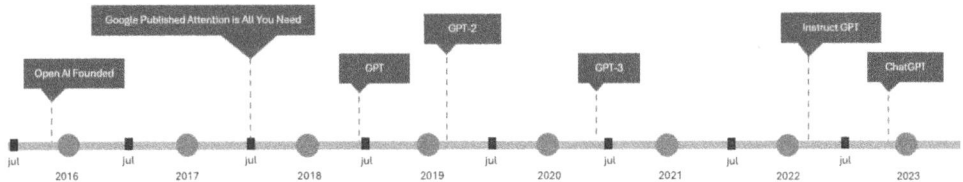

***Figure 3-1.*** *Significant milestones of Generative AI*

CHAPTER 3  TRANSFORMER ARCHITECTURE AND LARGE LANGUAGE MODELS

As shown in Figure 3-1, it all started in 2015 when OpenAI was founded by Sam Altman, Elon Musk, Greg Brockman, Peter Thiel, and others. In 2017, researchers from Google Brain published the paper, "Attention Is All You Need," introducing the Transformer architecture, which laid the groundwork for subsequent groundbreaking LLMs with a shift from sequential to self-attention mechanisms, allowing the models to consider all the words in a sequence simultaneously. In 2018, OpenAI unveiled the generative pre-training (GPT) model, built on the Transformer framework and trained on a vast text corpora. Building on this foundation, the following year saw the release of T5, which took a novel approach by reframing every NLP task as a text-to-text challenge—highlighting the model's flexibility and wide-ranging potential in language processing. The year 2020 marked a major leap with the launch of GPT-3, a massive-scale language model showcasing exceptional performance across tasks like text generation, summarization, and translation, all powered by the Transformer architecture. Advancements continued in 2022 with Google's release of the Progressive Language Model, which brought improved contextual comprehension and refined capabilities. Then in 2023, Google introduced Bard, expanding the lineup of cutting-edge language models and further pushing the frontiers of AI-generated language. The next section dives deeper into why the Transformer architecture outperforms older models such as RNNs, CNNs, and LSTMs in natural language processing applications.

## The Transformer vs. RNN vs. CNN

Transformers were introduced (by Vaswani et al.) to address the problem of sequence transduction, or neural machine translation, which ultimately refers to any task that transforms an input sequence to an output sequence, including speech recognition, text-to-speech transformation, and so on. Models must be able to store and retrieve information from memory in order to perform sequence transduction. For example, let's say that we are translating the following sentence from English to French:

"The Beatles were an English rock band formed in Liverpool in 1960, comprising John Lennon, Paul McCartney, George Harrison and Ringo Starr. The band received many accolades, including seven Grammy Awards, four Brit Awards, an Academy Award (for Best Original Song Score for the 1970 documentary film Let It Be) and fifteen Ivor Novello Awards."

In this example, the word "the band" in the second sentence refers to the band "The Beatles" introduced in the first sentence. While reading, you know that "the band" mentioned in the second sentence is referring to the "The Beatles" and this relationship is important for translation. There can be many such examples where words in some sentences refer to words in previous sentences. The underlying model needs to figure out these sorts of dependencies and connections for translating sentences.

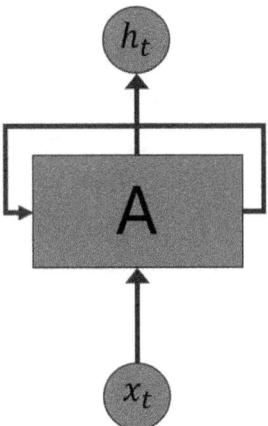

*Figure 3-2.* *A recurrent neural network*

As shown in Figure 3-2, recurrent neural networks have loops in them that allow them to persist information while processing inputs $X_t$ and outputs $h_t$. While processing, loops allow information to be passed from one step to the next. RNNs can be thought of as multiple copies of the same network, as shown in Figure 3-2, where each network is passing a message to a successor. Figure 3-3 depicts the unrolled version of the loop.

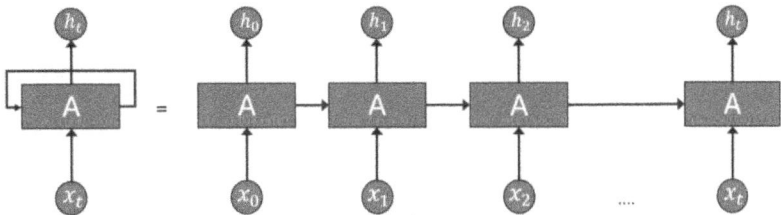

*Figure 3-3.* *Unrolled recurrent neural networks*

As illustrated in Figure 3-3, the linked-chain structure of RNNs makes them well-suited for handling sequential data and lists. When applied to language translation, for instance, an RNN processes input by feeding each word into the network, one at a time, passing along contextual information from previous words through hidden states. In a sequence-to-sequence model, each word is interpreted independently, with the encoder passing a hidden representation to the decoder, which then generates the output sentence.

To understand where RNNs fall short, consider the issue of long-term dependencies. Consider the sentence: "the rainbow in the ...." It's clear that the next word is likely "sky," and since the needed context is nearby, RNNs handle this scenario effectively. For further challenging sentences like: "I grew up in Germany... I speak fluent ....", predicting the word "German" requires remembering the reference to "Germany," which appears earlier in the sequence. RNNs struggle in such cases because, as the distance between the relevant information and its point of use increases, the ability to retain that context weakens. The core issue is that with each step in the sequence, RNNs transform the information they carry forward by applying a function. This transformation can overwrite important data without distinguishing what should be preserved. As a result, the longer the sequence, the more likely it is that valuable context is lost along the way—making RNNs less effective for tasks that depend on long-term context.

In contrast to RNNs and LSTMs, CNNs are trivial to parallelize (per layer) and, with ability to exploit local dependencies, they can address these challenges. CNNs can work in parallel where each word that comes as input can be processed at the same time and does not necessarily depend on the previous words to be translated. This is true even when the distance between the output word and the input is in the order of log(N), which is the height of the tree generated from the output. This is in contrast to the distance of the output of an RNN and an input, which is on the order of N. Models such as ByteNet and ConvS2S use CNNs that are easy to parallelize, which isn't possible with RNNs, although they seem to be better suited to sequence modeling. But the key challenge with CNNs is that their ability to determine the problem of dependencies between positions decreases rapidly with distance, which makes it critical to find another approach that can parallelize these sequential data. Transformers were created by combining CNNs with attention. Transformers perform better due to the attention mechanism helping them look at all the input and output words simultaneously and figuring out the long-term connections between words across the entire sentence in parallel, allowing for higher-quality long-distance context.

The primary advantage of the Transformer architecture lies in its ability to support parallelization. Unlike RNNs, which handle one word per time step, Transformers allow each word in the input sequence to move independently through the encoder. While the self-attention mechanism still introduces interdependencies—because each word considers all others to determine relevance—once this layer completes, the following feedforward network has no such constraints. This allows each word's path to be processed simultaneously during this stage. This capacity for parallel execution is especially beneficial in the encoder portion of the Transformer, where each token can be handled in tandem after the attention scores are computed. However, this same feature doesn't provide much advantage in the decoder, which is designed to generate output sequentially, producing one token at a time and thereby relying on previously generated tokens.

This list quickly summarizes the key strengths of the Transformers mechanism:

- Presents a completely new approach to encode each position and apply the attention mechanism in order to connect two distant words, which can then be parallelized, thus accelerating learning.

- To calculate the attention score, the Transformer architecture compares the score to all other words (their scores) in the sentence. The result of these comparisons is a score of attention for each word of the sentence. These attention scores determine the contribution of the other words to the next representation.

- Using attention blocks ultimately helps draw connections between any parts of the sequence, so long-range dependencies are not a problem and are treated as any other short-range dependencies.

- There is a significant reduction in gradient vanishing or explosion related challenges. The entire sequence is trained simultaneously, and only a few more layers are added. So gradient vanishing or explosion is rarely an issue.

- Requires fewer steps to train than an RNN.

- No recurrence in the Transformer networks allows parallel computation for every step, which enables it to effectively capture long-range dependencies in the input sequence.

So far, the chapter has gone through a detailed analysis explaining how the Transformer architecture addresses the challenges and shortcomings of neural network-based models like RNNs, LSTMs, and CNNs in natural language processing. Each of these models has different architectures and strengths and even though the Transformer is well-suited to parallel computation and the handling of long-range dependencies in

CHAPTER 3  TRANSFORMER ARCHITECTURE AND LARGE LANGUAGE MODELS

the input sequence, CNNs and RNNs have their own set of strengths. They are well-suited to solve problems involving spatial data, such as images and analyzing temporal and sequential data. After a comprehensive comparison of the Transformer architecture with other neural networks, the next section focuses on explaining the key components of the Transformer architecture.

## Key Components of the Transformer Architecture

The Transformer model is designed to convert an input sequence into a corresponding output sequence, excelling particularly with sequential data such as text. It has shown outstanding performance in tasks like machine translation, text summarization, and text generation. This cutting-edge deep learning framework has significantly transformed the landscape of natural language processing, thanks to its capability to capture and manage long-distance relationships within text. The key components—tokenizer, embedding layer, positional encoding, transformer blocks, attention mechanism, feedforward layers, and the final softmax layer—work in harmony to help the model predict the next word in a sentence with impressive precision. See Figure 3-4.

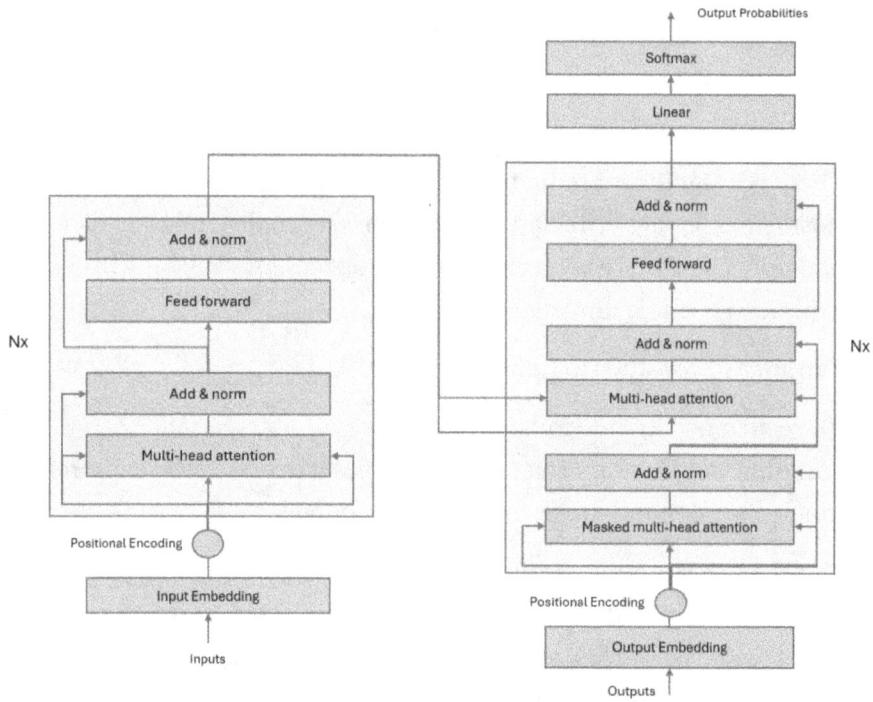

*Figure 3-4. The Transformer architecture*

# Tokenization

- Tokenization is the first step and consists of a large dataset including tokens, words, punctuation signs, and so on. The tokenization step takes every word, prefix, suffix, and punctuation, and sends them to a known token from the library. Once tokenized, each token is converted into numbers/unique IDs representing a position in a dictionary or model's vocabulary consisting of all the possible words the model can work with. The vocabulary is established during pre-training and should contain thousands if not millions of unique tokens. For example, if the sentence is "Write a poem." then the four corresponding tokens will be generated as shown in Figure 3-5. The tokenizer is the initial key component and it helps the model identify the underlying structure of the text. It handles variations in the language and handles words with multiple meanings or forms more efficiently. The choice of tokenization is influenced by the task and language being processed and can become a major factor in determining the effectiveness of the model.

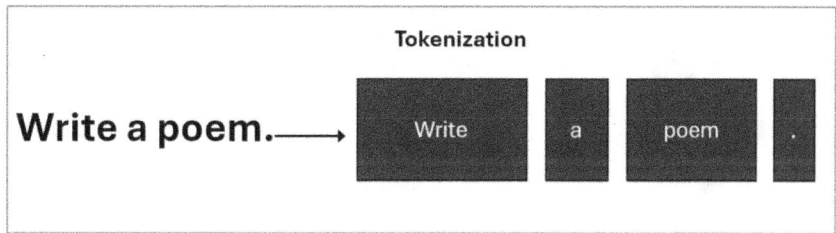

*Figure 3-5.* *Tokenization*

# Embedding

- Once the input text is tokenized, tokens are considered inputs for the machine learning models. But models can only interpret numbers, not text, so these inputs need to be converted into a numerical format known as *input embeddings*. They represent words as numbers that machine learning models can then process. Embeddings are like a dictionary that help the model understand the meaning of words by placing them in a mathematical space, where similar words are placed near each other. The embedding vectors are learned during training, and they allow the model to process the input sequence in a continuous vector space, where similar words are represented by similar vectors helping the model to understand the relationships between them. The input sequence is first encoded into a sequence of embeddings, which are high-dimensional vectors representing the meaning of each word in the sequence. Encoding the input sequence starts with mapping each word in the sentence to its corresponding embedding vector. This is done using a pre-trained embedding matrix, where each row of the matrix represents the embedding vector of a specific word.

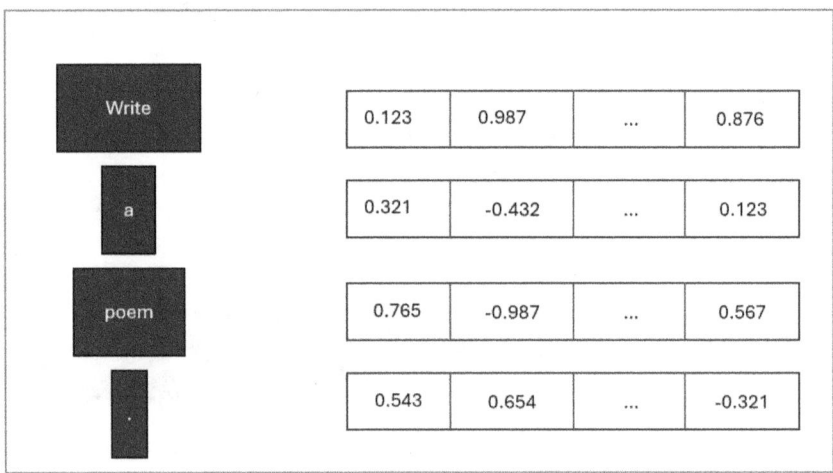

*Figure 3-6. Embedding*

Figure 3-6 depicts the embedding of the sentence "Write a poem." where the tokens are <Write>, <a>, <poem>, and <.>, which we have already tokenized in the previous segment. Each of these will be sent to a long vector, which results in four vectors. Here, each word has been matched to a token ID, and each token is mapped to a vector.

# Positional Encoding

The Transformer architecture does not use any explicit recurrence or convolution, which means it does not have a built-in understanding of the order of the input elements. According to the Vaswani et al., to overcome this limitation, the Transformer architecture uses a technique called *positional encoding*, which basically adds a dimension to the input by encoding the position of each element in the input. Positional encoding helps the model understand the order of the elements and accurately process sequential data, especially the sequence of the words in a sentence, which is significant in understanding the meaning of the text. These embeddings provide information about the relative position of each token in the sequence, allowing the model to distinguish between different positions. As depicted in Figure 3-7, the vectors corresponding to the words "Write", "a", "poem", and "." become the modified vectors that carry information about their position, labelled "Write (1)", "a (2)", "poem (3)", and ". (4)".

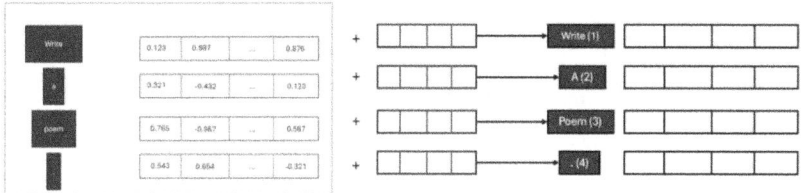

***Figure 3-7.*** *Positional encoding*

Positional encoding to the input embedding is only added in the Transformer architecture, not any other architectures/models such as RNN, LSTM or GRU where the processing of the input is sequential by default. Since words appear sequentially, the recurrent models need not care about the ordering of the words, because they know which word came first, second and so on. But in Transformer-like models, all the words in the input are passed at same time. The attention mechanism takes the weighted average of inputs to calculate the attention score. There is no way that input order is retained/learned at any other place in the architecture. Therefore, it's important to send this critical information of word order through the input embedding of the words. That is the only reason to add positional encoding to the Transformer input.

In order to differentiate between different positions in the input sequence, the positional encoding uses both sine and cosine functions of different frequencies to encode positional information. Sine and cosine functions, being periodic in nature, help represent positions as continuous signals that repeat in predictable cycles. This enables the model to learn relative positions and distances between tokens. According to Vaswani et al., the reason for using both sine and cosine functions is to allow the model to capture different patterns and avoid aliasing effects.

$$PE_{(pos,\ 2i)} = \sin\left(\frac{pos}{10000^{\frac{2i}{d_{model}}}}\right)$$

$$PE_{(pos,\ 2i+1)} = \cos\left(\frac{pos}{10000^{\frac{2i}{d_{model}}}}\right)$$

Here, *pos* signifies the specific position of a word in a sequence, while $d_{model}$ denotes the size of the model's hidden layer or embedding vector. The index *i* represents the dimension in the positional encoding vector, and the condition $0 \leq 2_i \leq d_{model}$ ensures that this index remains within the allowable dimensional range.

Each position in the sequence holds a unique positional encoding vector. Realizing $2i/d_{model} \leq 1$, the wavelengths form a geometric sequence from $2\pi$ to $2\pi * C$, where *C* is a constant used to control the total number of oscillations in the signal. The authors of the paper Vaswani et al. considered a large integer (e.g., 10,000).

According to the explanation mentioned in that paper, this function was chosen based on the hypothesis that it would allow the model to easily learn to attend to relative positions, since for any fixed offset k, $PE_{(pos+k)}$ can be represented as a linear function of $PE_{(pos)}$. Furthermore, due to the sinusoidal nature of these functions, the model can learn relative positions for any offset *k*. In other words, $PE_{(pos+k)}$ can be represented as a linear function of $PE_{(pos)}$ (think of the rotation matrix).

In easier terms, the reasoning behind using sine for even indices and cosine for odd indices is to ensure that the positional encodings have different properties. Sine and cosine functions are periodic, but they have different phases. By using both, the positional encoding can represent different positional information in a unique manner, and they can work together to capture complex patterns in the data. The division by increasing powers of 10,000 allows the model to distinguish between elements based on their relative positions in the sequence. Different frequencies are used to capture different ranges of positional information effectively. By using both sine and cosine functions, the positional encoding is designed to be continuous and smooth, which helps the model generalize well to sequences of different lengths and positions. It also avoids the problem of ambiguous positional encodings that may arise if you only used one type of function for all dimensions. (Ambiguous positional encodings occur when different positions in a sequence have indistinguishable or very similar positional encoding vectors.)

Transformers use a smart positional encoding scheme, where each *position/index* is mapped to a vector. Figure 3-8 illustrates positional encoding for the sentence, "I am a robot", where each row of the matrix in the encoded sequence is combined with its positional data, ensuring a distinct vector for every sentence. As a result, sentences containing the same words in a different arrangement receive unique vector representations.

| Sequence | Index of token | $i = 0$ | $i = 0$ | $i = 1$ | $i = 1$ |
|---|---|---|---|---|---|
| I | 0 | $PE(0,0) = \sin\left(\frac{0}{1000^{\frac{0}{4}}}\right) = \sin(0) = 0$ | $PE(0,1) = \cos\left(\frac{0}{1000^{\frac{0}{4}}}\right) = \cos(0) = 1$ | $PE(0,2) = \sin\left(\frac{0}{1000^{\frac{2}{4}}}\right) = \sin(0) = 0$ | $PE(0,3) = \cos\left(\frac{0}{1000^{\frac{2}{4}}}\right) = \cos(0) = 1$ |
| am | 1 | $PE(1,0) = \sin\left(\frac{1}{1000^{\frac{0}{4}}}\right) = \sin(1) = 0.841$ | $PE(1,1) = \cos\left(\frac{1}{1000^{\frac{0}{4}}}\right) = \cos(1) = 0.540$ | $PE(1,2) = \sin\left(\frac{1}{1000^{\frac{2}{4}}}\right) = \sin\left(\frac{1}{100}\right) = 0.01$ | $PE(1,3) = \cos\left(\frac{1}{1000^{\frac{2}{4}}}\right) = \cos\left(\frac{1}{100}\right) = .999$ |
| a | 2 | $PE(2,0) = \sin\left(\frac{2}{1000^{\frac{0}{4}}}\right) = \sin(2) = 0.909$ | $PE(2,1) = \cos\left(\frac{2}{1000^{\frac{0}{4}}}\right) = \cos(2) = -0.416$ | $PE(2,2) = \sin\left(\frac{2}{1000^{\frac{2}{4}}}\right) = \sin\left(\frac{2}{100}\right) = 0.02$ | $PE(2,3) = \cos\left(\frac{2}{1000^{\frac{2}{4}}}\right) = \cos\left(\frac{2}{100}\right) = 0.999$ |
| robot | 3 | $PE(3,0) = \sin\left(\frac{3}{1000^{\frac{0}{4}}}\right) = \sin(3) = 0.141$ | $PE(3,1) = \cos\left(\frac{3}{1000^{\frac{0}{4}}}\right) = \cos(3) = -0.990$ | $PE(3,2) = \sin\left(\frac{3}{1000^{\frac{2}{4}}}\right) = \sin\left(\frac{3}{100}\right) = 0.03$ | $PE(3,3) = \cos\left(\frac{3}{1000^{\frac{2}{4}}}\right) = \cos\left(\frac{3}{100}\right) = 0.998$ |

***Figure 3-8.*** *Positional encoding sequence for "I am a robot" with d = 4 (embedding dimension) and n = 100 (maximum sequence length)*

As shown in Figure 3-8, the positional encoding vectors possess $d_{model}$ dimensions. This is necessary, as the positional encoding vectors must be able to add elementwise with the $d_{model}$-dimensional word embedding vectors in order to be later fed into the encoder and decoder stacks of the Transformer architecture.

# Attention

To summarize briefly, you've encountered three essential components of the Transformer architecture so far: the tokenizer, embedding, and positional encoding. These elements work together to transform incoming words into tokens (tokenization), convert those words into numerical representations (embedding), and then encode the position of each word in the input sequence (positional encoding). Ultimately, this results in a vector for every token that is fed into the model.

# CHAPTER 3   TRANSFORMER ARCHITECTURE AND LARGE LANGUAGE MODELS

The next step is the Attention mechanism, as introduced by Vaswani et al., which is a core element of Transformer models and a major factor in their success. Similar to attention mechanism in humans, the methods help overcome the weakness of using information from RNN hidden layers. Attention allows the model to focus on specific parts of the input while processing it. Unlike traditional RNNs, where the input is processed sequentially, one element at a time, the Transformer architecture enables the model to attend to various parts of the input in parallel. Attention mechanisms mirror the way humans process language, where we capture relationships between words and assess the importance of those relationships. Beyond resource efficiency, Attention is critical for a model's ability to grasp the semantic meaning of raw sensory data.

*Figure 3-9. Attention mechanism*

As depicted in Figure 3-9, while interpreting this sentence, the word "green" has a strong attention relationship with "apple" and "apple" shares a strong attention relationship with "eating." This attention data is a vital step in interpreting the meaning of the sentence, and the Transformer architecture efficiently implements this mechanism in a neural network architecture. The Attention mechanism made its debut in 2014 in the domain of computer vision, with the goal of identifying which parts of the input a neural network concentrates on while generating predictions. This marked an early attempt to explain the outputs of CNNs. By 2017, attention mechanisms were incorporated into Transformer networks for language modeling. Since then, Transformers have outperformed RNNs in prediction accuracy, becoming the state-of-the-art model for NLP tasks. Unlike RNNs, which process words sequentially and face challenges with long-term dependencies, Transformers process the entire sentence simultaneously, allowing each word to assess what it should focus on. Being one of the most critical components of the Transformer architecture, the Attention mechanism basically focuses on different parts of the input sequence to identify potential dependencies and relationships by using three core components—Query, Key, and Value.

According to paper, "Attention Is All You Need," published by Vaswani et al., the mechanism compares the Query to the Keys, producing a similarity score, which is then used to weigh the values. This is finally summed to produce the output of this mechanism. Being similar to the concepts of relational database, where a query is being used to retrieve data by matching a key-value pair, the Transformer architecture works similarly. Imagine searching for something on YouTube, which stores its videos as pairs of video titles (Key) and video files (Value). When you type a search term into the YouTube search box (the Query), YouTube compares the search Query to the Keys of all videos, calculates the similarity, and ranks the Values (videos) according to the highest match. Ultimately, the Query, Key, and Value vectors are learned representations, not direct matches like in a database, allowing the model to compute contextual relevance dynamically.

## Multi-Attention

The previous section explored how to calculate a single attention matrix. This section extends this concept by computing multiple attention matrices instead of just one. But why compute several attention matrices? Rather than relying on a single attention function, the model uses multiple sets of learned linear projections to project the Queries, Keys, and Values **h** times. Each of these projection feeds into a separate "head," where the Attention mechanism operates in parallel. Each head produces a unique output, and all outputs are then concatenated and passed through another linear projection to produce the final output.

This setup allows the model to attend to different parts of a sequence simultaneously, capturing a variety of relationships and dependencies between words and phrases. By doing so, the model develops more nuanced and comprehensive representations of the input, leading to improved accuracy and performance. Multi-head attention has been a key innovation in helping language models understand and generate text with greater precision.

CHAPTER 3   TRANSFORMER ARCHITECTURE AND LARGE LANGUAGE MODELS

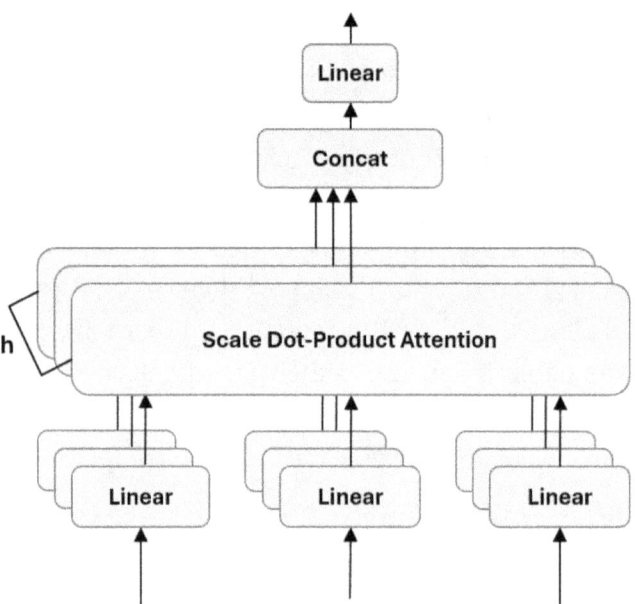

*Figure 3-10. Multi-attention*

As illustrated in Figure 3-10, within the Transformer architecture, the attention mechanism performs multiple operations in parallel. Each separate instance is referred to as an *attention head*. The Attention mechanism splits the Query, Key, and Value tensors into $N$ distinct sections, with each section processed independently by a different head. The outputs from all heads are then combined to produce a final attention score. This technique, known as *multi-head attention*, greatly improves the model's capacity to learn diverse linguistic patterns and relationships.

## Masked Multi-Head Attention

Inside the Transformer architecture, masked multi-head attention plays a key role by helping the model act like a spotlight and focus on different parts of the sentence. Masking ensures that the decoder attends only to previous tokens, enforcing autoregressive generation and preventing information leakage from future tokens. It's special because it doesn't let the model look at words that come later in the sentence. This ultimately helps the model perform tasks like talking or translating words into another language by understanding and generating sentences step by step. For instance, suppose you're trying to learn how to write a story based on a bunch of sentences, and you want to predict what the next sentence should be. But if you cheat and look at all the sentences at once, you might just copy the answer instead of actually learning how to write a good story. This is exactly what the masking helps the transformer with. A masked multi-head attention layer inside the decoder enables it to focus on various portions of the input sequence as it generates the output at each step. On the other hand, cheating-proof masking is absent on the encoder side, and while the self-attention mechanism performs a comparable function, it introduces a key distinction by blocking positions from attending to those that follow. This ensures that each word in the sequence remains uninfluenced by any future tokens.

## Feedforward Network (FFN)

The feedforward component of the Transformer architecture is a basic type of neural network where information flows in a single direction—from input to output—without looping back or forming cycles. This FFN layer takes the output from the multi-head attention mechanism and first applies a linear transformation, then a non-linear activation function, followed by another linear transformation. Essentially, once the attention mechanism captures the context and inter-word relationships, the FFN layer applies a uniform set of transformations to enhance and process this contextual data further. If the Attention mechanism is seen as the process of selecting the key ingredients for a recipe, the FFN ensures that those ingredients are fine-tuned and blended smoothly. Depending on whether the FFN is located in the encoder or decoder, its output may vary. The feedforward operation is a crucial element of the Transformer architecture, allowing the model to recognize and learn intricate patterns and connections within the data. Without it, the Transformer would be far less powerful and versatile. The feedforward operation is highly parallelizable, making it an excellent candidate for modern hardware, as computations for each node in a layer can be conducted independently from other nodes in the layer. This allows these calculations to be distributed across multiple processing units, such as CPU cores or GPU processors, thereby enabling high scalability and leveraging modern hardware effectively. The feedforward operation complements the Transformer's self-attention mechanism, and this synergy between the two operations contributes to the model's final output.

## Add & Norm Layer

The next crucial component in the Transformer architecture is the Add & Norm layer. This layer performs a residual connection by adding the original word embedding to the output from the multi-head attention. After the addition, it applies normalization to ensure the resulting embedding has a mean of zero and a variance of one. This output is passed to the feedforward block, which also includes an Add & Norm layer at its output. The Add & Norm layer is strategically placed after each self-attention and feedforward layer, performing two key functions. First, it establishes the residual connection through addition, referred to as the Add functions, and second, it enforces layer normalization, known as the Norm function. In essence, the output from the multi-head attention's linear transformation is not passed directly to the next layer. Rather than replacing the original input, it is combined with it through a residual connection within the multi-head attention block. This mitigates the vanishing gradient issue often encountered in deep neural networks. By offering an alternative route for gradients during backpropagation, it becomes easier to train deeper models. After the addition step, the resulting vector undergoes feature-wise normalization. This normalization step is designed to stabilize the training dynamics, enabling the model to learn more quickly and efficiently. The Add & Norm layer maintains a consistent distribution of activations across layers, which is especially critical in architectures as deep as Transformers.

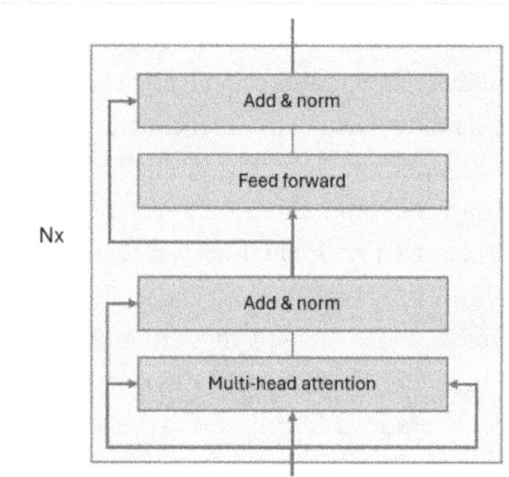

*Figure 3-11. Encoder block*

## Encoder

The architecture of the encoder stack, as shown in Figure 3-11, is designed to be structured and adaptable, allowing the Transformer to handle input data efficiently while striking a balance between performance and complexity. By incorporating multi-head attention and uniform layering, the model can capture intricate relationships within the data, enhancing its overall modeling strength. In simple terms, the encoder's job is to transform an input sequence into a sequence of continuous representations, which are then passed to the decoder. According to the paper published by Vaswani et al., the encoder is built using a stack of $N = 6$ identical layers, each containing two key sublayers. The first sublayer features a multi-head self-attention mechanism, which has been discussed in detail previously. This mechanism uses multiple attention heads, each working on a uniquely projected version of the input Queries, Keys, and Values. These projections are processed in parallel, and their results are combined to form the final output. The second sublayer is a feedforward neural network made up of two linear transformations with a Rectified Linear Unit (ReLU) activation in between.

Across all six encoder layers, each word in the input sequence undergoes the same kind of linear transformation. However, the parameters—specifically the weights ($W_1$, $W_2$) and biases ($b_1$, $b_2$)—are distinct for every layer. Additionally, each sublayer incorporates a residual connection, allowing the input to bypass the sublayer and be directly added to its output. This is immediately followed by a layer normalization step, expressed as follows:

$$layernorm(x + sublayer(x))$$

Positional encoding vectors, which have the same dimensions as the input embeddings, are generated using sine and cosine functions at various frequencies. These vectors are then added to the input embeddings to incorporate information about the position of each word in the sequence.

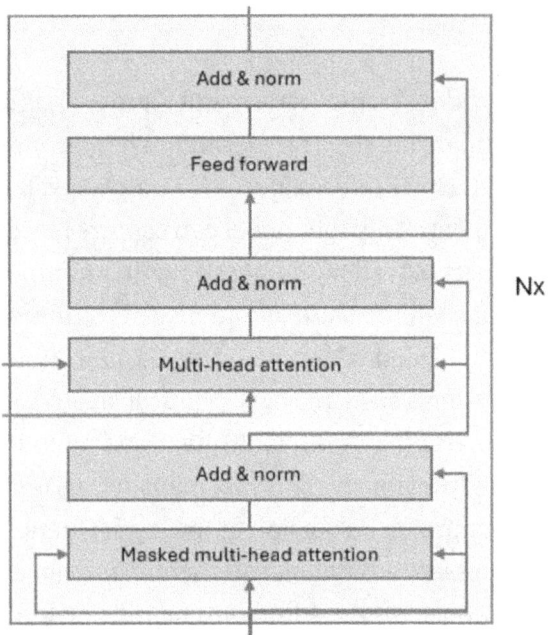

*Figure 3-12. Decoder block*

## Decoder

At the final stage of the decoder, depicted in Figure 3-12, a linear layer followed by a Softmax function transforms the decoder's output into a set of word probabilities. Similar to the encoder, the decoder consists of a stack of $N = 6$ identical layers. Each of these layers includes three distinct sublayers. The first sublayer takes the decoder's previous output, integrates positional encoding, and applies multi-head self-attention. Unlike the encoder, which attends to all the input tokens at once, the decoder can only attend to earlier tokens in the sequence. This limitation enforces a left-to-right generation process, ensuring each word prediction is based solely on prior words. The enforcement of this constraint during the multi-head attention step is achieved by applying a mask to the scaled dot product of the Q and K matrices. The second sublayer employs another multi-head attention mechanism, but in this case, the queries come from the decoder while the keys and values are derived from the encoder's output. This arrangement allows the decoder to selectively attend to relevant elements of the input sequence. The third sublayer is a feedforward neural network, functioning the same way as its counterpart in the encoder. Each of these sublayers includes a residual connection and is followed by layer normalization, mirroring the structure used in the encoder. Additionally, the decoder also uses positional encoding on its input embeddings, following the same method applied in the encoder.

Up to this point, the chapter has explored the major components and building blocks that make up the Transformer architecture. You have seen how they work together to deliver high-quality results in natural language processing and content generation. The upcoming section shifts focus to the different types of Transformer models, categorized by their use of encoder and decoder structures.

# Types of Transformers

Since its introduction in 2017, the Transformer model has served as a catalyst for a wave of innovations built upon its core architecture, extending far beyond natural language processing (NLP) into diverse domains such as protein folding prediction, cheetah locomotion training, and time series forecasting. Despite the vast array of Transformer variants that have emerged, they all share a common backbone rooted in the original Transformer framework. Some of these models utilize only the encoder or decoder components, while others integrate both. Gaining insight into the unique characteristics of the various Transformer family members and their practical implementations allows you to better understand the scope and strength of these powerful deep learning tools. Transformer model variants can generally be grouped into three main categories, discussed in the following sections.

## Encoder-Only Models

The encoder-only transformer is a streamlined version of the Transformer architecture that relies solely on the encoder component, excluding the decoder entirely. These models are tailored for tasks centered on text comprehension rather than text generation. Unlike models that both understand and create text, encoder-only models specialize in interpreting language—much like a reader who excels at analyzing and understanding but not writing or speaking it. They are particularly well-suited for applications such as sentiment analysis, text classification, and named entity recognition. In this model type, the input text is first converted into a continuous vector format via an embedding layer, which is then processed through multiple identical encoder layers. Each encoder layer includes two subcomponents: a multi-head self-attention mechanism and a feedforward neural network. The output from the final encoder layer consists of a series of hidden vectors, each corresponding to a specific token position in the input.

These hidden vectors serve as powerful features for a wide variety of NLP tasks, including language modeling, text classification, and entity recognition. A prominent example of an encoder-only model is BERT (Bidirectional Encoder Representations from Transformers). BERT adopts an encoder-only architecture but enhances it with two novel training tasks: masked language modeling and next sentence prediction. In masked language modeling, a random subset of tokens is replaced with a mask, and the model learns to predict the masked tokens using contextual information from the rest of the sentence. This task equips the model with the ability to deeply understand word relationships. In next sentence prediction, the model is trained to determine whether a pair of sentences appear consecutively in a document, allowing it to better grasp inter-sentence relationships and document-level coherence. Some more relevant examples of encoder-only Transformer architecture include:

- **RoBERTa (Robustly Optimized BERT Pretraining Approach):** A variant of BERT that only uses only the encoder part of the Transformer architecture and is pre-trained on a larger corpora of text data and fine-tuned to perform a variety of NLP tasks.

- **ELECTRA (Efficiently Learning an Encoder that Classifies Token Replacements Accurately):** Uses the encoder-only Transformer architecture, which uses a novel pre-training method called replaced token detection. It trains a discriminator to differentiate between replaced and original tokens.

- **ALBERT (A Lite BERT):** A lightweight variant of BERT that uses the encoder part of the Transformer architecture and is capable of reducing the number of parameters while maintaining the same or better performance on downstream tasks.

- **DistilBERT:** A distilled version of BERT that is smaller and faster but still maintains most of BERT's performance and uses only the encoder part of the Transformer architecture.

# Decoder-Only Transformer Models

Unlike encoder-only models that are built to understand and interpret language, decoder-only models are specifically designed for text generation. Their primary role is creation rather than comprehension. As a variation of the Transformer framework, a decoder-only model processes an input sequence of tokens by first embedding it into a continuous vector space through an embedding layer. This embedded input then moves through a stack of identical decoder layers. Each decoder layer is made up of three sub-layers: a multi-head self-attention mechanism, a multi-head cross-attention mechanism, and a feedforward neural network. The multi-head self-attention mechanism allows the model to selectively focus on different parts of the input it has already seen, while the multi-head cross-attention mechanism enables it to reference external hidden states, such as those from an encoder. The feedforward layer introduces non-linearity by further transforming the attention outputs. The output from the final decoder layer is a sequence of hidden representations, suitable for tasks like language generation and summarization. In recent developments, decoder-only architectures have gained significant traction and now serve as the backbone for state-of-the-art language models such as GPT-4 and Falcon. These models distinguish themselves by generating rather than analyzing text, setting them apart from encoder-only counterparts. What makes decoder-only models particularly powerful is their capacity to produce human-like language—capable of telling stories, answering questions, and maintaining fluid, natural conversations. This creative strength renders them ideal for numerous use cases, including chatbots, virtual assistants, content generation, narrative writing, and abstractive summarization. Some examples of decoder-only models in the Transformer architecture include:

- **Mistral 7B:** Designed as a decoder-only architecture, Mistral 7B mirrors the decoder portion of the original Transformer model. Like many of today's leading language models optimized for text generation, it operates without bidirectional context. Introduced in October 2023 by Mistral AI, a prominent French company known for its contributions to open-source AI, Mistral 7B represents a shift toward streamlined, high-performance generative models.

- **T5 (Text-to-Text Transfer Transformer):** T5 combines the encoder and decoder sections of the Transformer architecture but is also capable of functioning in a decoder-only mode. It is trained across a broad spectrum of NLP tasks, including summarization, translation, and question answering, and it is designed to produce text outputs based on given input sequences.

- **BART (Bidirectional and Auto-Regressive Transformer):** A pre-trained Transformer model that is trained on a variety of NLP tasks, such as summarization, machine translation, and text generation and uses both the encoder and decoder parts of the architecture.

## Encoder-Decoder Transformer Models

The encoder-decoder Transformer model combines both components of the original Transformer architecture—an encoder and a decoder—and is especially suited for tasks that require transforming one sequence into another, such as translation, summarization, and answering questions. In this setup, the encoder first processes the input sequence and transforms it into a series of hidden vectors, which serve as the foundation for the decoder to construct the output sequence.

To begin, the input is embedded into a continuous vector format via an embedding layer, then passed through several identical encoder layers. These layers use multi-head self-attention to help the model concentrate on various segments of the input, allowing it to understand relationships across the entire sequence and handle inputs of different lengths effectively. Once the final encoder layer completes its processing, it outputs hidden representations that are delivered to the decoder.

The decoder, structured as a stack of identical layers, includes three key sub-layers in each layer: a multi-head self-attention module, a multi-head cross-attention module, and a feedforward neural network. The self-attention mechanism enables the decoder to reference earlier tokens in the output sequence as it generates new ones. The cross-attention module, on the other hand, connects the decoder to the encoder's hidden states, allowing it to incorporate insights from the input sequence when forming the output. Encoder-decoder transformer architecture-based model types include:

- **GNMT (Google Neural Machine Translation):** A prime illustration of an encoder-decoder Transformer in action is Google's GNMT system, which facilitates translation across multiple languages. In this setup, the encoder processes the input text in the source language and converts it into a series of hidden vectors. These vectors are then passed to the decoder, which produces the translated output in the target language.

- **BERT2BERT:** Built on the encoder-decoder Transformer framework, BERT2BERT is designed specifically for text summarization. It takes a full document or source text as input and outputs a condensed summary, effectively distilling key information using pre-trained BERT models for the encoder and the decoder.

- **T5:** Developed by Google in 2019, T5 adopts an encoder-decoder structure and is versatile enough to handle a wide array of NLP tasks. It can be fine-tuned to perform translation, summarization, question answering, and other tasks, treating all of them under a unified text-to-text format.

After a detailed explanation of the different types of transformers, the next section covers the potential benefits that you can expect when using the Transformer architecture.

# Benefits and Limitations of the Transformer Architecture

In terms of natural language processing, the introduction of the Transformer architecture is of monumental importance. This section covers their benefits and limitations.

## Benefits

This section outlines some of the key benefits of the Transformer architecture:

- **Parallelization:** This feature leads to faster training times and more efficient hardware utilization. The self-attention mechanism in the Transformer architecture allows for parallelization of training. Unlike sequential models, such as recurrent neural networks (RNNs), which process sequences element by element, the Transformer architecture can process all elements simultaneously. This results in quicker training and better use of hardware resources.

- **Capturing long-range dependencies:** The self-attention mechanism in Transformers enables the capture of extensive dependencies within sequences. This capability is particularly useful for language understanding tasks, as it allows the model to capture relationships between words or tokens over long distances.

- **Scalability:** Transformers exhibit impressive scalability, with their performance improving consistently as data and computational resources increase. This scalability has made Transformers the preferred architecture for training on large datasets and achieving outstanding results in various NLP tasks.

- **Flexibility and modularity:** The Transformer architecture is highly modular and flexible, allowing easy adaptation to different tasks. Pre-trained Transformer models can be fine-tuned for specific applications, making them versatile for a wide range of natural language understanding tasks, such as machine translation, text summarization, and sentiment analysis.

- **Transfer learning and pre-training:** Transformers can be excellent choice for transfer learning scenarios in the NLP field. By utilizing pre-trained models on large datasets for language modeling, they can be fine-tuned for specific downstream tasks with smaller datasets.

- **Attention mechanism:** Attention mechanism in Transformers allows the model to focus on different parts of the input sequence, enhancing its ability to understand context and relationships. This mechanism is both more expressive and computationally efficient compared to traditional sequential models.

- **Reduced vanishing gradient problem:** Transformers mitigate the vanishing gradient problem often encountered in deep neural networks during backpropagation. The attention mechanism helps maintain non-zero gradients for distant elements in the sequence, improving gradient flow throughout training.

- **Interpretable representations:** The attention mechanism provides interpretability, allowing analysts and researchers to identify which parts of the input sequence have the most influence on predictions. This transparency is crucial for applications that require interpretability.

- **State-of-the-art performance:** Transformer based models like BERT (Bidirectional Encoder Representations from Transformers) and GPT (Generative Pre-trained Transformer) have achieved state-of-the-art performance across various benchmarks and competitions, demonstrating their effectiveness across a wide range of NLP tasks.

## Limitations

This section covers some of the key limitations of the Transformer architecture:

- **Computational complexity:** Transformers, especially large models like GPT-3, can incur significant computational costs during training and deployment. These expenses can be a major barrier to their adoption in real-world applications, particularly for smaller organizations or individuals without access to substantial computing resources.

- **Long-term dependencies:** Transformers may face difficulties in effectively modeling long-term dependencies within sequences, particularly when these dependencies span multiple tokens.

- **Attention bias:** Transformers rely on attention mechanisms to focus on the most relevant parts of the input sequence. However, these mechanisms can sometimes exhibit bias, leading to suboptimal outcomes.

- **Interpretability:** Transformers present challenges in terms of interpretability due to their end-to-end training approach, which lacks the clear, interpretable intermediate representations found in some other neural network architectures.

- **Limited models:** While transformer models have achieved remarkable results across various natural language processing tasks, there is still a need for models that can generalize to new domains or languages. Current Transformer models may struggle to generalize to low-resource languages or highly specialized domains with limited training data.

Despite these downsides, the Transformer architecture remains a powerful and widely used tool in NLP, and research is ongoing to mitigate its computational requirements and improve its interpretability and robustness.

# Conclusion

Generative AI, driven by the Transformer model, represents a transformative paradigm shift in natural language processing and creative expression. It was introduced by Vaswani et al. in their seminal paper, "Attention Is All You Need." By leveraging the innovative attention mechanism, the Transformer architecture allows machines to understand context and generate human-like text with exceptional precision and coherence. The attention mechanism, a cornerstone of the Transformer architecture, assigns significance to each word relative to others in the sequence, emphasizing those most appropriate to the current context. In language generation, this capability is particularly powerful. Instead of relying solely on previous words to predict the next one, the Transformer model evaluates all words and determines their relevance. This approach allows the model to capture complex relationships, nuances, and dependencies within sentences, leading to greater accuracy and coherence in language generation. This chapter explored the Transformer architecture's potential use cases, benefits, and limitations. In summary, the Transformer architecture has significantly impacted NLP, driving advancements in areas such as language translation, text classification, and language generation. With ongoing progress in deep learning research, the Transformer model is set to remain at the forefront of NLP innovations for the foreseeable future.

# CHAPTER 4

# Large Language Models (LLMs)

Large language models (LLMs) are a type of Generative AI technology that have gained significant attention in recent years. Trained on massive amounts of data, these models are capable of generating human-like text and carrying out complex tasks with remarkable accuracy. After comprehensively explaining Generative AI and the foundation model, this chapter introduces the concept of LLMs, followed by their significance in the area of NLP, history, architecture, key components, and adaptation methodologies.

## Large Language Models

Language plays a crucial role in human communication, self-expression, and interactions with machines. The growing demand for machines to handle increasingly complex language tasks—such as translation, summarization, information retrieval, and conversational interaction—has driven the development of generalized models. Recent advances in language models are largely attributed to the introduction of transformers, greater computational power, and the availability of vast amounts of training data. These factors have enabled the revolutionary creation of LLMs, which can perform at near-human levels on various tasks. LLMs are deep learning models, specifically transformer-based, and they are pre-trained on massive datasets and aligned with human preferences through meta-training. They are termed "large" because they consist of hundreds of millions to billions of parameters, which define the model's behavior. They are trained on extensive corpora of text data.

The backbone of LLMs is a revolutionary neural network architecture called the Transformer architecture, which was introduced by Vaswani et al. from Google in 2017, in their seminal paper called "Attention Is All You Need." Since its inception, the

# CHAPTER 4   LARGE LANGUAGE MODELS (LLMS)

Transformer architecture has become the dominant model for machine translation and other natural language processing tasks, such as text summarization, question answering, and natural language inference, along with image and multimedia content processing. The large scale of these models allows them to capture more subtle patterns in language, improving their ability to understand and generate text, while the vast pre-training data equips the models with knowledge from diverse text sources. Pre-training equips the model with universal language knowledge, while meta-training aligns LLMs to act according to the user's intentions. Starting with models like GPT-1 and BERT, and advancing to more recent models like DeBERTa, pre-trained language models have made significant strides, reducing the amount of labelled data required to train task-specific models. These pre-trained language models follow the "pre-train then fine-tune" paradigm, where the model is first pre-trained and later adapted for downstream tasks through fine-tuning.

But task-specific fine-tuning to make pre-trained models adapt to new or specific-task always requires labelled data. This results in the creation of separate copies of the pre-trained model for each task, which increases both development and deployment costs. To address these limitations, the research community has focused on developing more advanced models, such as LLMs, that can generalize to unseen tasks without the need for task-specific training. The era of LLMs began with GPT-3, whose success spurred the development of other LLMs such as PaLM, Chinchilla, GLaM, LaMDA, Gopher, BLOOM, LlaMA, and others. LLMs represent a distinct class of pre-trained models that are achieved by scaling up the model size, the pre-training corpus, and the computational power, as illustrated in Figure 4-1.

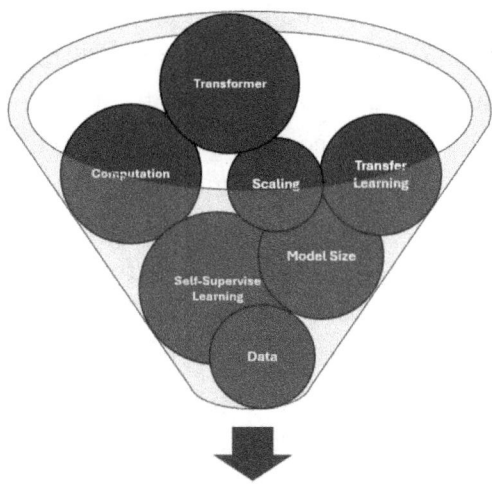

***Figure 4-1.*** *A large language model (LLM)*

Now that you have been introduced to LLMs, the next section explores the evolution of LLMs over the last few decades.

# The Evolution of LLMs

The origins of LLMs stem from the rise and development of neural network-based methods in natural language processing. Early NLP systems relied on rule-based techniques and statistical models to process language, but these methods often struggled to understand the context of a specific discourse. Over the years, NLP has evolved through various stages, starting all the way from statistical to neural language modeling followed by the pre-trained language model stage to today's large language models. In the 1940s, Warren McCulloch and Walter Pitts introduced the concept of artificial neural networks (ANNs). The 1950s and 1960s saw the development of the first language models, which included both early neural networks and rule-based models. However, they were limited in their capabilities and faced challenges in handling the complexities of advanced language tasks. In the 1980s and 1990s, statistical language models were introduced in the fields of NLP and machine learning (ML) to capture and quantify statistical patterns and relationships within language data. These models outperformed early neural networks and rule-based systems in terms of accuracy and could process large datasets with ease. However, despite their success in various

NLP applications, statistical language models struggled with predicting semantic relationships between concepts and understanding the full context of language. A major breakthrough occurred in the mid-2000s with the introduction of word embeddings, a method for representing words in a continuous vector space that captured semantic relationships among words and at the same time reduced computational costs by mapping words to a lower-dimensional space. While not classified as LLMs, word embeddings played a significant role in advancing natural language understanding and laid the groundwork for more complex models. The introduction of neural language models in the mid-2010s further advanced LLMs, utilizing deep learning to learn language patterns from large datasets and employing artificial neural networks to understand, generate, or predict human language. In 2016, Google introduced its first large neural language model, which utilized deep learning techniques. Known as the Google Neural Machine Translation (GNMT) model, it was trained on vast amounts of multilingual data, marking a major milestone in machine translation.

The Transformer architecture was introduced in 2017, and it not only modernized NLP but also played a key role in the development of models like BERT (Bidirectional Encoder Representations from Transformers) and GPT (Generative Pre-trained Transformers). Transformer models use a self-attention mechanism to evaluate the relative importance of individual words in a sentence, capturing complex relationships in the text. The Transformer model was developed to address limitations in earlier models, such as RNNs (Recurrent Neural Networks) and LSTM (Long Short-Term Memory) networks. Transformer models offer significant advantages, including their ability to capture long-term dependencies in language and train concurrently on multiple GPUs with vast parameters, enabling the creation of much larger models. Following the success of BERT, numerous variations and subsequent models, such as RoBERTa, T5, and DistilBERT, were developed to tackle diverse tasks across multiple domains. In 2018, OpenAI introduced the first version of the GPT model, known as GPT-1. It was considered to be a major advancement in the field of natural language processing. GPT-1 demonstrated the ability to generate contextually relevant text, showcasing the transformative potential of transformers in NLP. GPT-2, the successor to GPT-1, was designed to address the shortcomings of its predecessor. In 2020, OpenAI released GPT-3, trained on a massive dataset and capable of generating highly coherent and natural text. After the success of GPT-3, OpenAI developed successor models like InstructGPT, Codex, ChatGPT, and GPT-4. Meanwhile, Google introduced models such as GLaM, PaLM, PaLM2, LaMDA, and Bard. DeepMind created models like Gopher, Chinchilla, AlphaCode, and Sparrow. Figure 4-2 shows the evolution of different LLMs over the years.

CHAPTER 4  LARGE LANGUAGE MODELS (LLMS)

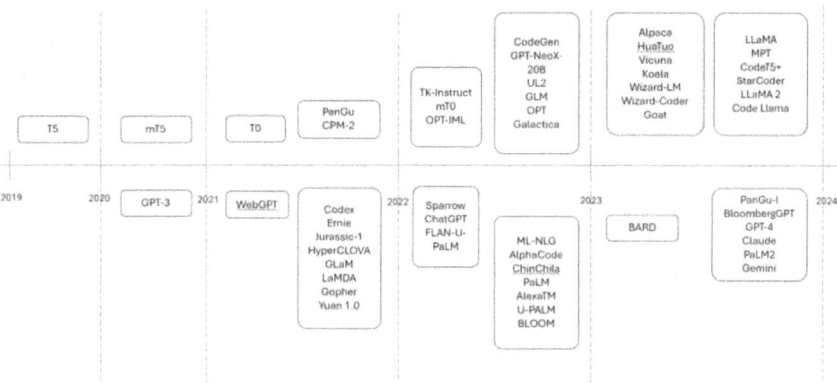

*Figure 4-2.  Evolution of LLMs*

A comprehensive introduction followed by explaining the significance and evolution of LLM has set the context, and the next section dives deeper to explain the LLM architecture and its associated components.

# The LLM Architecture

The Transformer architecture introduced by Vaswani et al. in their seminal paper called "Attention Is All You Need" in 2017 laid the foundation for today's LLMs, letting neural networks process sequential data more efficiently instead of relying on iterative methods. LLMs today utilize an attention-based mechanism to capture global input-output dependencies. The model is capable of handling inputs of varying lengths and can dynamically adjust its focus depending on the sequence length. As a result, it has become the go-to architecture in many fields, often replacing sophisticated recurrent or convolutional neural networks with much more efficient structure. Chapter 3 explains each building blocks of the Transformer architecture in detail. This list briefly recaps each component of the Transformer architecture in the context of LLMs:

- **Tokenization:** The tokenizer is the first component in the Transformer model pipeline and it converts the raw input into tokens, which are basically numerical representations of individual words or sub-words. Characters, sub-words, symbols, or words may serve as tokens, contingent upon the language model's dimensions and nature. Various tokenization algorithms are utilized in LLMs, including WordPiece, UnigramLM, and Byte Pair Encoding.

- **Input embedding:** Tokenization initiates the process of transforming input text into meaningful elements where each token is assigned a unique numerical identifier, connecting linguistic content to a numerical form. This numerical form is referred to as an *input embedding*. These input embeddings are the numerical counterparts of words, which the models then process. Similar to a dictionary, these embeddings help the model grasp the meaning of words by positioning them in a mathematical space, where related words are located closer to one another. The model is trained to generate embeddings that represent words with similar meanings using vectors of equal dimensions.

- **Encoder:** The encoder in the Transformer architecture is a critical component. It interprets the input sequence. It consists of multiple layers that work together to interpret input sequence and each of these multiple layers is basically a combination of the Attention mechanism and a feedforward network. Inside the Transformer architecture, the primary role of the encoder is to perform tasks like text classification (e.g., sentiment analysis), named entity recognition, and question answering.

- **Positional encoding:** As part of the Transformer architecture, positional encoding plays a critical role in providing positional information for each token in the input sequence. This information is key to understanding the order of the input sequence, especially for NLP-related tasks like understanding language. As transformers process information in parallel and independently, position encoding helps the model understand the position of the elements in the input sequence.

- **Self-attention:** In contrast to conventional sequential models, Transformer models rely on self-attention mechanisms, which enable them to determine dynamically, the relative relevance of various items in a input sequence. According to the seminal paper "Attention Is All You Need" published by Vaswani et al., this mechanism enables the model to capture contextual information and long-range dependencies, leading to a deeper comprehension of intricate patterns. This ultimately helps drive the interpretation of the input sequence by taking the entire context and the importance of different words relative to other words into consideration.

- **Multi-head attention:** This is the self-attention mechanism that can be run in parallel and multiple times (heads) with concatenated results linearly transformed to produce the final output. In this kind of Attention mechanism, each attention head processes a unique projection of the input, and their outputs are concatenated and linearly transformed to produce the final representation. Consequently, this enhances the representation of the input contexts, as it merges information from distinct features of the Attention mechanism within a specific range, which could be either short or long. This approach allows the attention mechanism to jointly function, resulting in better network performance.

- **Feedforward neural network:** A feedforward neural network is critical in the Transformer architecture. It processes the information collated from the previous layer using the Attention mechanism. Made up of connected layers and activation functions, this network adds non-linearity to the model and helps it capture more complex relationships in the data. The feedforward network is comprised of two linear layers with a ReLU activation function in between. It basically allows the model to extract higher-level features or deeper meaning from the input data more compactly and represent the input more usefully.

- **Layer normalization:** After each sub-layer like feedforward and self-attention, layer normalization is applied to normalize the output from the previous layer and help stabilize the learning process throughout the architecture. Normalization not only helps stabilize but also prevents the model from amplifying undesired features or gradients during training (i.e., it fuels the stability and efficiency of the transformer architecture).

- **Decoder:** The primarily role of decoder is generating an output sequence based on the encoded information. Similar to the encoder, the decoder consists multiple layers with self-attention and feedforward components. The decoder also applies the Attention mechanism to generate meaningful output based on positionally encoded information from the input sequence. The positional information helps the decoder effectively capture the structure within the sequences. The decoder also has an attention mechanism that helps improve the output's quality by leveraging contextual information received from the encoder. The dependency between the encoder-decoder in a transformer is significant where the encoder processes the input sequence based on the representation, and the decoder provides the desired output sequence.

- **Linear layers and Softmax:** Linear layers are fully connected neural network layers that transform the output embedding into a higher dimensional space. This step is required to convert the output embedding into the original input space. This transformation enhances the expressiveness of the representation, allowing the model to capture more complex patterns and relationships in the data. Besides, the Softmax function generates a probability distribution for each output token in the developed vocabulary, allowing you to generate probabilistic output tokens.

- **Output embedding:** Similar to input embeddings, output embeddings assist the model in interpreting the order of words in an input sequence. According to the seminal paper by Vaswani et al., 2017, the output embedding, along with the masked multi-head attention section, ensures that predictions at any position can only rely on the known outputs from earlier positions. In other words, it ensures that the model looks only at the past, not the future, when making predictions.

Chapter 3 and this section covered the key components involved in the LLM architecture and how they play a crucial role in the formation of the language models. This next section dives deep into the development process of language models by exploring the steps involved in their learning and development process.

# The LLM Development Process

Harnessing the power of LLMs doesn't mean you have to train them from the ground up, which can be technically tricky and extremely resource intensive. The effectiveness of LLMs in NLU and NLG tasks hinges on a sophisticated interplay of various tasks involved in its development. This includes pre-training, fine-tuning, data augmentation, prompt engineering, and evaluation, along with others. These key components of LLM development collectively empower these models to understand and generate human-like text:

- **Pre-training:** Pre-training is the foundational phase in the development of LLMs, where they are exposed to extensive and diverse text corpora. This phase equips LLMs with a broad understanding of language, covering aspects like grammar, syntax, semantics, and general world knowledge. During pre-training, LLMs are trained to predict the next word in a sequence, which helps them learn patterns and dependencies within language. Key factors such as the choice of training data, the scale of the dataset, and the duration of training significantly impact the model's proficiency. While pre-training provides LLMs with a general understanding of language, fine-tuning hones their abilities for specific natural language understanding and for natural language generation tasks. Pre-training serves as the foundation for an LLM's capabilities. Through pre-training on large collections of text, LLMs pick up the key abilities needed to understand and produce language. The model's overall performance heavily depends on how big and how good that training data is. To pre-train LLMs successfully, it is essential to carefully design model architectures, leverage acceleration techniques, and optimize training methods. In comparison to smaller-scale language models, LLMs have a greater need for high-quality data during pre-training, and their overall capacity is heavily dependent on the scale and preprocessing of the pre-training corpus.

- **Fine-tuning:** During this phase, the model undergoes additional training, but now on a smaller, more targeted dataset that may be either labelled or unlabeled, depending on the specific task at hand. This dataset is tailored to the application in which the LLM will be used, such as medical terminology for healthcare or legal language for legal applications. Fine-tuning enables the model to adjust its pre-trained parameters to better understand and generate text that is aligned with its intended use case. This stage requires fewer resources compared to pre-training, both in terms of data volume and computational power, due to the narrower learning scope.

- **Prompt engineering and context management:** Prompt engineering is a vital component of working with language models like GPT. This practice involves designing the input prompt to effectively steer the language model toward generating the desired output or completion. Achieving optimal results often requires several iterations of refinement, a process known as *prompt engineering*. Managing context is also crucial in natural language generation tasks, ensuring that LLMs produce text that is coherent and contextually appropriate. Techniques such as providing explicit context or using specific instructions help guide the generation process to yield more accurate results. LLMs can be prompted in various ways, including these:

    - **Zero-shot prompting:** In this style of prompting, the LLM doesn't need any examples to answer questions. As zero-shot learners, LLMs are capable of handling queries they haven't encountered before. In the context of zero-shot prompting, no example needs to be included as part of the input prompt for reference and LLMs can still respond without seeing examples.

- **In-context learning:** In contrast to zero-shot prompting, this pattern of prompt engineering, which is also known as *few-shot learning,* requires multiple input and output combination samples to be included in the input prompt. In this context, the LLM basically generates responds based on the demonstration of input and output combinations. For instance, providing input-output pairs like 'Input: Translate "hello" to French. Output: Bonjour' enables the LLM to learn from context and generate similar translations.

- **Chain-of-Thought (CoT):** LLMs can also be tailored to perform reasoning-oriented tasks, analysis and planning, and solve logical problems by deploying one of the diverse prompt engineering techniques called Chain-of-Thought (CoT). CoT is a special prompt engineering technique that prompts LLMs through demonstrations of reasoning information combined with inputs and outputs. This can ultimately help the model generate outcomes by performing step-by-step reasoning.

- **Parameters:** Parameters represent key variables in the LLM's neural network, which can bring variations to the output generated by the LLM. These parameters represent the weight and biases being used to learn the relationship between input and output parameters and you can tune them necessarily to influence the creativity, diversity, and quality of the delivered text. Some of the well-known LLM parameters include top-p, temperature, no. of tokens, presence and frequency penalty, and so on. The more parameters there are, the more complex and diverse the LLM is. The list of parameters has changed significantly over the years and different LLMs have varying numbers of parameters, ranging all the way from a few billion to hundreds of billions. For instance, OpenAI's GPT-4 and Google's PaLM-2 are known for their large-scale parameter counts, while smaller models focus on efficiency.

- **Reinforcement learning with human feedback (RLHF):** RLHF plays an important role in how LLMs are developed and fine-tuned. It works especially well for tasks where the goals are tricky to describe or hard to measure directly. For instance, it's challenging to mathematically define what constitutes "funny," but humans can easily evaluate and rate jokes produced by a LLM. By converting this human feedback into a reward function, the LLM's joke-writing capabilities can be significantly improved. In a 2017 paper, Paul F. Christiano from OpenAI, along with researchers from OpenAI and DeepMind, demonstrated the success of RLHF in training AI models for complex tasks such as Atari games and robotic locomotion. RLHF is especially helpful when standard reward systems don't quite work. Take training a customer service chatbot, for instance. Traditional reinforcement learning might just reward it for finishing a conversation, which could lead to quick but unhelpful replies. RLHF, however, involves human feedback on the chatbot's responses, considering not just content but also tone and helpfulness. This feedback is incorporated into the reward model, refining the chatbot's performance to better address customer needs.

- **Retrieval-augmented generation (RAG):** LLMs have demonstrated remarkable achievements, yet they continue to encounter notable limitations, especially in tasks that demand domain-specific knowledge or rely heavily on accurate, up-to-date information. A key challenge for LLMs is the generation of "hallucinations" when presented with queries that extend beyond their training data. To address these issues, RAG has been developed as a technique to enhance LLMs by incorporating relevant information retrieved from external knowledge sources. By leveraging semantic similarity calculations to find pertinent document chunks, RAG allows LLMs to reference external knowledge and thus significantly reduces the chances of generating incorrect information. This integration has contributed to the widespread adoption of RAG, positioning it as a critical technology for advancing chatbot functionality and improving the applicability of LLMs in real-world scenarios.

- **Fine-tuned models:** In addition to various methods of prompt engineering and RAG-based techniques, fine-tuning is one of the potentiation options to tailor LLM for specific use cases, especially catering to enterprise business processes. Fine-tuning LLMs on specific knowledgebases and updated weights requires no additional training or examples to address queries related to the relevant context. Fine-tuning LLMs can provide effective solutions, including high ROI, lower privacy risks, and lack of token size constraints. It also leads to better latency, as the model already absorbed the entire context. Although fine-tuning may look attractive in some contexts, fine-tuning an LLM can be highly resource intensive and preparing data in the right format can be time consuming. Also fine-tuning does not guarantee the prevention of hallucinations, biases, or inaccuracies.

Even though adoption of LLMs can be driven by various means and can vary case to case, RAG is one of the most promising and futuristic techniques. The next section discusses its significance.

# Why RAG?

In the world of conversational AI, LLMs are like encyclopedias packed with general knowledge. They cover a wide range of topics but often fall short when it comes to detailed, local information—like the specifics of a company's internal system or the details in a niche research paper. To answer any question, an LLM has to go through a heavy computational process, blending the input with millions (or even billions) of parameters that make up the model. And training an LLM for this magnitude of computational process is orders of magnitude harder. Training an LLM means running multiple iterations of the process to determine the best value for the parameter within the model.

Different algorithms can calculate the best weights, but this requires an iterative process of running the model on given input and then backpropagating an adjustment so that the answer improves. This process is repeated multiple times with many inputs and eventually the model gets trained. While model inference can take seconds, training the model may take weeks and massive clusters of GPUs. Also, updating the model with any new or updated information is massively costly and most companies don't have the resources to support the model training process and cannot simply inject new information.

Sending new information through prompts is also limited, due to limitations in the length of context window, which potentially comes in sizes of 10K, 20K, or more (although much larger context windows are becoming available in the recent times).

This is where introduction of RAG in the context of conversational AI is considered to be a significant paradigm shift. With RAG, providing additional and updated knowledge to LLMs is much easier and more cost effective. It requires no additional training. RAG was introduced by researchers at Meta in 2020, combining the natural language generation (NLG) abilities of LLMs with an information retrieval (IR) system to produce more accurate and useful responses. RAG has two phases—retrieval and generation. Retrieval is where the underlying algorithms perform the searches to retrieve snippets of information relevant to the user prompt. Generation produces relevant responses to user's query based on the retrieved context. RAG helps deliver a more precise response by injecting a vast array of external information sources in addition to the model's internal knowledge—through conversational AI in a cost-effective manner.

Being empowered by RAG, today's LLM-based bots can deliver responses in much more personalized way without any human written scripts and retrain of the model on fresh examples. By simply uploading the latest documents or policies, LLMs can immediately start acting on them to retrieve the required information in open-book mode and deliver responses. Even though RAG is a highly simplified approach, higher latency and ethical considerations regarding data retrieval can still be a concern in many contexts.

Understanding RAG's importance has set the context for the next set of discussions, and the next section discusses the components that lay the foundation of the RAG architecture.

# The Key Components of RAG

This chapter as thus far explained the potential value of RAG as a key technique toward curving LLM into an enterprise context without any need to retrain or tune. This section discusses the key components that act as the foundation of this technique. The key components are discussed in the following sections.

# Embedding

Embedding is one of the most notable components in the RAG technique. It basically takes care of syntactic and semantic relationships of words and phrases present in the input. Embedding basically creates vector representations of the user prompts and resources from the given knowledgebase within a continuous and high-dimensional space. In a vector space, things that have similar meanings or are used in similar contexts are positioned close to one another. This makes it easier later on to find and retrieve information that's semantically related to what the user is asking. However, it all depends on the embedding model and how good the vocabulary of the embedding model is. Each embedding model is trained using its own unique vocabulary—for instance, BERT has a vocabulary of about 30,000 words. Even if a word isn't in its vocabulary, the model still needs to calculate a vector for it. To make this work, many models split words into smaller sub-words and treat those as separate tokens, or they combine the vectors of the sub-words to form one overall embedding.

In the context of RAG LLMs, various types of embeddings can be used, including Word2Vec, GloVe, and BERT embeddings, each with unique characteristics. For example, Word2Vec picks up on word meanings by looking at which words show up together, while BERT embeddings—built using Transformer models—go a step further by understanding the meaning of words based on the context around them. Embeddings are categorized into two categories—word and sentence embedding. Word embedding represents an $n$-dimensional vector space representation of words, where semantically similar words (e.g., "boat" and "ship") are positioned closer together in the vector space based on the training data. Sentence embedding is quite similar to Word embedding; it embeds the whole sentence instead of words.

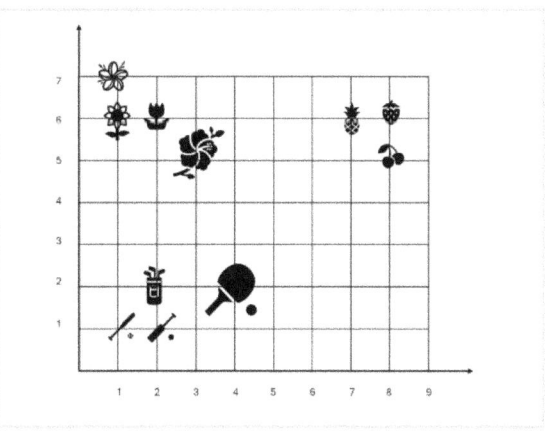

***Figure 4-3.*** *Embedding*

## CHAPTER 4   LARGE LANGUAGE MODELS (LLMS)

Embedding, demonstrated in Figure 4-3, shows that similar words appear close to each other, and words that are different appear far away from each other. For example, in the embedding in Figure 4-3, the coordinates for lotus are [2, 6], which are close to rose [2, 7], but far from orange [8, 6]. A new word like *hibiscus* might be placed somewhere near the upper left, while a word like *racquet* could end up closer to the lower left of the plane.

## Vector Databases

As part of the RAG technique, embeddings produced by LLMs consist of numerous features, making their representation complex and difficult to manage. An embedding essentially captures various dimensions of data, allowing AI models to recognize relationships, patterns, and hidden structures. Managing vector embeddings with traditional scalar-based databases poses challenges, as these databases aren't equipped to handle the scale and complexity involved; this is what triggered the paradigm shift and introduced vector databases. Vector databases are crafted to support the query and storage of multidimensional vector embedding structures in an optimized manner.

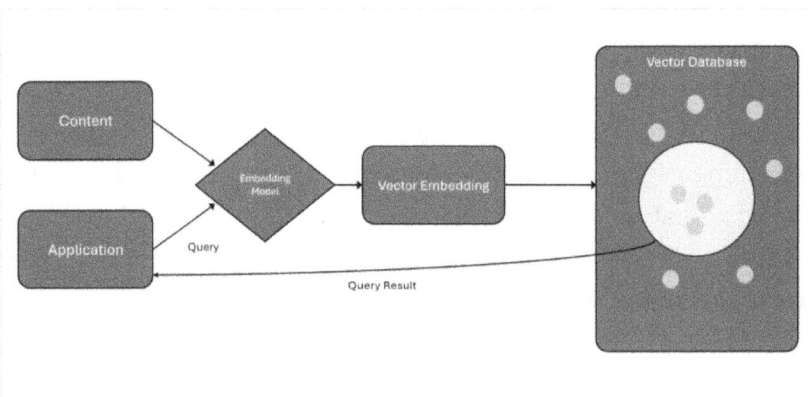

***Figure 4-4.*** *Vector database*

As depicted in Figure 4-4, vector databases allow for easy searching, high performance, scalability, and efficient data retrieval by comparing values and finding similarities between vectors. According to Wikipedia, a vector database—also known as a vector store—is a type of database that holds vectors (which are fixed-length lists of numbers) along with other kinds of data. These databases often implement Approximate Nearest Neighbor (ANN) algorithms, enabling users to search the database with a query vector to retrieve the most closely related records. Vector databases are designed to store and query high-dimensional vector embeddings efficiently, supporting fast similarity searches using Approximate Nearest Neighbor (ANN) algorithms.

In the field of ML, a vector is essentially a collection of numerical values representing the features or characteristics of multi-dimensional objects, such as words or images. For LLMs, an embedding model generates these embeddings—vectors that encapsulate the most important features of a data point. For instance, in natural language processing, a model might generate embeddings for words or sentences. These embeddings are useful for tasks such as clustering, classification, and anomaly detection. Vector databases are highly efficient for storing and querying these embeddings, making them ideal for a wide range of ML applications.

## Similarity Searches

The next most pivotal component that empowers the RAG technique is its vector-searching capability, which drives swift and accurate data-driven decisions. Similarity searching is essential for picking out the most relevant matches from the many vectors stored in the vector database. With the exponential growth in the multi-dimensional enterprise, data saved in the vector database requires efficient and precise mechanism for data retrieval. Similarity searching addresses this exact need by ensuring efficient comparison and ranking of vectors with speed and very low computational resources.

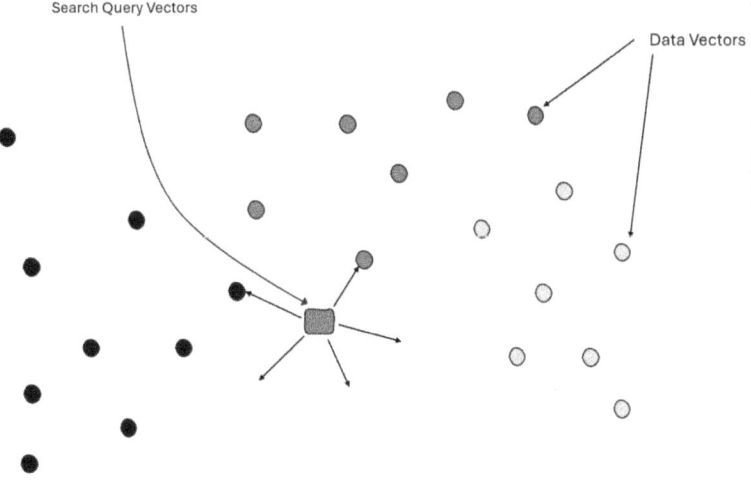

***Figure 4-5.*** *Vector search*

Similarity measures basically apply mathematical methods to determine how similar vectors are placed in the vector space. Figure 4-5 shows this concept. Based on the similarity measure, the vectors most similar to the given query vector are retrieved from the vector database based on comparison. In this context, the result obtained from the vector database depends on the choice of similarity measure.

When running a search, the first step is to turn the search query into a vector embedding using the same LLM or method that was used earlier to embed the data stored in the vector database. Next, the system compares the query embedding with the stored data embeddings by calculating the distance between them to find possible matches. But not all the data will be useful—only the vectors closest to the query are picked as candidates. Keeping the number of these closest matches to a set limit can also help improve accuracy. At present, there are different ways to measure the distance between the vectors. The Cosine Similarity method looks at the angle between two vectors; the Euclidean Distance method measures the straight-line distance between them; and the Dot Product method considers both the magnitudes and the angle. Reranking the steps based on how relevant the returned results are helps improve the overall quality of what RAG retrieves.

## How RAG Works

Since the inception of LLM, RAG has become one of most adopted techniques, empowering LLMs to anchor the generated response based on information curated through different search algorithms. RAG basically combines the query and retrieved context passed to the LLM in the form of a prompt to facilitate a more informed and contextually grounded response.

The evolution of RAG in the context of large models can be understood through several distinct phases. Early RAG efforts focused on enhancing LLMs with external knowledge during inference, evolving to include fine-tuning techniques. RAG research began to focus on supplying LLMs with better information during inferences to handle more complex, knowledge-intensive tasks, driving rapid advancements in the field. As RAG research advanced, its scope expanded from merely improving the inference phase to also incorporating fine-tuning techniques for LLMs, enabling further performance gains. RAG follows a structured process, often referred to as the "Retrieve-Read" framework, which consists of three key stages—indexing, retrieval, and generation.
In the indexing phase, raw data from various formats such as PDF, HTML, Word, and

Markdown is cleaned, extracted, and converted into a unified plain text format. This is followed by a segmentation, which basically converts the text into smaller and manageable chunks, and this ultimately helps win over the contextual limitation of LLMs. These chunks are encoded into vector representations using an embedding model and stored in a vector database, facilitating efficient similarity searches during retrieval.

During the retrieval phase of RAG, the model basically converts the user query into a vector representation by leveraging the same encoding model applied at the indexing phase followed by calculating the similarity score between indexed text chunks vectors and query vectors. This is further followed by retrieval of the top $K$ chunks with the highest similarity. These retrieved text chunks then go into the generation phase as the expanded context.

During the generation phase, the query and the retrieved documents are combined into a prompt that is provided to the LLM, which then generates a response. The model may choose its approach based on the task at hand—either drawing from its internal parametric knowledge or relying solely on the information retrieved from external documents. In the case of ongoing dialogues, the system can incorporate prior conversational history into the prompt, enabling effective multi-turn interactions.

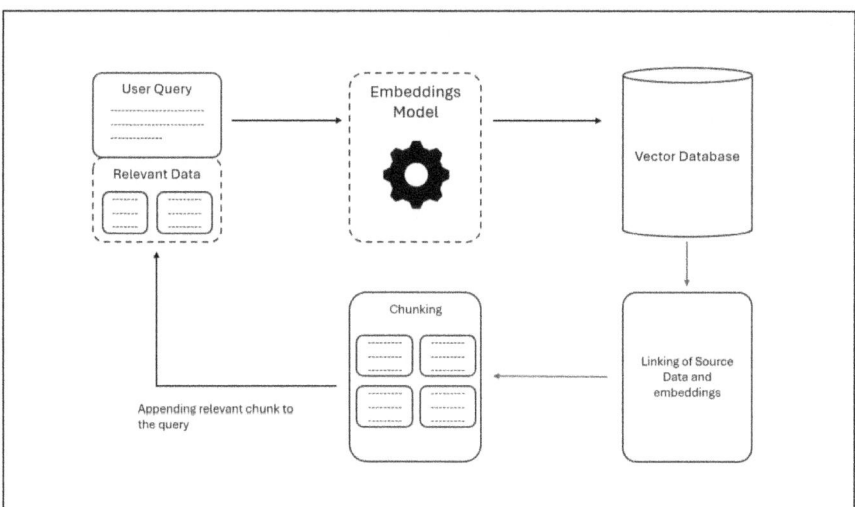

***Figure 4-6.*** *How RAG works*

Figure 4-6 is a representation of the underlying process flow of RAG, initiated based on a user query in the form of a simple prompt. Subsequent steps in the RAG workflow include the following:

- Query **processing**: The process begins with a user submitting a query, which can be a question, prompt, or any input requiring a response from the language model. RAG then converts the user's query into a vector representation. This vector is compared to those stored in the vector database using a relevancy search algorithm. The algorithm finds documents in the knowledgebase that have a similar meaning to the query.

- Embedding **model**: After the query is submitted, it's processed by an embedding model, which transforms the query into a numerical vector representation. Since language models work more effectively with numbers than with raw text, any external data must be converted into a format that the system can understand. The embedding model performs this conversion by representing the data as vectors, which are stored in a vector database.

- Vector **database** (DB) **retrieval**: The vector representation of the query is then used to search through a vector database, which contains pre-computed vectors representing potential contexts. The system pulls the most relevant context for the query by checking which vectors are most similar. This database is optimized for storing high-dimensional data and conducting fast similarity searches, making it an essential tool for retrieving the relevant information.

- Retrieved **contexts:** Once the relevant context is found, it's fed into the LLM as input. The LLM then uses this extra information to help create a more accurate and high-quality response.

- LLM **response generation:** The response generation part in the RAG workflow is all about the LLM using both the user prompt and the enhanced context to generate a response. The enhanced context provided to the LLM ensures that the response generated by LLM is not only based on its internal knowledge but also augmented with specific details from the provided context data.

- Maintaining **data freshness:** To keep the retrieved data up to date, the external data sources and their vector representations should be updated regularly. This can happen through automated real-time updates or periodic batch updates, depending on what the system needs.

- **Final response:** The LLM's final answer is shaped by the external data it retrieved along the way. This leads to a response that's more accurate, detailed, and relevant to the context.

# Conclusion

So far, you have learned how the field of LLMs has undergone a remarkable evolution, with extraordinary capabilities in NLP and a wide range of applications. Built on advanced neural networks and evolving Transformer architectures, LLMs have fundamentally transformed our approach to understanding and generating machine language. This chapter began with an introductory overview of LLMs, covering their evolution, architecture, and development processes. This chapter also covered details about the RAG technique embracing the accuracy and reliability of LLMs by establishing interactions with an external knowledgebase for relevant information before generating a response. This chapter also explained the key components in a RAG architecture and how these components interact with each other to drive the underlying process.

# CHAPTER 5

# Introduction to SAP Business AI Foundation

Integrating AI into enterprise systems has been a growing area of research, with numerous studies highlighting AI's potential to enhance decision-making, improve efficiency, and foster innovation. SAP Business AI has garnered attention for its ability to streamline AI integration within enterprise applications. The previous chapters explained Generative AI and associated concepts, including the Transformer architecture, LLMs, RAG, and other key components. This chapter shifts focus to bring AI into the enterprise context by leveraging SAP's Business AI offering on the SAP Business Technology Platform. Starting with a brief introduction to SAP Business AI, this chapter dives deep into SAP Joule, SAP AI's embedded AI assistant.

## SAP Business AI

The astonishing pace of breakthroughs in AI, and especially in Generative AI, has caught the world's imagination. While past general-purpose technologies like personal computers and the Internet took decades to reach widespread adoption, Generative AI's mainstream adoption is measured in months. As AI marches toward human-level capabilities on many intellectual tasks, leaders are pondering our future and racing to harness the benefits of this technology.

SAP is a pioneer in offering cutting-edge products and solutions for enterprise customers for decades, and it stepped into the world of Generative AI with a wide spectrum of products, services, and embedded AI capabilities across its product stack. With the introduction of the SAP Business AI offering, SAP has rejuvenated and re-aligned their entire AI offering with the latest and greatest in combination with classical AI/ML offerings on the SAP Business Technology Platform. The combination of SAP's robust business applications with advanced AI technology ultimately enables enterprises to make data-driven decisions, automate processes, and unlock new business opportunities. Additionally, an embedded AI copilot called *SAP Joule* is now empowering business users to perform business-oriented transactions based on simple natural language-based instructions.

The embedded capabilities of SAP Joule are integrated into SAP's product suite, including Financial Management, Supply Chain Management, Human Capital Management, Spend Management, and Customer Experience. This is not just limited to business users, but also to empowering full stack and citizen developers on the SAP Business Technology Platform to generate code, test data, test scenarios, and much more.

To complement embedded intelligence, SAP provides a pathway for Custom AI solutions built on top of its AI foundation. This allows enterprises to design, train, and deploy their own AI models and agents to tailor their unique needs and data. The AI foundation acts as the central operating system for AI, supporting the entire lifecycle from model development to deployment and monitoring, all while ensuring scalability, security, and compliance. This foundation is hosted on the SAP BTP offering a robust infrastructure for data connectivity, model governance, and AI service orchestration. Accompanied by required tools and services, such as SAP Business AI, AI Core, AI Launchpad, and Generative AI Hub, the AI foundation ensures a smooth and seamless integration of business AI applications into customers' existing landscape, realizing the full potential of AI.

Enhancing the entire architecture is SAP's strong network of AI ecosystem partnerships and investments. Collaborations with leading AI and technology providers—including Aleph Alpha, Anthropic, AWS, Cohere, Databricks, Google Cloud, IBM, Meta, Microsoft, Mistral AI, and NVIDIA—ensure that SAP remains at the forefront of AI innovation. These partnerships bring together the best in foundational models, cloud infrastructure, and machine learning capabilities, allowing SAP to deliver state-of-the-art AI solutions to its customers. Altogether, SAP Business AI combines orchestration, embedded intelligence, customization, and ecosystem strength to drive meaningful business outcomes in the AI era.

Now that you have learned what SAP Business is all about, the rest of this chapter dives deep into each of the components of Business AI, one by one, staring with Joule.

# SAP Joule

The world of SAP is abuzz with the arrival of Joule, a powerful Generative AI assistant that's changing the way businesses work with SAP systems. With the ability to simplify operations, deliver intelligent insights, and support faster, smarter decision-making, Joule is poised to reshape everyday enterprise workflows. But before exploring its full range of features, it's worth getting familiar with some key building blocks—like LLMs, SAP Build Code, prompt engineering, and the SAP Business Technology Platform (BTP). Joule isn't just another AI tool—it's SAP's answer to making user experiences more intuitive and productive. Inspired by the 19th-century physicist James Prescott Joule, its name reflects the idea of helping users achieve more with less effort. What also sets it apart is its strong emphasis on data privacy and accuracy, which makes it a trusted companion for enterprise-grade applications.

SAP's Joule AI copilot is designed to act like a smart, dependable assistant that helps businesses get more done in less time. What makes it unique is its ability to quickly generate content or surface useful insights by understanding the enterprise data and context through a simple natural language prompt. This reduces time spent on repetitive work and frees teams to focus on higher-value tasks. By delivering reliable insights, Joule helps teams make confident decisions, especially in fast-moving business environments. It's not just about saving time—it's about making a real, immediate impact. Due to having a better understanding of underlying business data and context of the business, Joule supports better outcomes by tailoring responses and suggestions to what actually matters to your goals. Whether the need is efficiency, clarity, or faster execution, Joule elevates everyday work and, more importantly, empowers decision-making and drives enterprise productivity at scale.

SAP's Joule AI copilot is evolving fast, and its latest capabilities highlight just how deeply it's being integrated into the SAP ecosystem. Designed to support users across a wide range of roles, Joule now comes with multi-language capabilities, making it easier for global teams to interact with SAP systems in their preferred language. It also brings AI-assisted document grounding, which helps reduce ambiguity, improve trust, and minimize hallucinations, which are especially important when making decisions based on critical business data. Joule's interaction patterns span transactional, navigational, and informational use cases, making it versatile in how it supports users. Whether you're a consultant needing faster insights or a developer working with CAP or ABAP, Joule is tailored to make your job easier. With skills and agents embedded across business processes and a growing list of capabilities—1,600 skills expected by Sapphire 2025—it's clear that SAP is investing heavily in making Joule a core part of the enterprise toolkit. And with mobile support, Joule ensures that assistance is always within reach, no matter where or how you work.

Behind the scenes, SAP Joule operates through a well-orchestrated system that combines intelligence, context, and enterprise-grade capabilities to deliver accurate and meaningful assistance. When a user enters a query through the interface, Joule doesn't just pass it on blindly—instead, it enriches the input by pulling in relevant context, referencing a catalog of business scenarios, and grounding the response with verified enterprise knowledge. This enriched query is then handled through dialogue management, where an LLM helps generate a precise and context-aware reply. What makes Joule particularly effective is its integration with SAP Cloud applications via a catalog of specialized "skills," allowing it to interact directly with systems like Cloud ERP, HCM, Supply Chain, BTP, and more. These backend function calls ensure that responses aren't just generic—they're tied to real-time enterprise data. The final answer is rendered back to the user in a conversational format, but it's backed by a sophisticated loop of grounding, reasoning, and real application logic that makes Joule a truly enterprise-ready AI copilot.

The next section covers AI Foundation, which basically provides the basis for SAP's entire AI product portfolio.

## SAP AI Foundation

As enterprise businesses are continuing to evolve every moment, the need to integrate AI has intensified. Enterprises must now process vast amounts of data, derive intelligent insights, and enhance operational efficiency across business processes. They are no longer skeptical about getting their hands on a growing range of smarter, more powerful tools and technologies, giving employees the ability to completely transform how they access, interact with, and make sense of enterprise data. Across the enterprise ecosystem, increasing complexity and exponential growth of business data have already underscored the need to advance AI driven decision-making tools across the enterprise. Meeting these demands is no longer futuristic but an immediate requirement and this is where SAP's next critical component comes in: SAP AI Foundation. SAP AI Foundation offers the required tools, service, APIs, and most importantly the required runtime to

CHAPTER 5 INTRODUCTION TO SAP BUSINESS AI FOUNDATION

build and host your enterprise AI solution. The AI foundation on SAP BTP is the basis for all AI capabilities across SAP's entire AI product portfolio and enables developers to assemble the right mix of AI and Generative AI services to meet their enterprise needs.

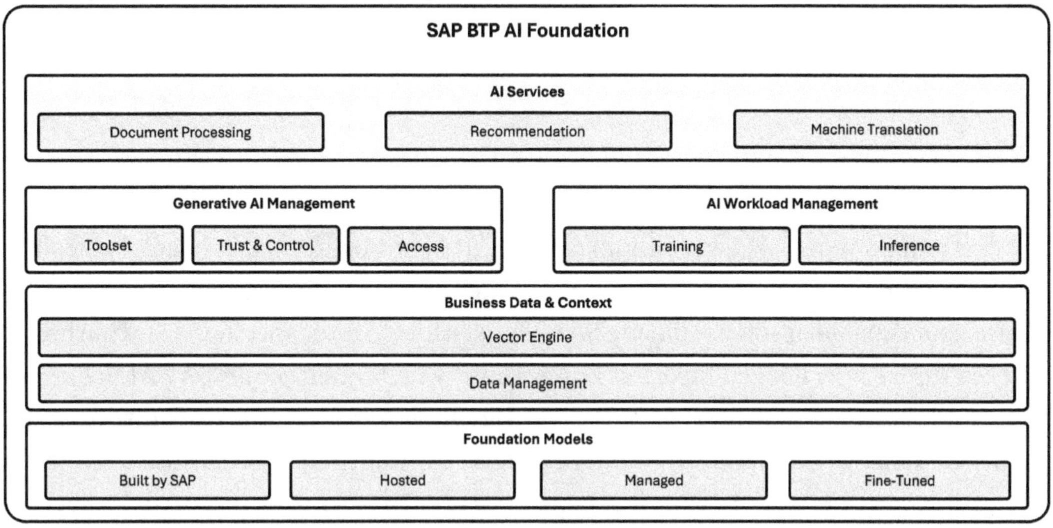

*Figure 5-1.* SAP AI Foundation

The AI Foundation on the Business Technology Platform, as shown in Figure 5-1, serves as a robust framework for integrating AI into business operations. It consists of several key components designed to streamline AI adoption and management. AI Services enable businesses to leverage capabilities such as document processing, recommendation systems, and machine translation to enhance operational efficiency and decision-making. Generative AI Management focuses on providing tools and frameworks for managing Generative AI, emphasizing trust, control, and accessibility to ensure responsible and secure usage. AI Workload Management addresses the critical aspects of training and inference, ensuring that AI models are optimized and effectively utilized. Business Data & Context is supported by advanced features such as a Vector Engines and comprehensive data management tools, enabling businesses to extract meaningful insights from their data. The Foundation Models built by SAP offer flexibility through hosting options, remote access, and fine-tuning capabilities, allowing organizations to adapt AI solutions to their specific needs. Lastly, Lifecycle Management ensures that AI systems remain sustainable and maintain their performance over time, offering end-to-end support for their integration into business workflows. Now that you

CHAPTER 5   INTRODUCTION TO SAP BUSINESS AI FOUNDATION

have a basic understanding of SAP AI Foundation, the next sections start diving deep into each of the components of the AI Foundation architecture that lay the groundwork in a top-down approach.

To accelerate the AI adoption and take advantage of pre-built offerings, SAP AI services are ideal ways for enterprises to kick off their AI journeys. The next section unearths more details.

## AI Services

The first component of AI Foundation, called SAP AI or Business AI Services, basically offers a rich collection of business-oriented AI services that are reusable, generic in nature, and capable of solving business challenges that are not specific to any business process, unlike fully fledged business applications with limited scope. SAP AI Business Services run on historical business data and are capable of addressing a wide range of business challenges, including document processing, information extraction, invoice processing, unstructured data processing, and more. These processes are typically manual and repetitive in nature. Automating these processes can ultimately help your organization and your employees focus more time and effort on strategic and value-creating work.

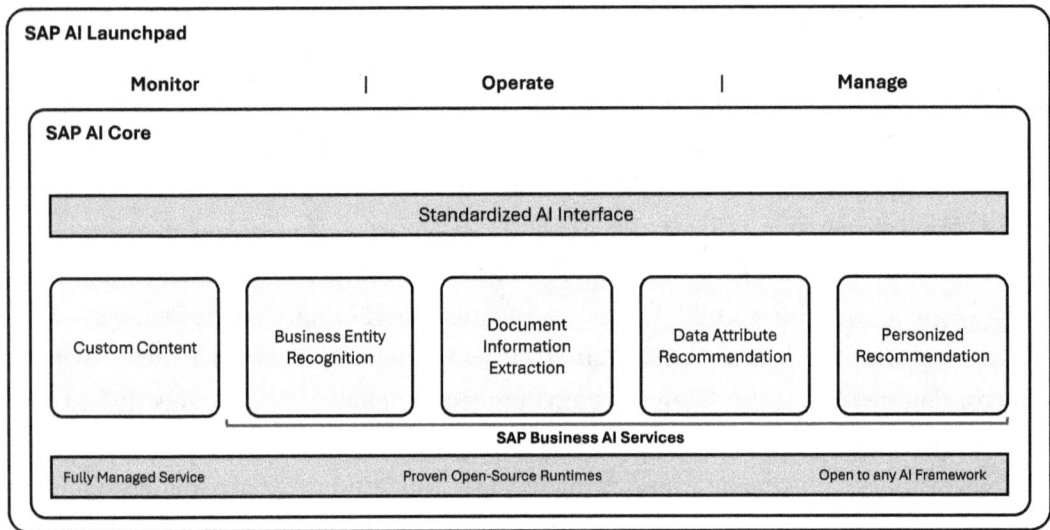

*Figure 5-2.* Business Service Portfolio of SAP AI Core

CHAPTER 5  INTRODUCTION TO SAP BUSINESS AI FOUNDATION

As shown in Figure 5-2, SAP AI Business Service Portfolio offers a spectrum of business services out-of-the-box to drive the intelligent processing of business documents or service tickets. It does this by extracting key information, entities, and attributes using AI.

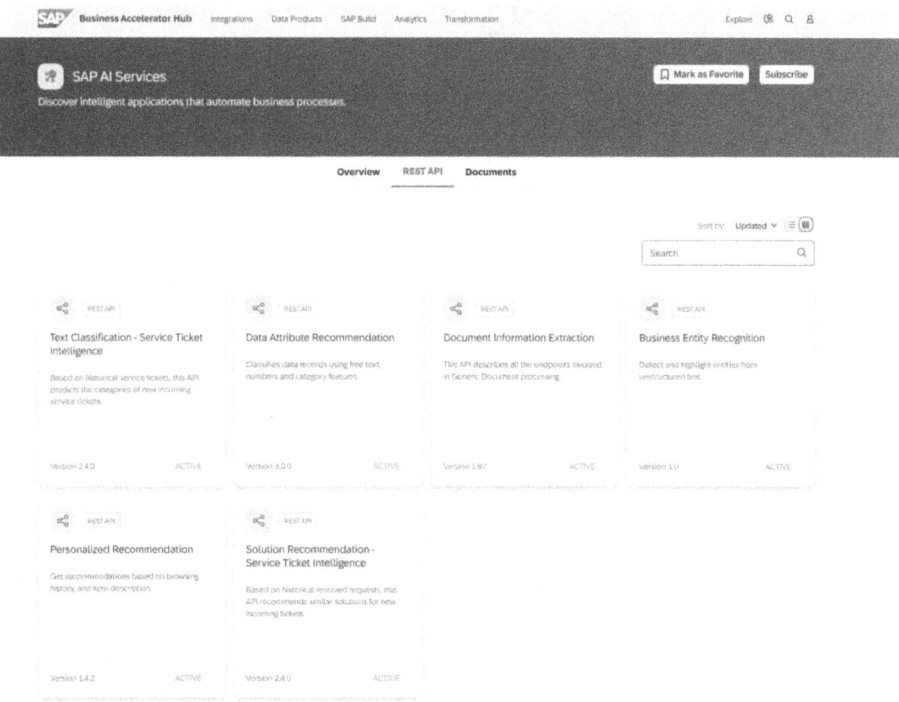

***Figure 5-3.*** *SAP AI Services from the Business Accelerator Hub*

Figure 5-3 shows a glimpse of AI Services from the Business Accelerator hub, which also includes detail documentation, API specifications, and provisions to test them. Even though it currently shows multiple services, some of these services (Data Attribute Recommendation, Service Ticket Intelligence, and Business Entity Recognition) are in the process of being sunset. At present, only SAP Document AI and Personalized Recommendation are available for consumption.

- **Document AI:** SAP Document AI is an intelligent solution designed to simplify and accelerate the processing of complex business documents avoiding tedious manual processing. Whether dealing with invoices, contracts, or forms, it can automatically extract key information from documents—no matter how the content is structured or where it appears. With built-in capabilities for both data extraction and enrichment, SAP Document AI can identify and match document content with relevant business records, enabling smarter automation and reducing manual effort. Its support for multitenancy ensures that it fits seamlessly into scalable, tenant-aware applications. SAP Document AI offers flexible service plans to meet diverse business needs, where the Base Edition provides core document processing features with support for high-volume uploads—up to 2,000 documents per hour per tenant. For advanced scenarios, the Premium Edition unlocks powerful features like Generative AI-based information extraction, offering deeper insights and greater automation.

- **Personalized Recommendations:** The Personalized Recommendation service, part of SAP AI Services, leverages advanced machine learning to deliver tailored suggestions that enhance user experience and drive business outcomes. By analyzing browsing behavior, item interactions, and contextual signals, the service provides highly relevant next-item and similar-item recommendations, smart search results, and affinity-based personalization. Whether it's guiding users to the next best action or surfacing products aligned with their preferences, this reusable service helps improve engagement, boost conversions, and support key business KPIs, while giving businesses full control over relevance and curation.

# SAP AI Core

SAP AI Core on the SAP AI Foundation is a cloud-native and extensible framework that has emerged as a powerful platform enterprise across the industry. SAP AI Core marks a significant leap toward bringing AI into the heart of enterprise applications, ensuring data privacy in a cost-effective manner. Built as a powerful platform on SAP BTP, it helps companies seamlessly add AI features and services into their SAP applications without added complexity.

CHAPTER 5  INTRODUCTION TO SAP BUSINESS AI FOUNDATION

With a wide range of tools to support decision-making systems, SAP AI Core empowers businesses to process data in real time, run deep analytics, and build predictive models. This empowers organizations not only to tackle today's challenges but also to quickly act on new opportunities. A major benefit of using SAP AI Core within SAP BTP is that it lets customers manage the execution and operation of their AI solutions in a consistent, scalable way—without being tied to any specific cloud provider. This reduces vendor lock-in and helps democratize enterprise-grade AI.

With SAP AI Core as a service on SAP BTP, SAP is offering a wide spectrum of features and services, ranging from built-in machine learning models, services, standardized AI interface, AI API, SAP AI Core SDK. It also has running pipelines, inference requests, multi-tenancy, and required runtimes to all the latest Generative AI related offerings, including embedded AI assistants across multiple product stacks, partner foundation models, orchestration, and many more. With the introduction of Generative AI related offerings, SAP AI Core is no longer limited to conventional machine learning features limited to classification or extraction-oriented processing. Generative AI Hub on SAP AI Core offers a central cockpit for developers—not just AI experts—to create, operate, monitor, and orchestrate all possible Generative AI driven enterprise solutions, enabling scalable innovation for teams across the business.

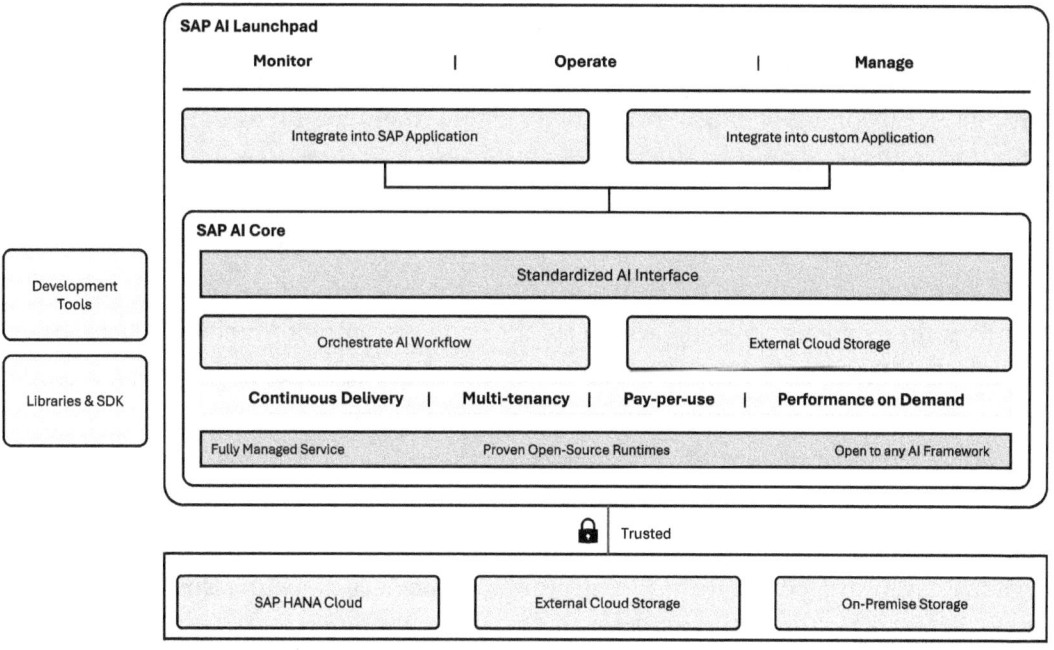

*Figure 5-4.* SAP AI Core

CHAPTER 5  INTRODUCTION TO SAP BUSINESS AI FOUNDATION

As depicted in Figure 5-4, SAP AI Core lets you administer almost every stage of the enterprise AI implementation cycle by offering end-to-end solution without the need to understand the underlying dependencies and set up productive environments for training. Key capabilities include AI scenario creation, model training, deployment, and inferencing, including support for tenant isolation and multi-tenancy.

With SAP AI Core, customers can focus on outcomes rather than on the technical heavy lifting. It offers a fully managed service that takes care of all dependencies and removes the hassle of setting up and maintaining your own training and serving infrastructure. Instead of dealing with the underlying complexity, you get straightforward API endpoints that make it easy to integrate AI into your business applications. SAP AI Core relies on Kubernetes clusters to manage and run containerized applications used in training and deploying AI models.

Being powered by the Kubernetes cluster, SAP AI Core lets you easily deploy container-based AI solutions along with auto-scaling and scale-to-zero like features. This creates a cost check and runs most resource-hungry use cases at scale. These clusters are designed to allocate resources based on real-time needs. For instance, tapping into GPU nodes when handling intensive AI workloads or complex ML pipelines that demand varied resources at each stage. In this context, the Kubernetes setup brings speed and agility, allowing containers running AI code to scale up or down easily depending on demand. Not being limited to only SAP's AI related offering, AI Core also provides the required runtime to bring and host your own AI model or scenario, which is a great advantage. Customers willing to bring their custom AI models on AI Core can take advantage of its model training and inferencing process though reusable templates, which can further be shared with different teams for training based on their own data.

Being hosted on SAP BTP, it has seamless integration with SAP HANA Cloud and other product stack and other hyperscalers. This eases the integration related effort required for sourcing data, which is especially relevant for AI related use cases. Additionally, integration with data science tools to ship AI scenarios to the secure and productive environment ensures a faster go-to-market time.

SAP AI Core is built to simplify and manage the full lifecycle of machine learning models—from data preparation to deployment—while giving users control and flexibility. It starts by connecting to an object store to load training datasets and then organizes everything through "resource groups," which act as secure, isolated spaces. These resource groups help separate datasets, training templates, and other assets, so different teams or tenants can work independently without risk of overlap. Once the dataset is registered, users create a configuration that links the input data with the training logic—called an *executable*. These executables are grouped under what SAP calls a "scenario," which is a way to organize related ML components for a given business case. Although a scenario isn't technically a namespace, it helps keep projects tidy and manageable. When the training starts, SAP AI Core handles the workflow, using containerized pipelines and selecting from a range of predefined infrastructure options based on resource needs—like more CPUs, GPUs, or memory. This makes it easy to scale depending on how heavy the training job is. Once the training is done, the final model is automatically stored in the same connected object store and registered in SAP AI Core, ready to be deployed. And through SAP AI Launchpad, users can monitor training progress, view logs, and check results, all in one place. It's a setup that brings structure to ML operations without getting in the way of experimentation or scale.

After a model has been trained and has picked up the patterns hidden in the dataset, the next step is deployment. Once deployed, the model can start accepting new data and return prediction for each input, known as *model serving* or *inferencing*. To support this inferencing phase, a Kubernetes cluster can be set up with containers that run on CPUs, which are more cost-effective, or GPUs for higher performance.

The next section covers comprehensive details about the features offered by each of the segments inside SAP AI Launchpad.

## SAP AI Launchpad

All the features discussed so far in the context SAP Business AI are powered by a single launchpad, known as SAP AI Launchpad on SAP BTP. The SAP AI Launchpad acts as a single-entry point to let you manage the lifecycle of all your Business AI-oriented use cases, models, and scenarios deployed across the enterprise, through a centralized cockpit. Basically, it is a multitenant software-as-a-service (SaaS) application on SAP BTP through which customers and partners can manage their AI use cases or scenarios across multiple instances of AI runtimes. The AI runtimes in this context are not limited to AI Core. SAP HANA, Data Intelligence, Business Services, and various partner offerings can be managed through this unified interface.

The integration between SAP AI Launchpad and supported AI runtimes is facilitated by a standardized interface, called *AI API*, which is designed to manage key AI components like training scripts, datasets, models, and model servers across different runtime environments. The AI API is extended and tailored to support more complex workflows, including the use of Argo workflows and serving templates. These are centrally managed under the concept of an executable, which acts as a bridge between the pipeline definitions and how they actually run. To recognize and handle these templates correctly, specific metadata attributes must be included as part of the workflow and serving templates.

As shown in Figure 5-5, the AI Launchpad has a simple user interface with capabilities to manage, monitor, and analyze deployed models and their outcomes, including a wide range of API support. With a holistic view of the metrics generated by the underlying AI runtime, you can access tooling around ML lifecycle management and data science activity containers to access SAP and open-sourced integrated apps and tools.

*Figure 5-5. SAP AI Launchpad*

SAP AI Core uses resource groups, as shown in Figure 5-5, to logically separate machine learning resources and workloads in a single tenant. These resource groups act as virtual containers that help keep related assets—like datasets, configurations, and execution results—organized and isolated. While elements like scenarios, executables, and Docker Registry Secrets are shared across all resource groups within a tenant, the grouping helps define boundaries for how resources are used and managed. When a new tenant is onboarded, SAP AI Core automatically sets up a default resource group. Additional groups can be created or removed later by the tenant administrator using the AI API, depending on how the workloads are structured or teams are split.

CHAPTER 5   INTRODUCTION TO SAP BUSINESS AI FOUNDATION

- **ML Operations:** Inside SAP AI Launchpad, the Machine learning operations (ML Ops) segment provides a structured and scalable approach to build, manage, and deploy AI workflows across the enterprise. At its core, it takes care of some of the most critical prerequisites of MLOps, including scenarios, configurations, executables, datasets, deployments, and schedules to enable teams to operationalize enterprise machine learning applications with consistency, automation, and traceability. Together, these components streamline the end-to-end lifecycle of machine learning projects, ranging from experimentation to production, along with support for collaboration, governance, and long-term scalability.

  - **Scenario:** In the context of SAP AI Core, a scenario represents the implementation of a specific AI use case within a user's tenant. It is a predefined collection of AI capabilities such as executables and templates that are required to run and manage that use case. Scenarios serve as reusable, structured blueprints that simplify the deployment and execution of AI workflows, ensuring consistency and efficiency across different projects or teams within the same tenant. Scenarios are also tightly scoped to a tenant, meaning they are set up and managed within the context of a single customer environment. However, once defined, scenarios can be reused across multiple projects or resource groups within that tenant, promoting consistency in how models are trained and deployed, while also speeding up implementation time. Figure 5-6, shows a glimpse of the Scenario section inside AI Launchpad. It depicts scenarios for RAG, orchestration, LLM access, and so on.

CHAPTER 5    INTRODUCTION TO SAP BUSINESS AI FOUNDATION

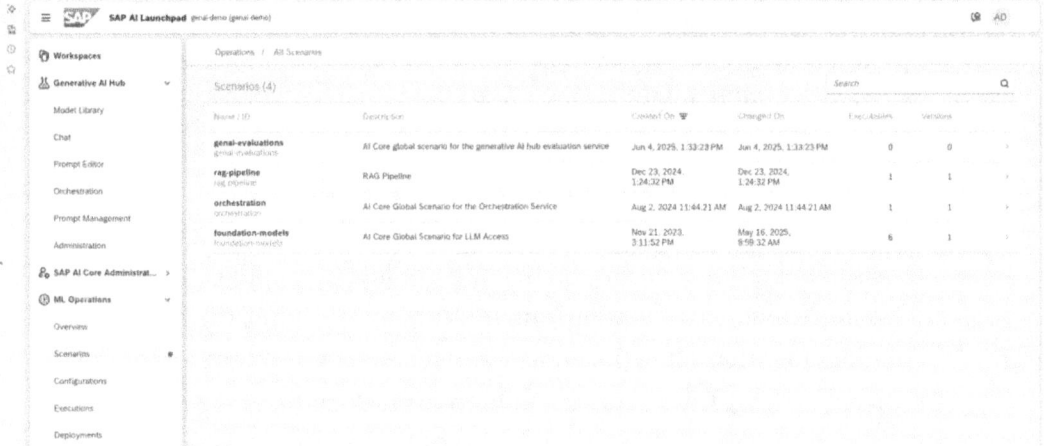

*Figure 5-6.  Scenarios*

- **Configurations:** Configurations inside SAP AI Launchpad, as shown in Figure 5-7, serve as operational blueprints that link the logic defined in an executable or template with the real-world data, parameters, and compute context needed to run it in a reusable and adaptable manner. Instead of modifying the executable or template for every new experiment or deployment, users simply create a new configuration tailored to the specific task. For example, the same training executable can be run on different datasets or with different model architectures just by changing the configuration. This helps maintain consistency in the pipeline logic while supporting flexibility in execution. Defining a new configuration inside SAP AI Launchpad is primarily driven by selection of a predefined scenario, relevant versions, and executables followed by input parameters and artifacts.

CHAPTER 5   INTRODUCTION TO SAP BUSINESS AI FOUNDATION

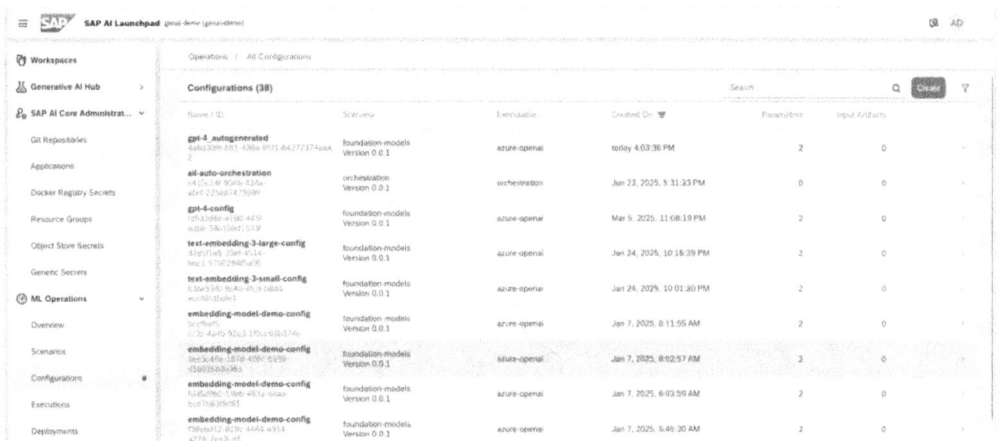

*Figure 5-7. Configurations*

- **Executions:** An executable is a reusable template that defines a workflow or pipeline for tasks such as training a machine learning model or creating a deployment. It contains placeholders for input artifacts (datasets or models) and parameters (custom key-pair values) that enable the template to be reused in different scenarios. In the context of SAP AI Core, executables are essential building blocks that standardize how AI tasks are performed. They provide a flexible structure that allows teams to define and run repeatable processes—whether it's model training, evaluation, or deployment—without rewriting the workflow each time. By using placeholders for inputs and parameters, executables can easily adapt to different datasets, models, and configurations, making them ideal across multiple use cases within the same environment.

CHAPTER 5   INTRODUCTION TO SAP BUSINESS AI FOUNDATION

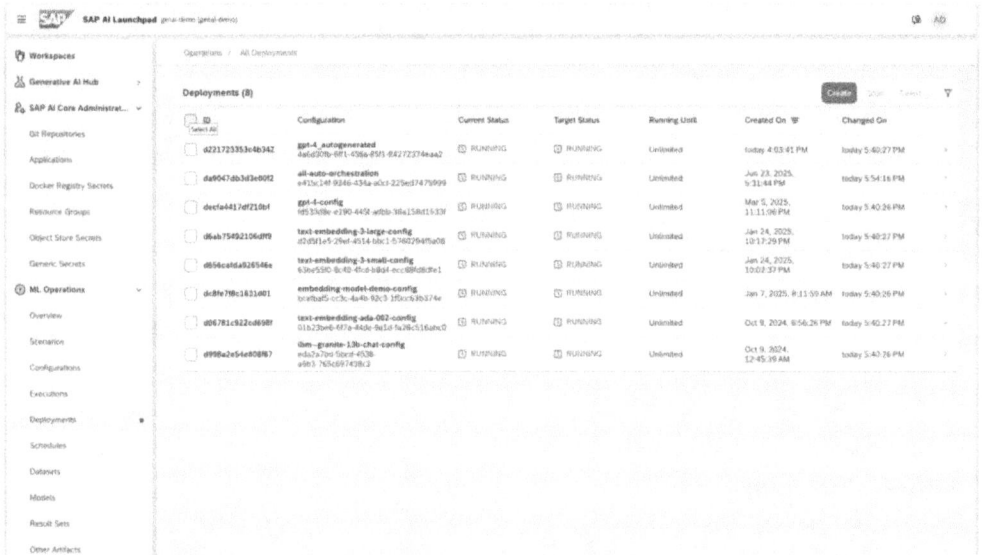

*Figure 5-8. Deployments*

- **Deployments:** Deployment is the process of making a trained machine learning model accessible for real-time or batch inference. Once a model has been trained and validated, it needs to be exposed so that other systems or users can interact with it, and this is where deployment comes in. As part of the deployment process, key information like the model name and version are essential to ensure clarity and traceability and post deployment. SAP AI Core generates a unique deployment URL, which acts as an API endpoint. This URL can be integrated into business applications, other AI pipelines, or shared across teams, enabling consistent and scalable access to the model's predictions. Each model version is deployed independently, so you can manage updates or rollbacks with minimal disruption. Figure 5-8 shows the list of different deployed models like GPT-4, text-embedding-3-large, and so on, inside the Deployments section of AI Launchpad.

- **Schedules:** Schedules are used to automate the repeated execution of workflows, most commonly for training jobs. Instead of manually triggering an execution each time, a schedule in place tells the system when and how often to run

CHAPTER 5  INTRODUCTION TO SAP BUSINESS AI FOUNDATION

it. This is particularly useful in scenarios where models need to be retrained on a regular basis, such as with updated data in production environments. By linking a prepared configuration to a schedule, SAP AI Core takes care of launching executions based on the defined timing. As long as the schedule remains active, executions will continue to run at the specified intervals. Once the schedule reaches its end timestamp, it becomes inactive, preventing any further runs.

- **Datasets:** Datasets are a core asset in SAP AI Launchpad, linking raw data to intelligent insights through structured, repeatable, and secure workflows. It serves as the source of truth for training models, evaluating performance, or running analytics, and is referenced within configurations to connect data to specific workflows. Each dataset is uniquely identified and versioned to ensure traceability and reproducibility across experiments. Since datasets may reside in various locations—like cloud storage, databases, or external APIs—access often requires specific credentials or libraries, which are securely handled through secrets. Metadata plays a critical role in describing the dataset's structure, helping templates and pipelines interpret and process the data correctly. Datasets can also be split into different parts for training, validation, and testing, and they often undergo preparation steps such as cleaning or augmentation before being used in production workflows.

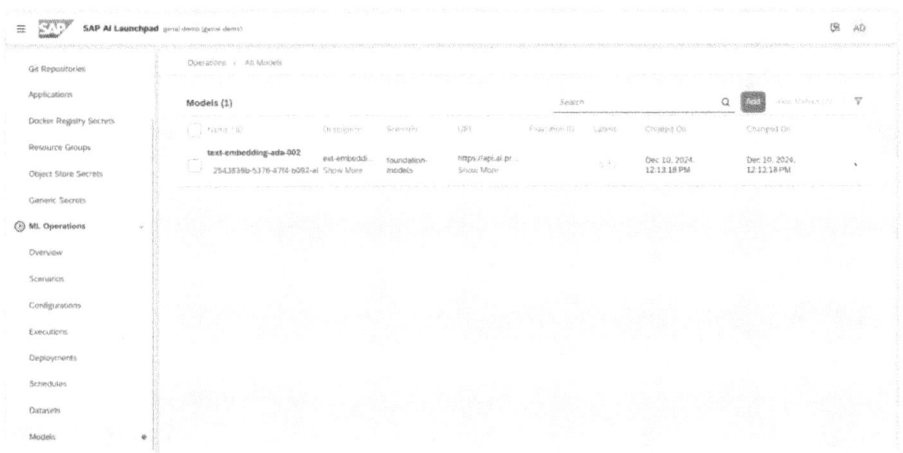

*Figure 5-9.* Models

117

- **Models:** As shown in Figure 5-9, the Models section hosts the ML models generated or procured through a definitive training process and can be of different types—including neural networks, decision trees, and clustering models—each suited to different AI tasks and data types. Each model is uniquely identified by a model ID, which is used in a configuration to bind the model as an input artifact to the serving executable for deployment. Models can be manually uploaded to the connected data storage or automatically generated and uploaded as the output of a training execution in SAP AI Launchpad. A model can consist of one or more files stored in a hyperscaler storage system, such as SAP AI Core's connected data storage or the data lake for SAP HANA Cloud. Models are managed and versioned artifacts that can be deployed to serving endpoints for production inference. Once trained, these models become the core component used to perform inference—applying its learned patterns to new data to generate predictions or insights.

- **Result sets:** In the context of SAP AI Core, a result set captures the outcomes of batch processing where a deployed model evaluates large volumes of input data in one go, instead of real-time prediction. These result sets are stored as artifacts and can be referenced later for validation, auditing, or downstream consumption in analytics or business workflows. Like other artifacts in AI Core, result sets are uniquely identifiable and versioned, ensuring traceability and reproducibility. They play an essential role in operationalizing AI, enabling teams to assess model performance at scale, integrate with decision-making systems, or feed back into the model improvement loop through error analysis or retraining efforts.

Now that you have an idea about the capabilities of the ML Operations segment inside SAP AI Launchpad, the next section talks about the AI Core Administration segment.

## SAP AI Core Administration

The SAP AI Core administration segment inside SAP AI Launchpad lets you manage all key components like Git repositories, applications, secrets, and resource groups to ensure secure, scalable, and efficient machine learning operations. The key components,

CHAPTER 5    INTRODUCTION TO SAP BUSINESS AI FOUNDATION

like Git repositories and applications, help manage versions and sync templates, while Docker Registry Secrets and Object Store Secrets securely connect to external containers and cloud storage. Resource groups provide isolated environments for managing workloads, whereas generic secrets offer flexible handling of sensitive data when system secrets aren't enough. Together, these features give administrators tight control over configurations, access, and orchestration across the AI lifecycle. Let's take a deeper dive into each of these components:

- **Git repositories:** Git repositories are used to version control your SAP AI Core templates. The GitOps onboarding to SAP AI Core instances involves setting up your Git repository and synchronizing your content. Git repositories, as shown in Figure 5-10, are managed by creating personal access tokens and registering them in SAP AI Core. Personal access tokens are a means of allowing and controlling connections to GitHub repositories without compromising your credentials. They also provide the traceability and collaboration that Git offers. By linking your repository using a personal access token, you ensure that changes to the AI Core templates are securely tracked, easily rolled back if needed, and seamlessly integrated into your development workflow. This also enables teams to maintain a single source of truth, helping to streamline model lifecycle management and promoting consistent deployment practices across environments.

*Figure 5-10.* Git repositories

119

CHAPTER 5　INTRODUCTION TO SAP BUSINESS AI FOUNDATION

- **Applications:** An application in SAP AI Core, as shown in Figure 5-11, refers to a configuration that links your Git repository to your AI Core instance, making it possible to automatically pull in and sync templates—like training or serving templates—directly from the repository. Setting up Applications is a way to tell SAP AI Core where to look and what files to keep track of. The application takes care of syncing, where it pulls the content for the first time, and after that, it keeps everything updated every three minutes. Or you can trigger the sync manually, ensuring the latest templates are always up to date in the AI Core environment. This helps maintain a smooth and consistent model lifecycle.

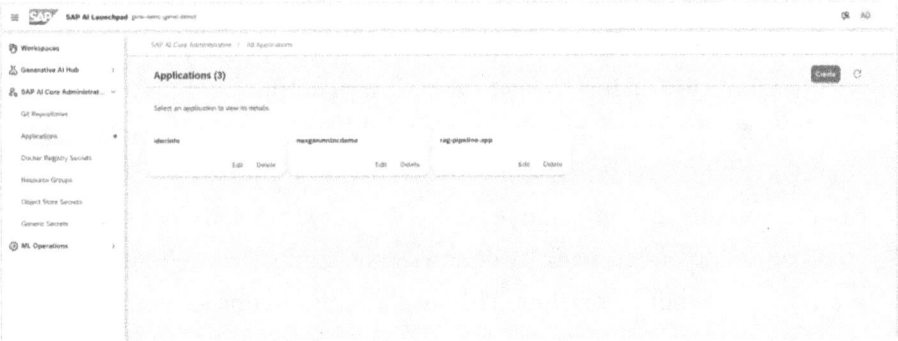

*Figure 5-11. Applications*

- **Docker Registry Secret:** Docker as a platform lets you bundle an application along with all its dependencies such as libraries, configuration files, and environment settings into a single, lightweight container that is portable across different computing environments. In this context, Docker Registry Secret lets you connect SAP AI Core to a Docker repository and manage Docker credentials. Docker Registry Secret, as shown in Figure 5-12, lets you authorize SAP AI Core to pull your private Docker images from your Docker repository just by simply specifying the name of the secret in the workflows to authenticate the Docker image pull. This ensures that the process is secure and seamless. It helps maintain a clean separation between code and credentials while allowing SAP AI Core to fetch and run containerized applications from your Docker registry without manual intervention.

CHAPTER 5  INTRODUCTION TO SAP BUSINESS AI FOUNDATION

*Figure 5-12.* Docker Registry Secrets

- **Resource group:** A resource group is a unique dedicated namespace or workspace environment, where users can create or add configurations, executions, deployments, and artifacts. In the context of SAP AI Core, resource groups play a critical role in organizing and isolating machine learning workloads. They do this by providing a structured environment to manage all runtime entities like training jobs, deployments, and artifacts—ensuring that each usage scenario remains logically and physically separate. When a tenant is onboarded, a default resource group is created automatically, which cannot be deleted. As an administrator, you have the flexibility to create, modify, or remove additional resource groups depending on the needs. Each runtime entity belongs to a specific resource group and isn't accessible across others, although some elements like scenarios, executables, and Docker Registry Secrets are shared across all resource groups within the same tenant.

- **Object Store Secrets:** Object Store Secrets are critical to connect SAP AI Core to a cloud object store and manage access to it. Connected cloud storage can potentially store datasets, models, and other cache files of the Metaflow Library relevant for SAP AI Core. Basically, it acts as a central storage space for handling large volumes of data required throughout the machine learning lifecycle. This ranges from raw datasets to trained models and temporary files used by the Metaflow Library during processing. To securely connect your AI Core environment to a cloud object store like Amazon S3 or Azure Blob object store secret, it is critical to authorize access without exposing sensitive information. Once configured, workflows in SAP AI Core can easily interact with the storage, making it a reliable and secure backend for managing the assets your ML pipelines depend on.

- **Generic secrets:** Generic secrets store sensitive information when system secrets aren't applicable. This is relevant to integration scenarios where SAP AI Core acts as an orchestration layer. SAP AI Core lets you use generic secrets at the main-tenant, tenant-wide, and resource-group levels. Generic secrets offer a flexible way to handle sensitive data like API keys or custom credentials where standard system secrets (such as those for object stores or Docker registries) aren't suitable. Generic secrets can be attached to containers during executions or deployments, either as environment variables or mounted volumes. One of their key advantages is support for tenant-wide secret rotation in long-running deployments without requiring restarts. However, managing generic secrets requires careful coordination, especially when tenant-wide and resource-group secrets share the same name, as local secrets can temporarily override the global ones. To avoid conflicts and maintain security, it's important to control access to the secrets endpoint and enforce a consistent secret-naming strategy. Each tenant can manage up to five tenant-wide secrets, and exceeding this limit will require cleanup or a quota increase.

Unearthing the details of SAP AI Core Administration segment inside SAP AI Launchpad can help show how you can leverage its various capabilities to manage the end-to-end AI model lifecycle.

# The Generative AI Hub

Introducing the Generative AI Hub as part of SAP BTP is a leap toward SAP's journey to accelerate the adoption of Generative AI in the context of enterprise application across the industry. According to SAP's official definition, the Generative AI Hub acts as a central cockpit for developers to build, run, and manage their Generative AI scenarios within the AI Foundation and Launchpad ecosystem. As depicted in Figure 5-13, it brings together a rich set of components and tools supporting the entire lifecycle of Generative AI based enterprise application development, including a dedicated user-friendly playground for model configuration, deployment, and model evaluation through prompting, a rich set of SDKs, templates, seamless integration with a wide spectrum of partner foundation models like OpenAI, Granite, Mistral, Bedrock, Granite, and so on.

The GenAI hub is designed to streamline the way businesses work with LLMs. Additional features like orchestration not only set it apart in terms of secure adoption and execution of LLMs for enterprise application but also enrich it with accurate contextual data sourced from SAP's HANA Cloud Vector Engine, Embeddings, Similarity Search and Knowledge Graph for most relevant response. At its core, the hub prioritizes trust, embedding compliance with technical, legal, and business standards across the AI workflow.

A major strength of the Generative AI Hub lies in its Trust & Control layer, which includes mechanisms like inference engines, content moderation, grounding, multi-tenancy, security, and data privacy features, essential for ensuring responsible AI usage in enterprise environments. Powered by self-supervised deep learning models trained on massive datasets, the Generative AI Hub enables enterprises to leverage advanced NLP capabilities, while still allowing for customization through domain-specific fine-tuning. Additionally, the AI Hub also includes a prompt registry to organize and share prompt templates across various projects.

CHAPTER 5   INTRODUCTION TO SAP BUSINESS AI FOUNDATION

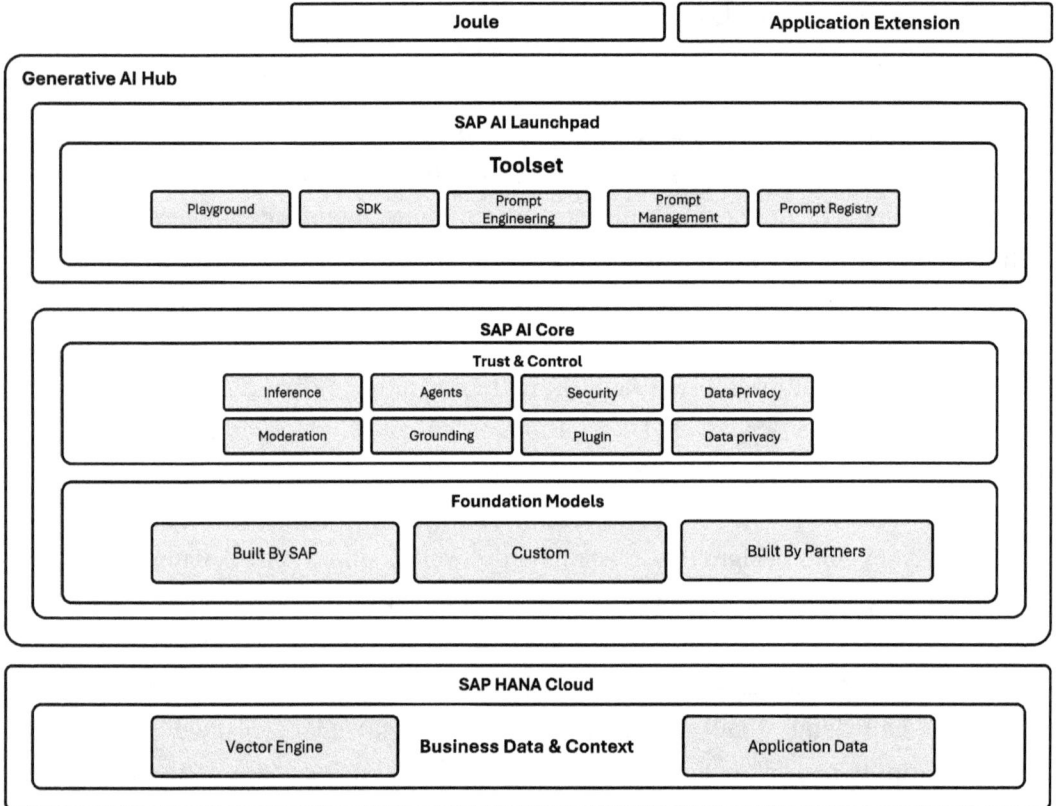

*Figure 5-13. Generative AI Hub architecture*

Overall, the Generative AI Hub is purpose-built to help businesses explore, experiment, and operationalize Generative AI with flexibility and control, bridging cutting-edge AI with real-world business needs. Ultimately, it empowers organizations to adopt Generative AI in a scalable, secure, and cost-effective way, transforming business processes with intelligence that is both contextual and responsible. In terms of Generative AI management, the next sections explain each part of the Generative AI Hub segment under the SAP AI Launchpad.

## The Model Library Section

The Model Library section of the Generative AI Hub is one of the most critical and essential sections for selecting your desired LLM that you want to leverage for building your business AI use case. Inside the Model Library, you can explore the list of partner foundation models, as shown in Figure 5-14.

CHAPTER 5  INTRODUCTION TO SAP BUSINESS AI FOUNDATION

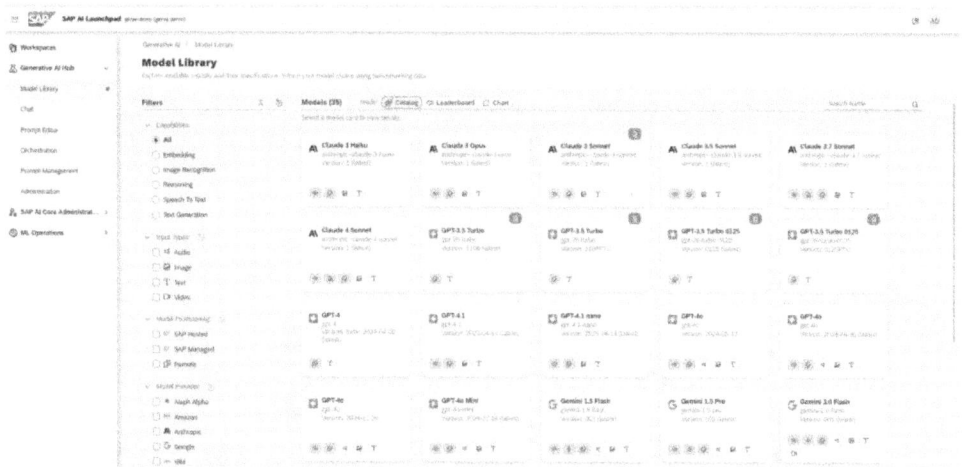

*Figure 5-14.* The Model Library section

As shown in Figure 5-14, the catalog mode lets users browse all available models along with their metadata, making it easier to compare options based on capabilities, providers, and compatibility. Each model also comes with a model card specifying input and output formats, supported modalities, cost considerations, and available performance metrics. Additionally, the leaderboard mode on the top presents benchmarking data, highlighting how models perform across various tasks and metrics. This helps users make confident and data-backed choices based on model performance.

## The Chat Section

After the Model Library selection, the Chat section is where users can engage directly with foundation models through a conversational interface. Basically, it is designed to streamline prompt testing and real-time experimentation, allowing users to quickly iterate on input phrasing, evaluate model responses, and fine-tune interactions, all without writing code. The Chat section is especially essential for business users or domain experts who want to explore Generative AI capabilities without needing deep technical expertise. By offering a simple yet powerful environment for testing and validation, the Chat section, as shown in Figure 5-15, bridges the gap between experimentation and deployment, accelerating the journey from concept to value.

CHAPTER 5   INTRODUCTION TO SAP BUSINESS AI FOUNDATION

*Figure 5-15.*  *The Chat section*

As part of the Model Settings tab, shown in Figure 5-16, Chat provides a set of adjustable parameters such as frequency penalty, presence penalty, max tokens, and temperature, all of which are essential for controlling the model's creativity, verbosity, and response length. Additionally, the streaming toggle at the bottom of the screen allows for real-time output streaming, enhancing the interactivity of the chat experience.

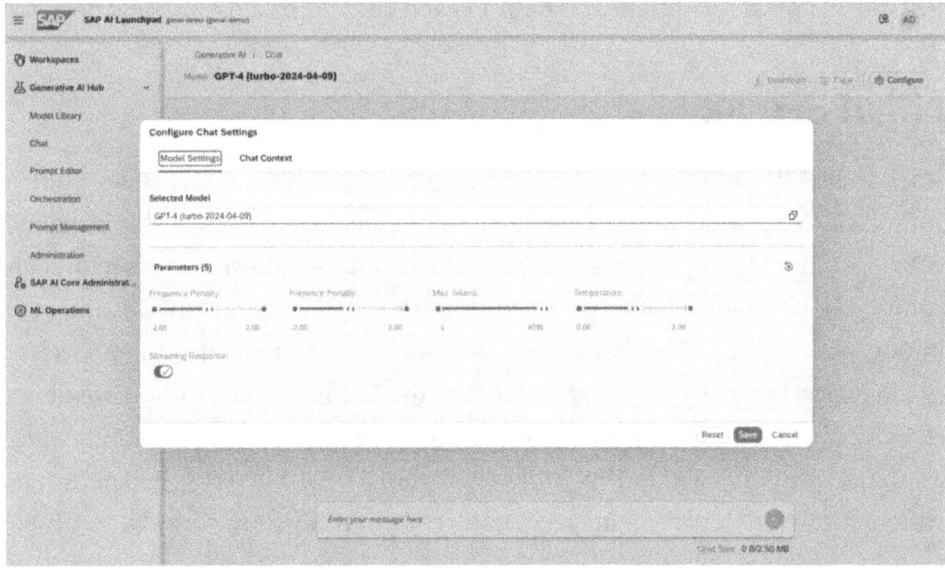

*Figure 5-16.*  *The Model Settings tab*

Users can also switch between models using the Chat Context tab, as shown in Figure 5-17, for deeper customization based on the use case. The Chat Context tab lets users define the conversational context for their chosen model. Also, the Context History slider helps users review the most recent messages sent to the model for evaluation, which ultimately helps balance contextual accuracy with performance.

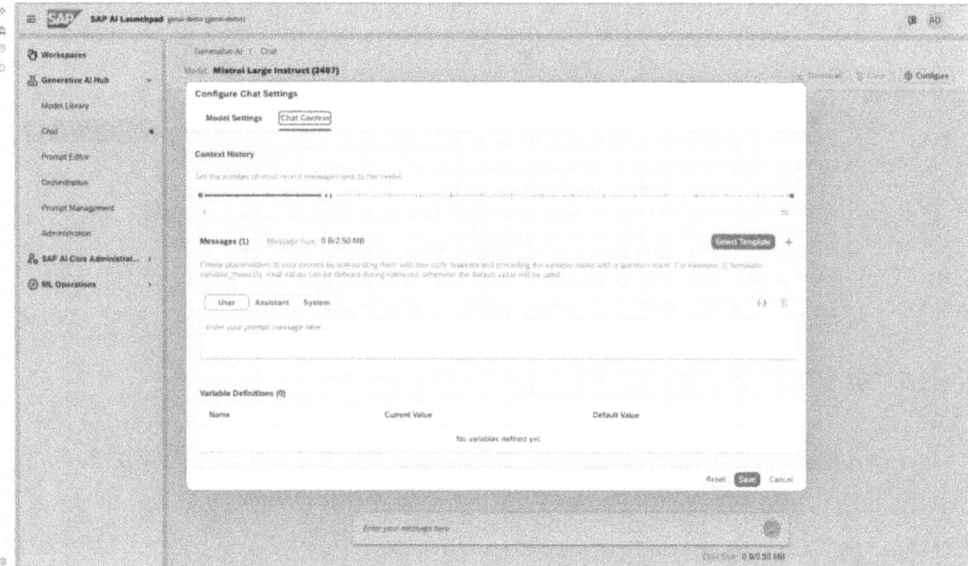

*Figure 5-17. The Chat Context tab*

## The Prompt Editor Section

The Prompt Editor section is one of the powerful features of SAP's Generative AI Hub. It assists users in creating, organizing, and testing prompt templates in a structured and reusable way. This kind of reusable prompt template can be applied across various business AI scenarios without the need to start from scratch each time. By using placeholders and variable definitions, templates make it easy to dynamically insert context-specific data—such as customer names, product IDs, or dates—into the prompt. This flexibility supports both personalization and scalability, enabling consistent and efficient prompt engineering for different business needs.

CHAPTER 5    INTRODUCTION TO SAP BUSINESS AI FOUNDATION

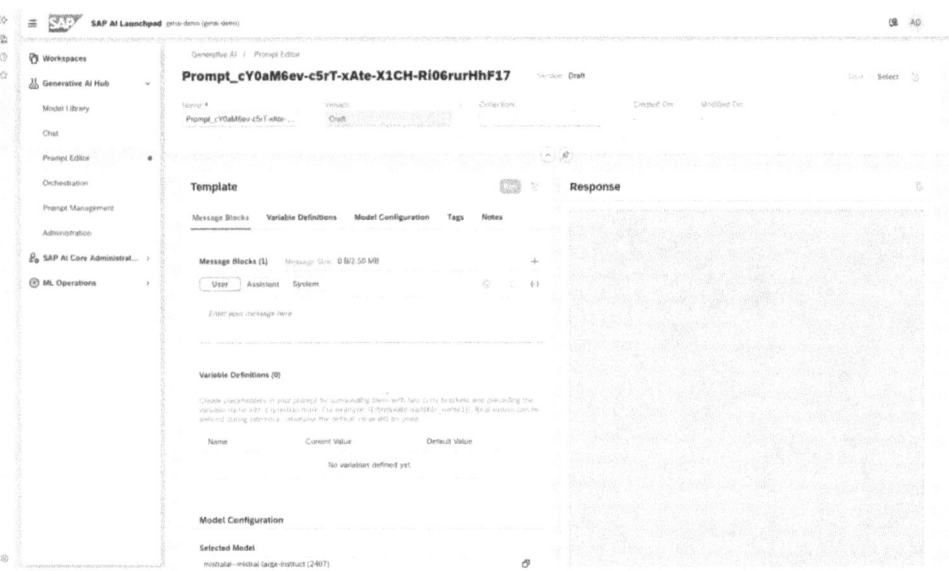

***Figure 5-18.*** *The Prompt template*

As shown in Figure 5-18, defining a new prompt template is primarily driven by the Template section, where users can define message blocks categorized by user, assistant, or system roles to simulate realistic interactions with the model. The Variable definition tab allows for dynamic input substitution using placeholders, which is especially useful for tailoring prompts across different business scenarios. Next is the Model Configuration area, as sown in Figure 5-19, where users can pick their preferred foundation model and associated model parameters, including Frequency Penalty, Presence Penalty, Max Token, and Temperature. This ultimately influences how creative or concise the model's responses will be. On the right, the Response panel displays the model's output when the prompt is executed, giving immediate feedback.

CHAPTER 5    INTRODUCTION TO SAP BUSINESS AI FOUNDATION

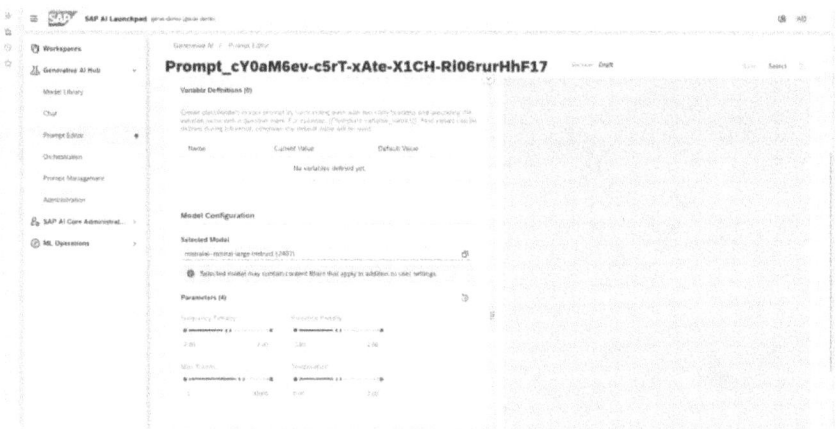

***Figure 5-19.*** *The Model Configuration area*

## The Orchestration Section

Before explaining how orchestration actually works, let's take a step back and look at why orchestration is so important in the context of business AI. Orchestration brings structure, control, and reliability to the way Generative AI interacts with enterprise data and users. Especially in the case of complex business environments, it's not always enough to just generate responses; you need to ensure that those responses are accurate, secure, and contextually relevant. Orchestration enables this by managing each stage of the AI workflow, starting all the way from grounding responses in real-time business data to enforcing data privacy through masking and ensuring compliance with safety and content-filtering rules. Basically, it bridges the gap between raw user input and enterprise-grade output by transforming, enriching, and validating data in between.

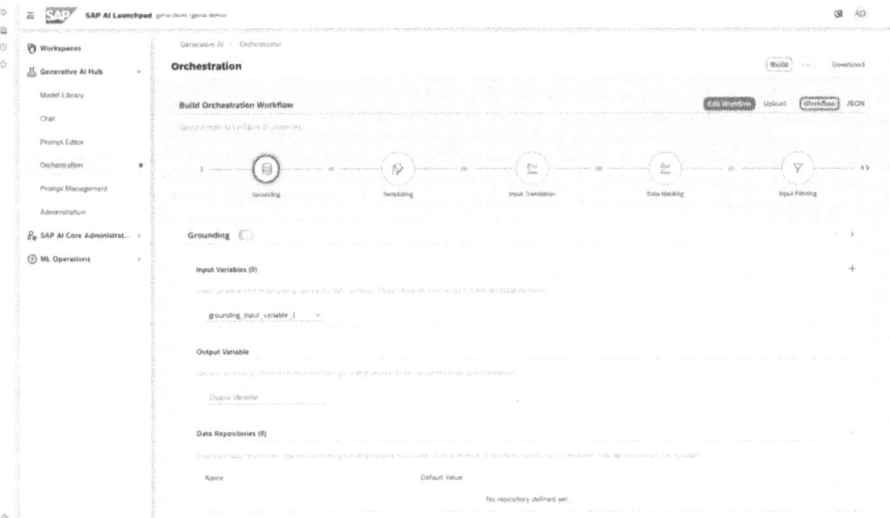

*Figure 5-20. Orchestration*

As shown in Figure 5-20, Orchestration enables users to design structured workflows that manage the end-to-end flow of data and logic across various stages of a Generative AI interaction.

- **Grounding:** Starting with Grounding, users can integrate external, contextually relevant, domain-specific, or real-time data into AI processes that are converted into vector representations to be stored in the HANA Cloud database. This ensures that generated responses are not only accurate but also tailored to enterprise-specific knowledge. You can currently source enterprise knowledge in the form of PDF, DOCS, HTML, TXT, JPEG, JPG, and MS Word from document repositories like MS SharePoint, AWS S3, and SFTP.

- **Templating:** Templating is the next significant step in orchestration, where users can map retrieved data into predefined prompt templates, making it easy to automate and standardize input formatting across different use cases.

- **Translation:** After templating comes the Input Translation step, which handles the conversions or transformations of user input into a format that the language model can interpret more effectively. The orchestration flow currently supports 35+ languages, including autodetection. Similar to the input side of translation, as part of the orchestration flow you can add the required translation on the output side of the workflow.

- **Data masking:** After translation comes the data masking step, as shown in Figure 5-21. It plays a critical role in terms of compliance and data protection by automatically redacting or anonymizing sensitive information before it is passed to the model. This safeguards business and personal data.

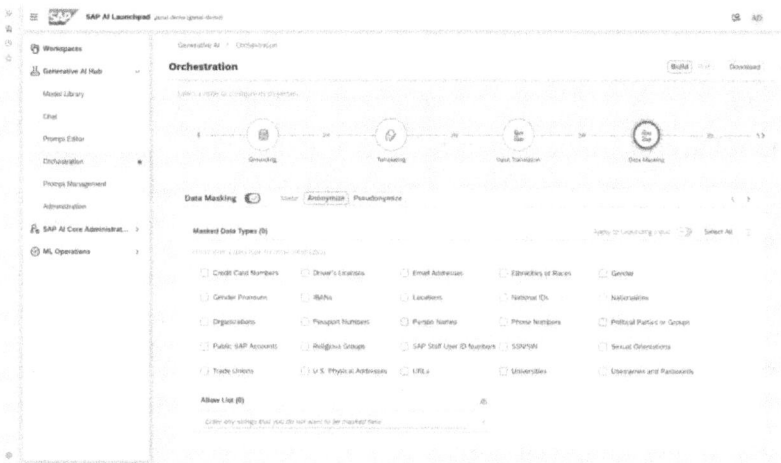

*Figure 5-21. Data Masking*

Data Masking inside the orchestration workflow supports a wide spectrum of masked data types, including personal names, email addresses, phone numbers, gender, political affiliations, national IDs, and more.

CHAPTER 5   INTRODUCTION TO SAP BUSINESS AI FOUNDATION

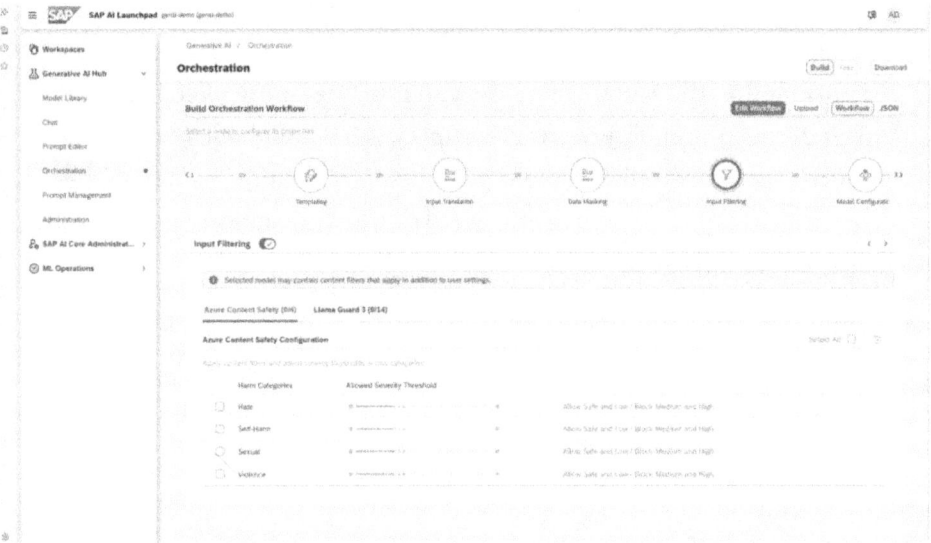

*Figure 5-22.  Input Filtering*

- **Input Filtering:** Input Filtering, as shown in Figure 5-22, enables users to set rules or validations to ensure that only permitted or relevant information is processed, adding another layer of control and security to the pipeline. This feature enables users to apply predefined content filters based on selected safety configurations—such as Azure Content Safety or Llama Guard 3. Users can define thresholds across multiple harm categories, including hate, self-harm, sexual content, and violence, with options to allow, block, or filter content based on severity levels like Safe, Low, Medium, and High. This proactive filtering mechanism ensures that only clean and appropriate inputs are passed to the model, helping organizations maintain ethical standards and prevent misuse. Similar to filtering on the input side, as part of the orchestration flow you can also add required filtering on the output side of the workflow.

Together, these orchestration components allow enterprises to build robust, responsible, and intelligent AI workflows, automating the journey from raw input to business-aware, AI-generated responses while maintaining trust, compliance, and flexibility throughout the process.

CHAPTER 5   INTRODUCTION TO SAP BUSINESS AI FOUNDATION

# The Administration Section

The Administration section of the SAP Generative AI Hub offers essential tools for managing user data and ensuring compliance. As shown in Figure 5-23, it allows administrators to monitor storage consumption through a clear visual progress bar, helping track usage against the allocated limit. The interface also supports manual user offboarding, where an admin can input a user's email ID to fetch and delete associated prompt data, maintaining data hygiene and control. Additionally, the Disclaimer Message tab enables organizations to create and manage custom disclaimers, ensuring transparency and governance over AI usage. This centralized view helps streamline administrative tasks with clarity and precision.

***Figure 5-23.*** *Administration: User Data section*

Additionally, the Disclaimer Message feature inside the Administration section also allows administrators to define a custom message that is displayed to all users of the Prompt Editor and Chat applications across the tenant. This message can be tailored to align with internal policies, such as guidelines on AI ethics, responsible usage, or data privacy practices. By setting up a disclaimer, organizations can proactively inform users about acceptable usage standards and ensure awareness of compliance requirements before interacting with Generative AI tools.

Now that you have a basic understanding of various components of AI Foundation on SAP BTP, the next section explains how you can take advantage of SAP's latest Vector Engine and Knowledge Graph related offerings on SAP Hana Cloud to obtain unseen insights from business data and its relevant context.

133

CHAPTER 5  INTRODUCTION TO SAP BUSINESS AI FOUNDATION

# Business Data and Context

The significance of business data and the right context, especially for enterprise scale AI solutions, cannot be overstated. Business data holds the real value; it captures transactions, processes, and relationships unique to the organization. Context ensures that AI models interpret this data meaningfully. This is where Knowledge Graphs and Vector Databases play a vital role. At one end, Knowledge Graphs bring structure and semantics to data by connecting entities and their relationships for deeper understanding. Vector Databases, on the other hand, enable similarity searching across unstructured data like text or images, helping AI systems retrieve the most relevant information quickly. To bring the best of both of these worlds, SAP has introduced Vector Databases and Knowledge Graphs as part of their SAP Hana Cloud offering. This empowers developers to build context-aware, intelligent queries that go far beyond keyword matching.

- **Vector Engine:** The SAP HANA Cloud Vector Engine, as depicted in Figure 5-24, is a powerful addition to SAP's multi-model database capabilities, especially tailored to support the growing need of Generative AI driven enterprise applications. Basically, it allows businesses to manage and analyze multi-dimensional vector data directly within the SAP HANA Cloud environment, enabling seamless integration of advanced use cases like semantic search, personalized recommendations, and similarity detection. By converting business data content sourced from various unstructured sources like documents, text, speech, and structured data into vector representations, the engine supports complex comparisons using methods like cosine similarity and Euclidean distance. Integrating Vector Engine into an enterprise application can help you unlock deeper and more context-aware insights that go beyond traditional databases offerings. Its ability to work natively with vector data positions it as a critical component for consultants and developers looking to embed real-time intelligence into enterprise workflows. As AI adoption accelerates across industries, the Vector Engine equips organizations with the tools to transform raw, unstructured data into valuable insights, enabling smarter decisions and more agile digital transformation strategies.

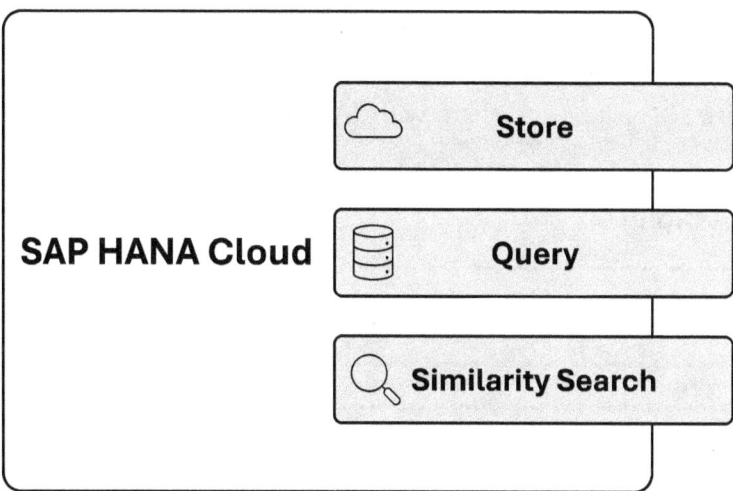

*Figure 5-24.* *The SAP HANA Cloud Vector Engine*

- **Knowledge Graph:** Knowledge Graph identifies different relationships between entities, such as people, places, or concepts, in a way that can be understood and processed by machines. SAP recently introduced Knowledge Graph as part of their SAP HANA Cloud offering to bring a transformative approach to enterprise data management. Knowledge Graph enables organizations to model and explore complex relationships between business entities in a highly intuitive and interconnected way. Unlike traditional relational databases that store data in isolated tables, Knowledge Graph represents data as nodes and edges, making it easier to trace how customers, suppliers, products, and transactions are linked. Being seamlessly integrated with SAP HANA Cloud's multi-model architecture and hosted on SAP BTP, Knowledge Graph functions as a unifying layer—breaking down data silos and supporting real-time, cross-application insights by leveraging industry standards like SQL, SQL Script, and SPARQL, allowing flexible and efficient querying across vast, distributed datasets. For consultants and enterprise users, this means that they can build intelligent applications that deliver greater visibility and actionable insights—whether it's tracking supply chain risks, mapping ESG dependencies, or enhancing compliance analytics. As enterprises move toward more connected, hybrid environments, SAP Knowledge Graph plays a pivotal role in delivering trusted, context-aware data that supports smarter decisions and aligns with SAP's broader data fabric strategy.

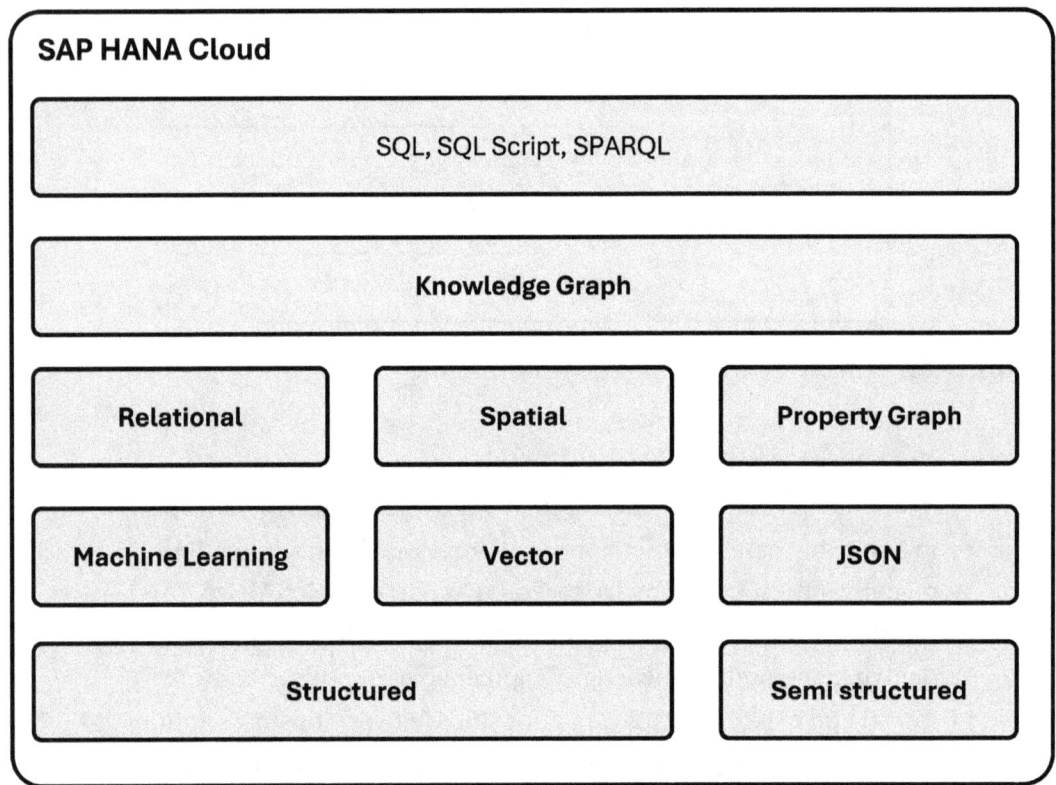

*Figure 5-25.* *SAP HANA Cloud Knowledge Graph*

As depicted in Figure 5-25, Knowledge Graph is positioned as a core component sitting alongside other data models such as relational, spatial, property graph, vector, JSON, and machine learning. It enables users to work across structured and semi-structured data, providing a unified view of diverse data types using standard query languages like SQL, SQL Script, and SPARQL. This makes it accessible and interoperable.

## Conclusion

This chapter explained SAP BTP Business AI and AI Foundation. Starting with a detailed introduction to SAP Business AI, the chapter covered various components of SAP's Business AI offering on SAP BTP, including AI Foundation, AI Services, AI Core, and SAP Joule. To quickly recap, SAP Business AI on SAP BTP has been crafted with a suite-first principle, ensuring a fully integrated AI approach that compounds value with every new capability. At the heart of this strategy is Joule, which is SAP's Generative AI copilot, designed to provide a unified AI experience across all business functions. On the other end, AI Services are specifically crafted for business processes and enable companies to quickly integrate AI functions into their SAP systems. Finally, SAP AI Core along with SAP AI Launchpad, not only provide the required foundation to host the entire Business AI offering but also offer a comprehensive platform and a central cockpit to build and manage enterprise-grade custom AI solutions. Last but not the least, Knowledge Graphs and Vector Databases introduced as part of SAP HANA Cloud offering on BTP help clients build context-aware, intelligent queries that go far beyond the keyword matching offered by traditional databases.

# CHAPTER 6

# Building Custom AI Applications Using SAP Business AI Foundation

In the previous chapters, you developed a solid understanding of the different dimensions and components of the Generative AI world, followed by an in-depth introduction to SAP's latest offering, Business AI Foundation for the Business Technology Platform. This foundation enables clients and stakeholders to kick-start their enterprise AI journey by providing the right blend of embedded AI capabilities, a wide range of foundation models, an AI assistant, and a robust runtime. This chapter leverages those components to develop an end-to-end enterprise AI use case using a step-by-step approach. It shows you not just how the platform works, but why it matters for real-world AI adoption and how it can meaningfully accelerate enterprise transformation.

## Use Case Identification

The first step of this journey of building an enterprise AI solution starts with identifying a possible use case that you can easily relate to common enterprise challenges and that can help you take advantage of various features and functionalities offered by the SAP Business AI Foundation. To gain a comprehensive understanding of various concepts introduced in the previous chapters, this chapter shows you how to develop an end user bot capable of answering various queries related to equipment maintenance. This is especially relevant in the context of industrial manufacturing.

While working in the field, maintenance technicians often struggle to access the various pieces of information they need—especially maintenance data—to carry out equipment repairs efficiently. With this data spread across disparate sources and silos,

CHAPTER 6   BUILDING CUSTOM AI APPLICATIONS USING SAP BUSINESS AI FOUNDATION

traditional AI-driven business applications often require multiple rounds of training and evaluation just to deliver reasonably accurate answers. This is where a RAG-based enterprise application powered by LLMs can truly ease the burden, overcoming the limitations of traditional machine learning and delivering relevant information from a continuously updating data corpus through simple, natural prompts—ultimately helping technicians work faster, smarter, and with greater confidence.

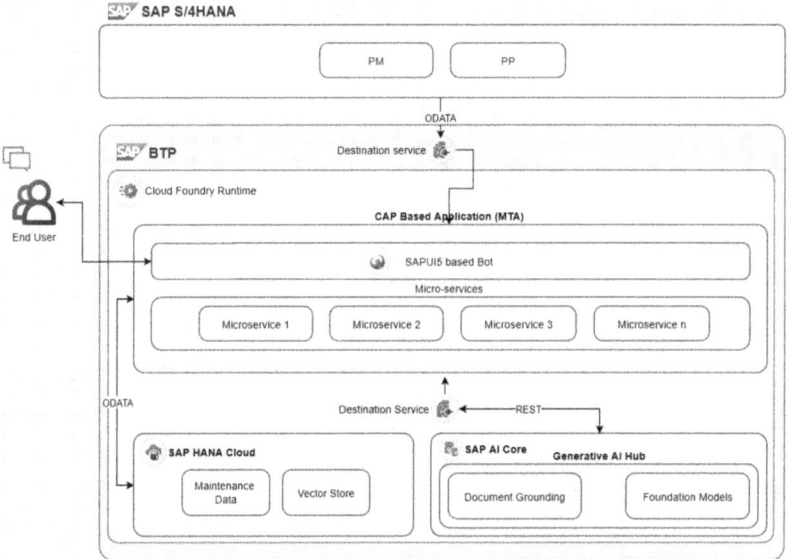

***Figure 6-1.*** *Solution architecture*

As depicted in Figure 6-1, the process starts with uploading maintenance data in the form of a PDF, triggering the process to covert the unstructured data from the PDF into sizable data chunks, followed by generation of the embeddings, which ultimately are saved into the SAP HANA Cloud Vector Engine database. After the embedding process, the maintenance technician submits a query in the form of prompts. The query is converted into embeddings using the LLM and sent to the vector database, where the system searches for similar information using techniques like Cosine Similarity or L2 Distance. The chunk with the highest similarity is retrieved, which is basically the vector database's response to the user query. Let's quickly chalk out the components that you need to deliver this use case:

- **SAP AI Launchpad:** SAP AI Launchpad acts as a central cockpit to manage the lifecycle of all your AI models and scenarios deployed across the enterprise, including a wide range of API support. To build the use case, you need access to the AI Launchpad link to your BTP global account. The Generative AI Hub, as part of AI Launchpad, lets you incorporate Generative AI into your AI activities in SAP AI Core. Booster driven setup is available for AI Launchpad, which can guide you through interactive steps to select, configure, and consume services on SAP BTP.

- **RAG technique:** RAG, being a popular technique for enhancing LLMs with information retrieved from external knowledge sources, plays a critical role in bringing maintenance-related data into the workflow, whether it comes from SOPs, log-books, or maintenance history in formats like PDF, HTML, or Word. You can think of the RAG technique as walking you through the process: first extracting and converting all those diverse source materials into a unified plain-text format, then segmenting it into smaller, manageable chunks that help overcome the contextual limitations of LLMs. These chunks are then encoded into vector representations using an embedding model and stored in a vector database, making it easy to perform fast and accurate similarity searches during retrieval.

- **HANA Cloud Vector Engine:** SAP HANA Cloud Vector Engine is a powerful addition to SAP's multi-model database capabilities, especially tailored to support the growing needs of Generative AI driven enterprise applications to manage and analyze multi-dimensional vector data. In the context of this use case, embeddings generated from unstructured maintenance data sources will be persisted using the SAP HANA Cloud Vector Engine.

- **LLM:** The LLM is the heart of any RAG-based application because it transforms raw, retrieved information into something that feels natural, relevant, and context-aware. In the context of this use case, the LLM plays a crucial role on the embedding generation side, converting chunks of documents and user queries into numerical vectors that capture their meaning, not just the words. Then comes the chat completion role, which is where the LLM shines. It not only interprets the user prompts but also acts on the best-matching document snippets retrieved from the vector store to craft a clear, coherent, and natural response.

CHAPTER 6   BUILDING CUSTOM AI APPLICATIONS USING SAP BUSINESS AI FOUNDATION

- **Document grounding:** Document grounding is the process of anchoring an LLM's responses to authoritative, organization-specific content so that answers are factually correct and contextually relevant. The document grounding component on Generative AI Hub plays a key role by sourcing the enterprise knowledge in the form of PDF, DOC, HTML, TXT, JPEG, JPG, or MS Word from document repositories like MS SharePoint, AWS S3, and SFTP. By ingesting and indexing these materials, the RAG pipeline can retrieve precise, up-to-date snippets from the specified knowledgebase whenever a query is made.

- **CAP LLM plugin:** The CAP LLM plugin is incredibly versatile, suitable for a wide range of applications across various industries. Whether automating customer service responses, optimizing HR recruitment processes, or ensuring compliance through data anonymization, the plugin provides the tools necessary for developing sophisticated, AI-driven solutions.

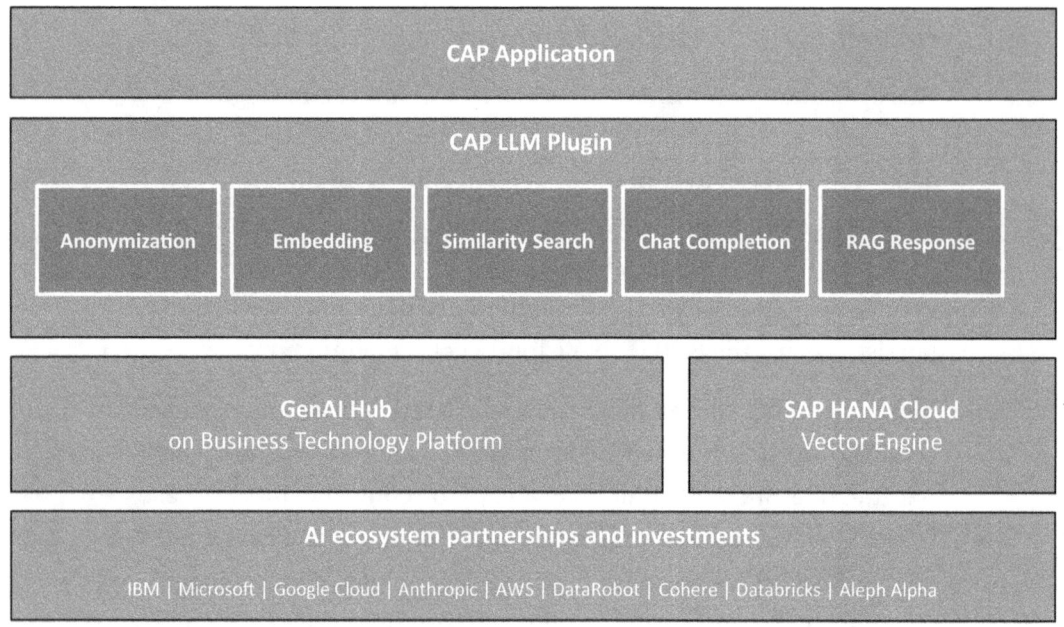

***Figure 6-2.*** *The CAP LLM plugin architecture*

- **Robust data anonymization:** Utilizing SAP HANA Cloud's advanced data anonymization techniques, the plugin enables developers to protect sensitive data seamlessly. With just a few annotations, such as @anonymize, developers can implement algorithms like k-Anonymity and l-Diversity, safeguarding data integrity and compliance.

- **Enhanced AI-powered functionalities:** The plugin connects directly to SAP AI Core, facilitating the generation of vector embeddings and performing similarity searches. This capability is crucial for applications that demand precise and insightful data analysis.

- **Simplified access to LLMs:** Through SAP AI Core, the plugin offers streamlined access to LLMs for tasks such as chat completion. This feature allows applications to deliver contextually appropriate AI-generated responses, enhancing user interaction.

- **Efficient RAG:** The plugin optimizes the RAG process by integrating functionalities of both SAP AI Core and SAP HANA Cloud Vector Engine into a single, streamlined method. This integration enables dynamic data fetching and utilization in AI operations, significantly boosting efficiency.

| Feature | Details |
| --- | --- |
| Embedding generation via SAP AI Core | Easily connect to embedding models via SAP AI Core and generate embeddings seamlessly |
| Similarity Search | Leverage SAP HANA Cloud's Vector Engine to perform similarity searches via the CAP LLM plugin |
| Chat LLM Access via SAP AI Core | Simple access to LLM models via SAP AI Core with a simplified method for chat completion |
| Streamlining RAG retrieval | Single method to streamline the entire RAG retrieval process leveraging SAP AI Core and the SAP HANA Cloud Vector Engine |
| Orchestration Service Support | Support for SAP AI Core orchestration service's harmonized chat completion APIs |

For more information related to the CAP LLM plugin and APIs, refer to https://github.com/SAP-samples/cap-llm-plugin-samples/blob/main/docs/api-documentation.md.

- **SAP AI Core SDK:** In addition to the CAP-LLM plugin, which is more open-source, SAP AI Core comes with its own set of libraries for JavaScript, Node.js, and Python, covering almost every aspect of building custom AI solutions.

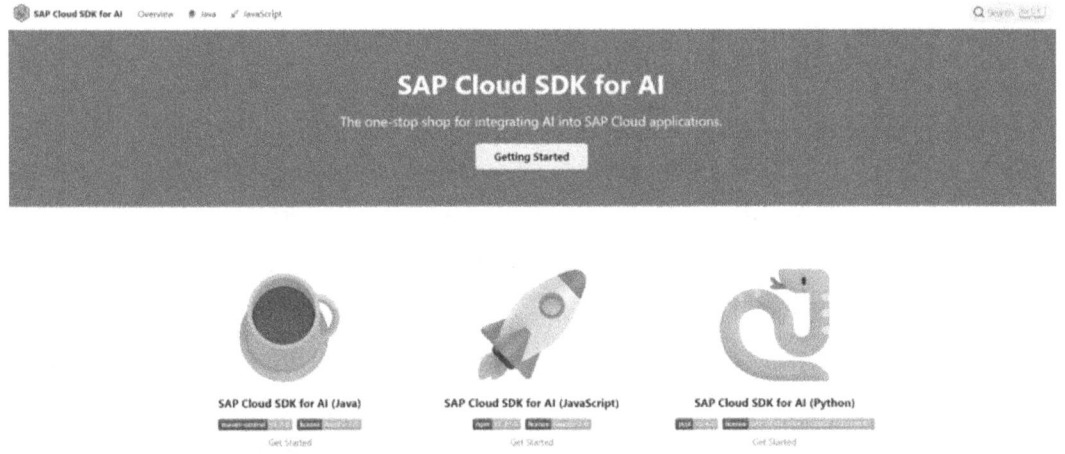

*Figure 6-3. SAP Cloud SDK*

- **SAP Cloud SDK (Java, JavaScript):** SAP Cloud SDK for AI is the official toolkit for working with SAP AI Core, the Generative AI Hub, and orchestration features. It enables you to integrate chat completion directly into your business applications, making it easier to deliver intelligent user experiences. Using the SDK, you can also take advantage of key AI Core capabilities, including but not limited to templating, grounding, data masking, content filtering, thus administrating the SAP AI Core instance more efficiently.

- **SAP Cloud SDK (Python):** The Python cloud SDK is delivered as three Python distributions, each serving a specific purpose. The sap-ai-sdk-base distribution can be leveraged to access the AI API through Python methods and data structures, while sap-ai-sdk-core allows you to interact with SAP AI Core for administration tasks and lifecycle management.

More details can be found at https://sap.github.io/ai-sdk/.

- **SAPUI5:** The SAPUI5 chat interface is the polished, user-facing layer that transforms the RAG system from a backend AI engine into a practical, interactive assistant embedded directly into the SAP business environment. With SAPUI5, you can design a conversational UI that not only looks and feels like a modern chat application but also integrates tightly with SAP systems and enterprise security standards. Users can type questions, upload documents, or even select from predefined prompts, and the interface passes these inputs to the RAG backend. Once the LLM processes the query—pulling context from embedded documents and grounding it in enterprise data—the SAPUI5 app displays the generated response in a clean, interactive format. What makes SAPUI5 especially valuable in this setup is its integration with SAP HANA Cloud, SAP BTP services, and other enterprise repositories to provide real-time data, user authentication, and role-based access control. It can also enhance the RAG experience with features like conversation history, document preview, or quick actions (e.g., "drill down" into the source document), giving users confidence that the answers are grounded in trusted enterprise content.

- **Node.js:** Node.js is a powerful open-source server-side JavaScript runtime environment that allows developers to build scalable and high-performing network applications. It provides a unique event-driven, non-blocking I/O model that makes it lightweight and efficient. The combination of Node.js and SAP BTP allows developers to leverage the power and flexibility of Node.js for building cloud-native applications that run on the SAP BTP Cloud Foundry environment, benefiting especially from Node.js's strong synergy with microservices, APIs, and real-time applications on BTP, which ties the technical architecture to clear enterprise advantages.

- **Business Application Studio:** SAP Business Application Studio (BAS), the successor to Neo-based SAP Web IDE, is a complete transformation of development environment for building modern, cloud-based applications that power the intelligent enterprise.

It offers developers an experience comparable to leading desktop IDEs, while also streamlining the entire process with productivity features like ready-to-use templates, guided wizards, visual editors, and rapid deployment options for a wide range of SAP applications, including CAP, MTA, Java, Noje.js, and SAPUI5. It significantly reduces the go-to-market time for enterprise applications.

- **SAP Destination service:** The SAP BTP Destination service lets you provides the details needed for your cloud application to connect with external systems or services. When working with on-premise systems, it is typically used alongside the Connectivity service. In Kubernetes environments, these connections are managed through the Destination service, the Connectivity Proxy, and the Transparent Proxy. For connections to other web applications, the Destination service can be used on its own without the Connectivity service.

- **Cloud Foundry Runtime:** On SAP BTP, the Cloud Foundry Runtime plays a critical role in building and running a RAG-based application because it gives you a flexible, managed environment to deploy all the moving parts of the pipeline—without getting bogged down in infrastructure management. In a RAG scenario, you typically have multiple backend services: a document ingestion pipeline, an embedding generator, a vector store integration, a retriever service, and the orchestration logic that connects everything to the LLM. Cloud Foundry lets you package these components into microservices (in Node.js, Python, Java, etc.) and run them in an isolated, scalable environment. You can bind these services to SAP BTP resources like SAP HANA Cloud (for storing metadata or document references) or object stores for raw file storage and connect securely to external repositories like SharePoint or AWS S3 for grounding data. The beauty of using Cloud Foundry is that it's language-agnostic and supports a polyglot development. That means your embedding generator might be written in Python using a machine learning library, while your orchestration service could

CHAPTER 6  BUILDING CUSTOM AI APPLICATIONS USING SAP BUSINESS AI FOUNDATION

be in Node.js—yet they can all be deployed and managed together under the same runtime. Plus, built-in environment management, service binding, and scaling capabilities mean that you can easily handle high query volumes without re-architecting your system, an abstraction that accelerates innovation cycles while maintaining enterprise-grade scalability and governance.

Now that you have read about the required services and tools for development, the next section explains how to pick the right LLM to build the enterprise use cases and how various offerings on SAP's Generative AI Hub can help.

# Choosing an LLM

SAP Generative AI Hub offers a diverse range of foundation models from leading AI providers like Open AI, Google, IBM, AWS, Mistral, Anthropic, and others, ensuring a secure, scalable, and enterprise-ready AI integration. Most of the partner foundation models offered through the Generative AI Hub are hosted and managed by SAP, but there are certain models like AWS Bedrock and GCP Vertex that only provide access to their model through endpoints. SAP hosted models are managed by SAP AI Core on SAP's own infrastructure. They physically reside in SAP's data centers or infrastructure environments, including provisioning, scaling, patching, monitoring, and security. In contrast, SAP managed models are hosted on isolated hyperscaler infrastructure and managed by SAP AI Core. Even though it runs on hyperscaler resources, SAP AI Core manages the entire lifecycle, including provisioning, scaling, updates, and monitoring. Table 6-1 offers a quick glimpse of the broad selection of models that enable businesses to choose the most suitable one for specific use cases.

*Table 6-1.* List of Available Foundation Models

| Global Scenario | Executable ID | Description |
| --- | --- | --- |
| foundation-models | azure-openai | The Azure OpenAI Service provides REST API access to OpenAI's LLMs. |
| foundation-models | aicore-opensource | Open-source models that are hosted and managed by SAP and accessed through SAP AI Core. |
| foundation-models | gcp-vertexai | GCP Vertex AI provides access to PaLM 2 and Gemini models from Google. |
| foundation-models | aws-bedrock | AWS Bedrock provides access to foundation models from Anthropic, Amazon, and other providers. |
| foundation-models | aicore-mistralai | Models from Mistral AI that are hosted and managed by SAP and accessed through SAP AI Core. |
| foundation-models | aicore-ibm | Models from IBM that are hosted and managed by SAP and accessed through SAP AI Core. |

Table 6-2 lists a comprehensive collection of language models along with their versions supported against each foundation models.

*Table 6-2.* List of Available LLMs in the Generative AI Hub

| Executable ID (Access Type) | Model Name | Version |
| --- | --- | --- |
| aicore-mistralai (sap-hosted) | mistralai--mistral-large-instruct | 2407 (latest) |
| aicore-mistralai (sap-hosted) | mistralai--mistral-small-instruct | 2503 (latest) |
| aicore-ibm (sap-managed) | ibm--granite-13b-chat | 2.1.0 (latest) |
| aicore-opensource (sap-managed) | meta--llama3.1-70b-instruct | 202409 (latest) |
| aicore-nvidia (sap-managed) | nvidia--llama-3.2-nv-embedqa-1b | 2 (latest) |
| aws-bedrock (AWS) | amazon--titan-embed-text | 1.2 |

(*continued*)

*Table 6-2.* (*continued*)

| Executable ID (Access Type) | Model Name | Version |
|---|---|---|
| aws-bedrock (AWS) | amazon--titan-embed-text | 2 (latest) |
| aws-bedrock (AWS) | amazon--titan-text-express | 1 (latest) |
| aws-bedrock (AWS) | amazon--titan-text-lite | 1 (latest) |
| aws-bedrock (AWS) | amazon--nova-pro | 1 (latest) |
| aws-bedrock (AWS) | amazon--nova-lite | 1 (latest) |
| aws-bedrock (AWS) | amazon--nova-micro | 1 (latest) |
| aws-bedrock (AWS) | amazon--nova-premier | 1 (latest) |
| aws-bedrock (AWS) | anthropic--claude-3-haiku | 1 (latest) |
| aws-bedrock (AWS) | anthropic--claude-3-sonnet | 1 (latest) |
| aws-bedrock (AWS) | anthropic--claude-3-opus | 1 (latest) |
| aws-bedrock (AWS) | anthropic--claude-3.5-sonnet | 1 |
| aws-bedrock (AWS) | anthropic--claude-3.5-sonnet | 2 (latest) |
| aws-bedrock (AWS) | anthropic--claude-3.7-sonnet | 1 |
| aws-bedrock (AWS) | anthropic--claude-4-sonnet | 1 (latest) |
| aws-bedrock (AWS) | anthropic--claude-4-opus | 1 (latest) |
| azure-openai (Azure) | text-embedding-3-large | 1 (latest) |
| azure-openai (Azure) | text-embedding-3-small | 1 (latest) |
| azure-openai (Azure) | text-embedding-ada-002 | 2 (latest) |
| azure-openai (Azure) | gpt-35-turbo | 1106 (latest) |
| azure-openai (Azure) | gpt-35-turbo-0125 | 0125 (latest) |
| azure-openai (Azure) | gpt-4o | 13-05-2024 |
| azure-openai (Azure) | gpt-4o | 2024-08-06 (latest) |

(*continued*)

*Table 6-2.* (*continued*)

| Executable ID (Access Type) | Model Name | Version |
|---|---|---|
| azure-openai (Azure) | gpt-4o | 20-11-2024 |
| azure-openai (Azure) | gpt-4o-mini | 18-07-2024 |
| azure-openai (Azure) | gpt-4 | turbo-2024-04-09 (latest) |
| azure-openai (Azure) | gpt-4.1 | 14-04-2025 |
| azure-openai (Azure) | gpt-4.1-mini | 14-04-2025 |
| azure-openai (Azure) | gpt-4.1-nano | 14-04-2025 |
| azure-openai (Azure) | o1 | 17-12-2024 |
| azure-openai (Azure) | o3-mini | 31-01-2025 |
| azure-openai (Azure) | o3 | 16-04-2025 |
| azure-openai (Azure) | o4-mini | 16-04-2025 |
| gcp-vertexai (Google) | gemini-1.5-flash | 002 (latest) |
| gcp-vertexai (Google) | gemini-1.5-pro | 002 (latest) |
| gcp-vertexai (Google) | gemini-2.0-flash | 001 (latest) |
| gcp-vertexai (Google) | gemini-2.0-flash-lite | 001 (latest) |
| gcp-vertexai (Google) | gemini-2.5-flash | 001 (latest) |
| gcp-vertexai (Google) | gemini-2.5-pro | 001 (latest) |
| aicore-alephalpha (sap-hosted) | alephalpha-pharia-1-7b-control | 202411 (latest) |
| aicore-opensource (sap-managed) | deepseek-ai--deepseek-r1 | * |

From advanced LLMs that can handle reasoning, summarization, and natural conversations, to specialized embedding models that power search, recommendation, and retrieval use cases, the portfolio covers a broad spectrum of needs. Enterprises can choose from instruction-tuned models for business process automation, lightweight models optimized for speed and cost, and high-performance models built for complex problem-solving. With options spanning multiple providers and architectures, this ecosystem ensures flexibility, scalability, and the ability to align the right model with the right task—whether it's conversational AI, content generation, knowledge retrieval, or domain-specific optimization.

In addition to a wide spectrum of partner foundation models, as expected SAP has introduced their specialized enterprise-oriented model for code generation and smart prediction. SAP has added two new unique models as part of Generative AI Hub known as SAP RPT-1 and SAP ABAP-1 where the RPT-1 model is tailored to make enterprise-oriented predictions faster and the ABAP-1 as the name implies is a dedicated foundation model for code generation and review related work.

The RPT-1 model is a outcome SAP's decade long research to deliver enterprise-oriented AI models and based on the foundation model called ConTextTab which is basically a semantics-aware, table-native in-context learning (ICL) model specially curated for tabular prediction tasks. Where most of the LLMs struggle to understand and interpret the tabular data, SAP RPT-1 works in two dimensions, meaning that both cross-column and cross-row attention are calculated for each cell. With SAP RPT-1 model, business scenarios requiring predictions are no longer needed to go through prolong training and testing life cycles and instead can generate accurate predictions much faster just by using a chunk of labeled data (tabular form column/row fashion data) and simple prompt engineering. Additionally, with SAP RPT-1, one single model can take of enterprise predictions in the area of across finance, supply chain, HR, and more, simply by seeing examples from a different domain in its respective context. For more information related to SAP RPT-1, you can refer here - https://help.sap.com/docs/sap-ai-core/generative-ai/sap-rpt-1?locale=en-US.

On the other end, to accelerate the coding related task SAP has introduced SAP ABAP-1 specially tailored for ABAP code generation, review, explanation etc. and interesting to know that SAP ABAP-1 also used internally for the SAP Joule for developers. The model is currently released for experimental purpose and not yet full scale production ready. For more details, you can refer here - https://help.sap.com/docs/sap-ai-core/generative-ai/sap-abap-1?locale=en-US.

With so many powerful models available, it can be overwhelming to decide which one best fits a specific use case. This is where the Prompting Playground in SAP's Generative AI Hub becomes invaluable. It allows teams to experiment with the same prompt across different models, compare the quality, tone, and relevance of the responses, and quickly identify which model delivers the most suitable outcome for their

CHAPTER 6   BUILDING CUSTOM AI APPLICATIONS USING SAP BUSINESS AI FOUNDATION

business scenario. By providing a safe, interactive environment for side-by-side testing and fine-tuning prompts, the playground takes the guesswork out of model selection and helps organizations make confident, data-driven choices.

As shown in Figure 6-4, the Generative AI Hub Model Library section lets you explore the wide spectrum of partner foundation models based on various capabilities like embedding, image recognition, reasoning, speech to text, and text-generation processing various input types like audio, image, text, and video.

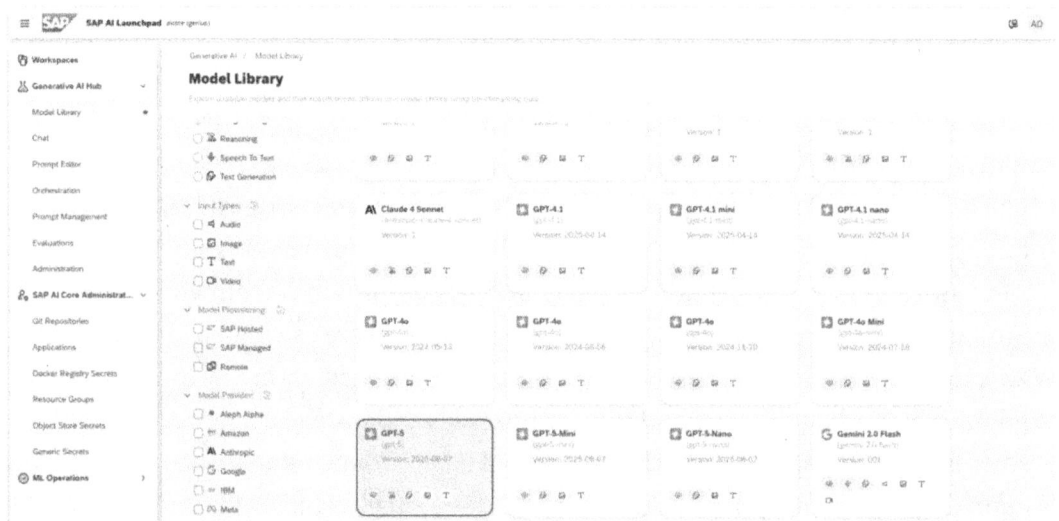

***Figure 6-4.*** *Model Library*

Clicking a model tile takes you to its model detail screen, displaying associated cost and properties associated with that model. Figure 6-5 shows the GPT-5 model tile.

CHAPTER 6   BUILDING CUSTOM AI APPLICATIONS USING SAP BUSINESS AI FOUNDATION

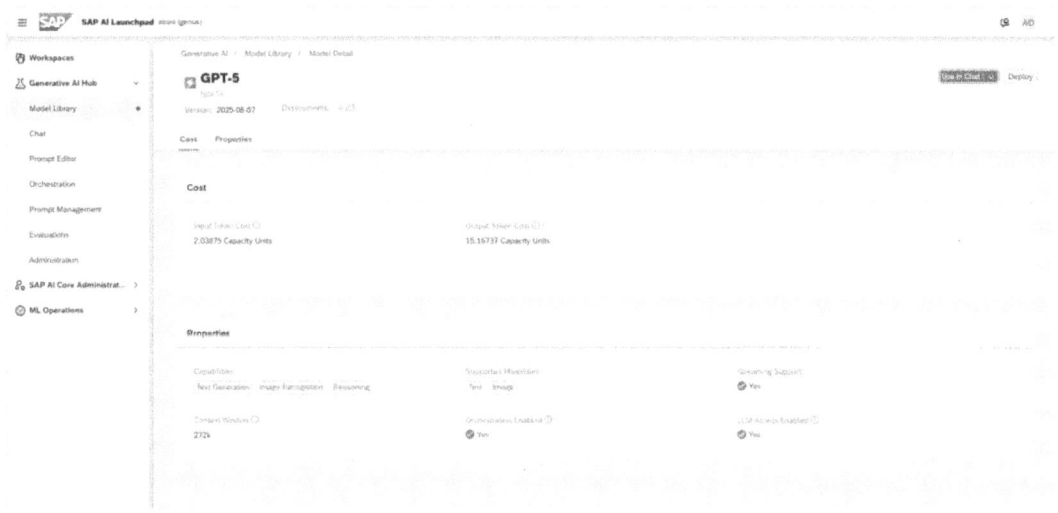

*Figure 6-5.* *Model Details*

Inside the model screen, as shown in Figure 6-6, you can choose the simple Use in Chat or Use in Prompt Editor option to play around with the selected model using relevant prompts.

*Figure 6-6.* *Use Model*

The Prompt Editor section of the Generative AI Hub is an ultimate playground to evaluate the capabilities of different LLMs through prompts. Prompts that you try as part of the evaluation exercise can be saved as templates for future reference across various business AI projects. The Template Editor, as shown in Figure 6-7, has multiple segments, including Message Blocks, Variable Definition, Model Configuration, Tag, and Notes.

153

CHAPTER 6   BUILDING CUSTOM AI APPLICATIONS USING SAP BUSINESS AI FOUNDATION

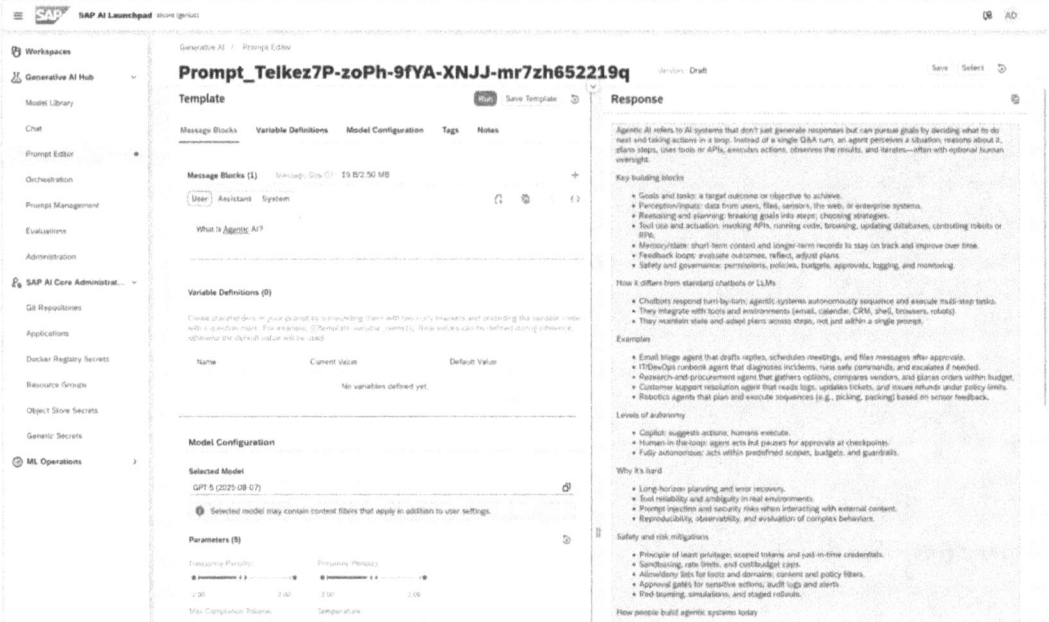

***Figure 6-7.*** *Text input prompt*

The Message Block section, as shown in Figure 6-7, allows you to structure and enter prompts in a clear and interactive way, including a provision to specify the role like User, Assistant, and System that the LLM should play when delivering the response. Each message block supports customizable inputs, making it easy to build, test, and refine prompts in a structured, reusable format. To try the capabilities, we have entered a very simple and generic prompt, "What is Agentic AI?". The LLM, which in this case is GPT-5, shows a comprehensive response about Agentic AI. In the same way, you can enter various prompts relevant for your use case and evaluate the model.

In the next attempt, we upload an image to see how well GPT-5 interprets it. As shown in Figure 6-8, we are using the image of an industrial ball bearing and requesting LLM to classify the image using prompt, "Classify the image and generate a description."

CHAPTER 6   BUILDING CUSTOM AI APPLICATIONS USING SAP BUSINESS AI FOUNDATION

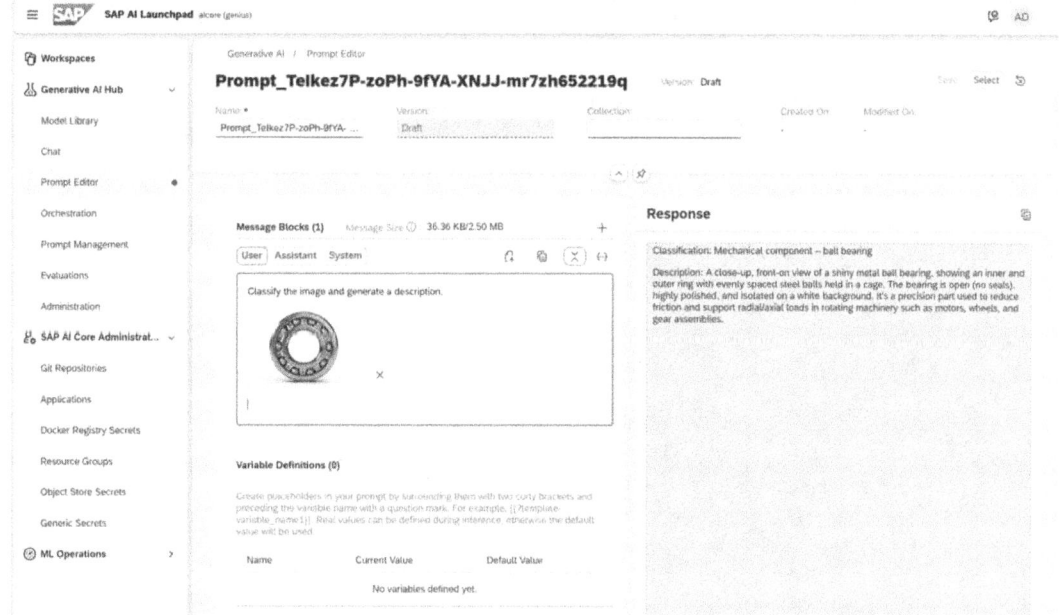

*Figure 6-8.   Image input prompt*

As shown in Figure 6-8, LLM not only classifies the image, but also generates a brief description of the ball bearing.

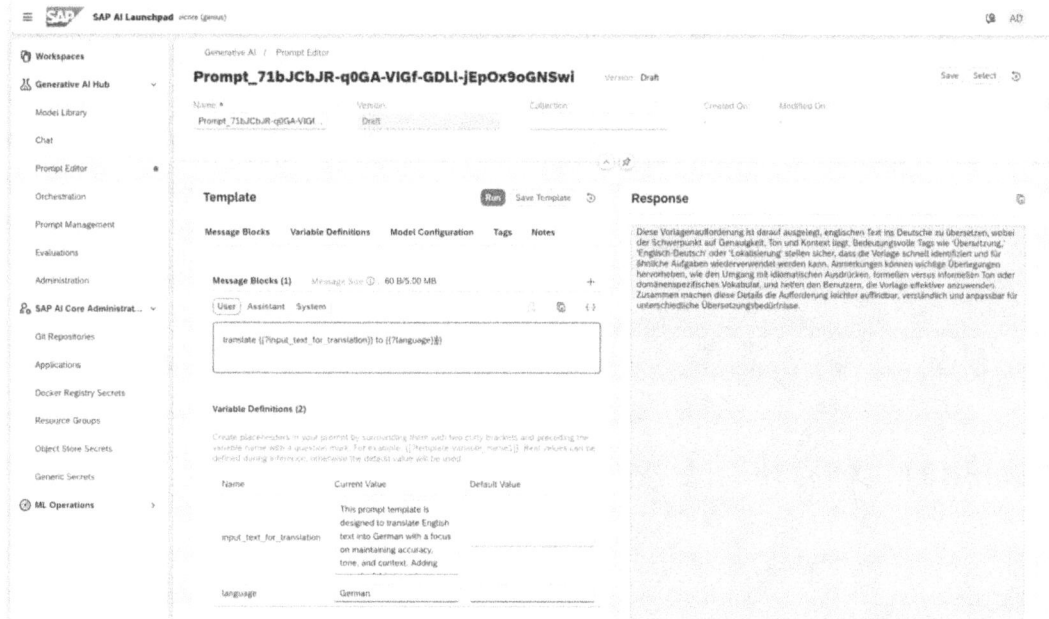

*Figure 6-9.   Translation through prompts*

155

CHAPTER 6   BUILDING CUSTOM AI APPLICATIONS USING SAP BUSINESS AI FOUNDATION

To evaluate further, let's try to perform some translation, as shown in Figure 6-9. In this case, instead of hardcoding the target text and language, we take advantage of the Variable Definitions section, as shown in Figure 6-10.

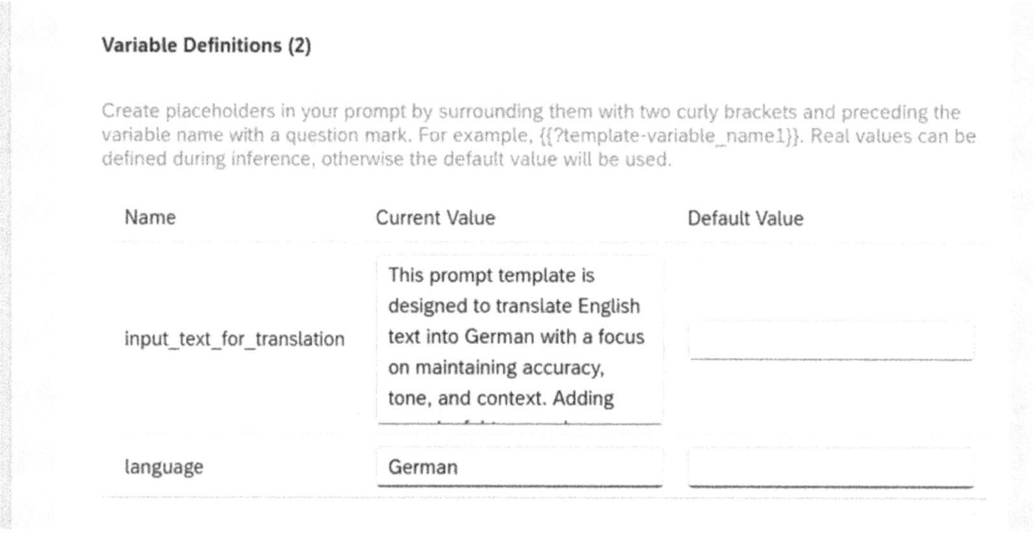

**Variable Definitions (2)**

Create placeholders in your prompt by surrounding them with two curly brackets and preceding the variable name with a question mark. For example, {{?template-variable_name1}}. Real values can be defined during inference, otherwise the default value will be used.

| Name | Current Value | Default Value |
| --- | --- | --- |
| input_text_for_translation | This prompt template is designed to translate English text into German with a focus on maintaining accuracy, tone, and context. Adding | |
| language | German | |

***Figure 6-10.*** *Variable Definitions*

The Variable Definitions section inside the Message Block tab lets you create placeholders for prompts, which are replaced at runtime with the actual values assigned to the variable. As shown in Figure 6-11, we have two variable definitions, including `input_text_for_translation` for storing the target text for translation and `language` for storing the target language to be applied for translation. Refer to the variable definitions with two curly brackets followed by a question mark and the variable name, as shown in Figure 6-11.

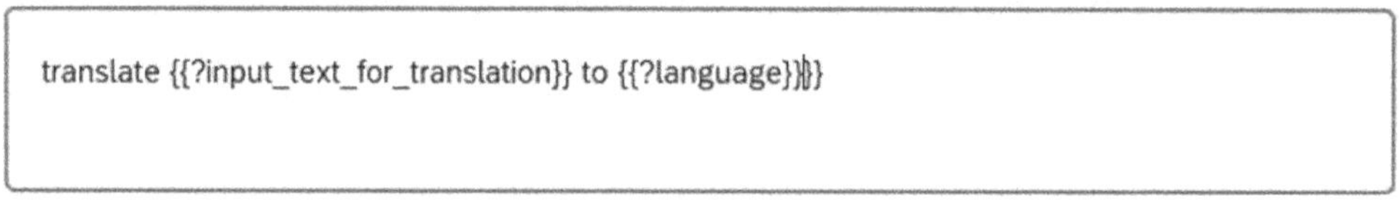

translate {{?input_text_for_translation}} to {{?language}}

***Figure 6-11.*** *Define Variable*

CHAPTER 6   BUILDING CUSTOM AI APPLICATIONS USING SAP BUSINESS AI FOUNDATION

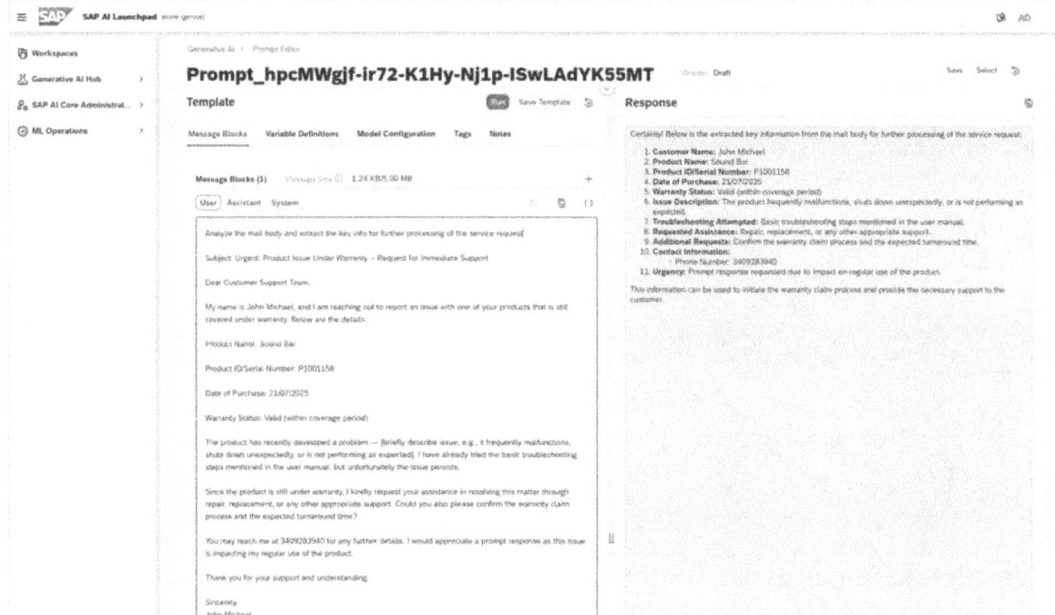

***Figure 6-12.***  *Information extraction sample*

Let's try some enterprise-oriented prompting, where we try to analyze an email to extract the key pieces of information present in the body of the email, as shown in Figure 6-12. The email contains key pieces of information from a customer wanting to know about the warranty status of a particular product ID. As shown in Figure 6-12, the LLM successfully extracts the key entities from the email content included in the prompt.

In the next evaluation attempt, we dive deeper to evaluate the application of the LLM in the context of real enterprise business challenges. We will try to evaluate a material description using the LLM and see what kind of outcome it delivers.

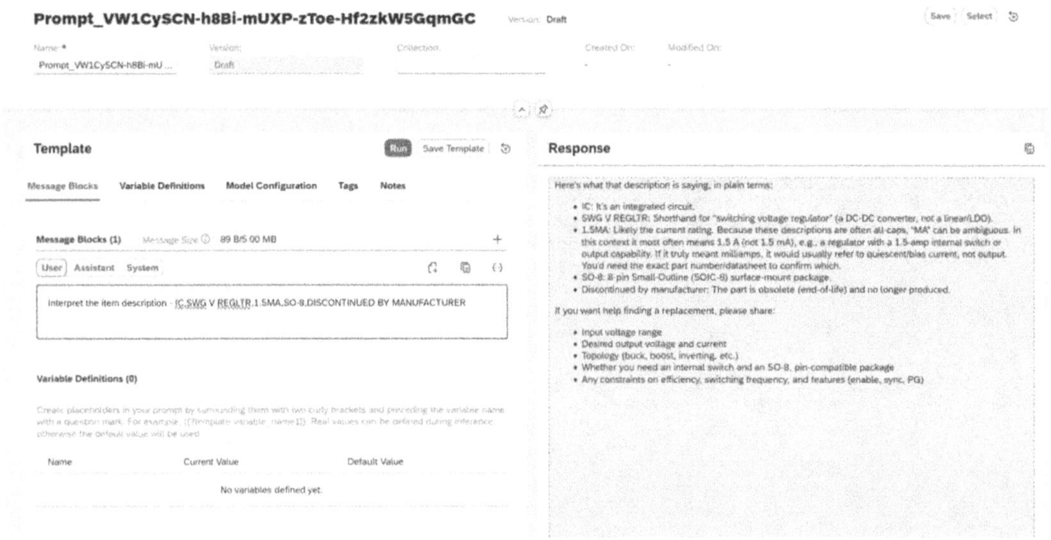

CHAPTER 6    BUILDING CUSTOM AI APPLICATIONS USING SAP BUSINESS AI FOUNDATION

*Figure 6-13.  Material description interpretation*

As shown in Figure 6-13, the LLM is not only able to interpret the material description but also understands the abbreviations in the description. The purpose of demonstrating different kinds of prompts is to trigger further enterprise-oriented use cases tailored to your needs.

*Figure 6-14.  Code generation*

Code generation, as shown in Figure 6-14, is another well-known capability of LLMs that you can use when building enterprise-oriented use cases for purposes like code migration, conversion, analysis, and review.

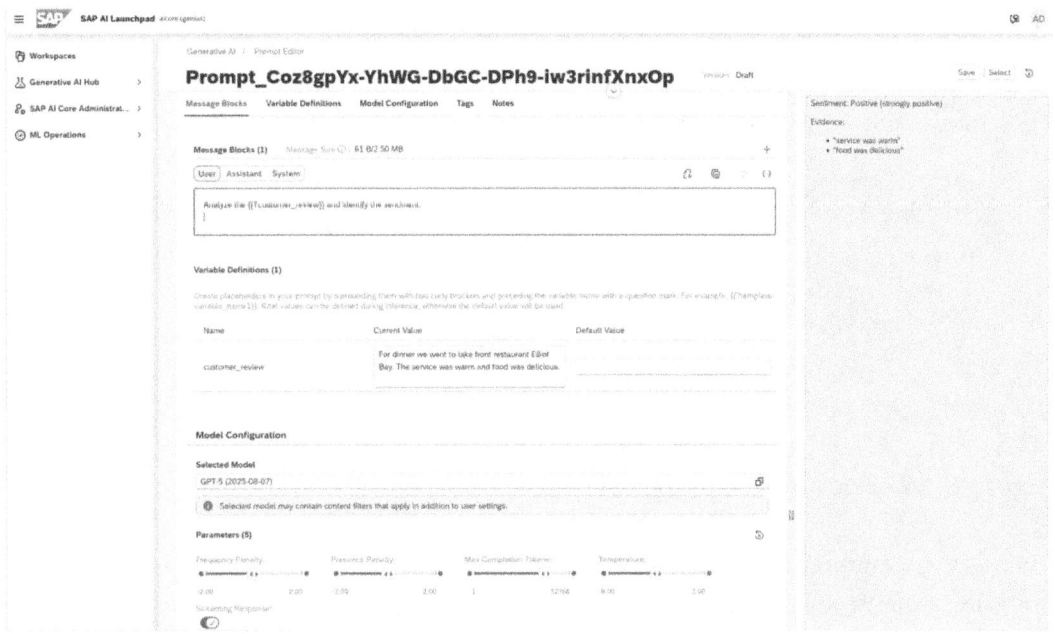

***Figure 6-15.*** *Sentiment analysis sample*

In the final stage of evaluation, let's try to apply the LLM in the context of sentiment analysis, which is a very common requirement across many industries. It helps with customer conversations and email feedback and ultimately help enterprises retain their customers and reduce the churn ratio.

The Model Configuration section, as shown in Figure 6-16, lets you choose or change the model and key parameters that can influence the response generated by the model. Key parameters, such as Frequency penalty, help reduce repeated words or phrases, which keeps responses concise and less redundant, while the Presence penalty encourages the model to introduce new ideas or topics, making answers more engaging and varied.

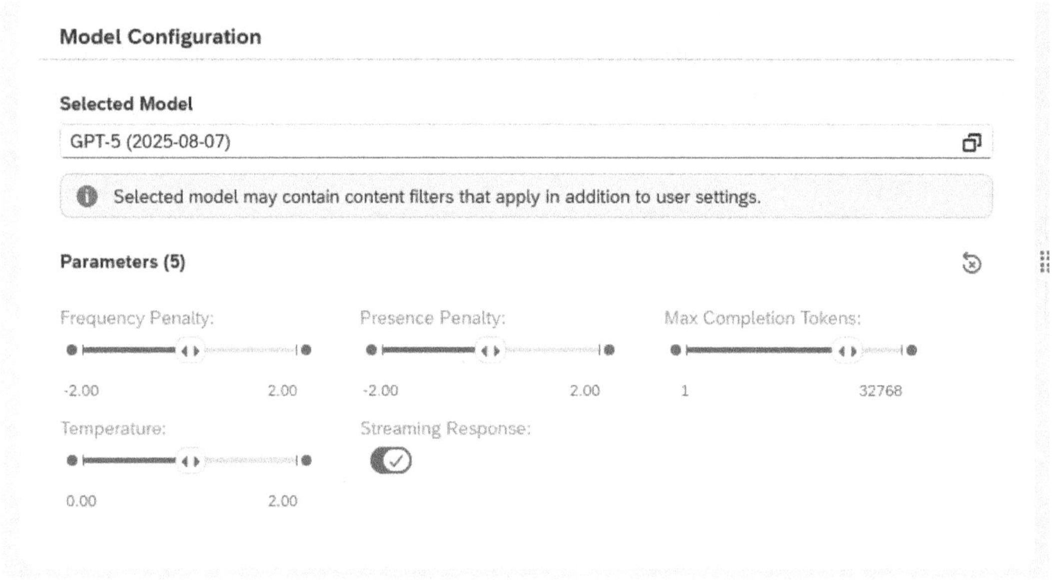

CHAPTER 6   BUILDING CUSTOM AI APPLICATIONS USING SAP BUSINESS AI FOUNDATION

**Model Configuration**

**Selected Model**

GPT-5 (2025-08-07)

ⓘ Selected model may contain content filters that apply in addition to user settings.

**Parameters (5)**

Frequency Penalty:
-2.00                2.00

Presence Penalty:
-2.00                2.00

Max Completion Tokens:
1                    32768

Temperature:
0.00                 2.00

Streaming Response:

*Figure 6-16. The Model Configuration section*

Adding meaningful tags and notes to the metadata of a prompt template helps make the prompt easier to manage, share, and reuse. Tags serve as quick identifiers that improve searchability, helping users filter and locate templates based on themes or use cases without having to go through each one manually. This not only improves clarity but also supports collaboration, as team members can quickly understand why a template was created and how it should be applied. Together, tags and notes turn a simple template into a well-documented resource that promotes consistency, avoids duplication, and makes prompt libraries more effective over time.

As shown in Figure 6-17, we assigned various tags like `sentimentanalysis`, `sentimentclassification`, and so on to the metadata segment, which will not only enrich the prompt template with additional details but will also help locate the results easily. The Notes field also helps maintain documentation for the template.

CHAPTER 6  BUILDING CUSTOM AI APPLICATIONS USING SAP BUSINESS AI FOUNDATION

*Figure 6-17. Prompt tags*

Prompts that you have tried and tested so far can be saved in the form of reusable templates, including variable definitions, and reused across projects, as shown in Figure 6-18.

CHAPTER 6   BUILDING CUSTOM AI APPLICATIONS USING SAP BUSINESS AI FOUNDATION

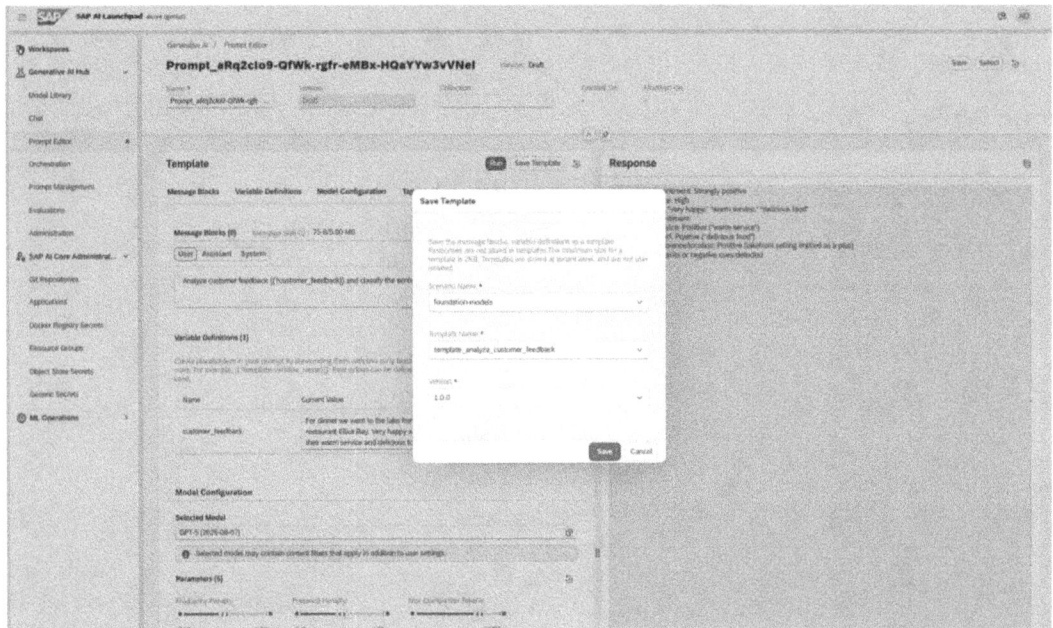

*Figure 6-18.   The Save Template dialog box*

Templates are saved under the Templates section, inside Prompt Management, as shown in Figure 6-19.

*Figure 6-19.   Saved templates*

Clicking a saved template loads the template details, including any revisions. You can open and edit the template using the Open in Prompt Editor option, as shown in Figure 6-20.

*Figure 6-20. Saved template details*

This section performed various experiments to show the potential of LLMs in the context of various enterprise contexts using SAP BTP Generative Hub-based chat and the Prompt Editor. The next section explains how to prepare a potential estimation for a SAP BTP-based Business AI project using SAP's latest discovery center.

# Preparing an Estimation

When preparing an estimation for a Generative AI–based enterprise project on BTP, it's important to balance technical and business dimensions. The clarity of the use case and the desired outcomes set the foundation, as vague objectives often lead to underestimating complexity. Data readiness is another major factor—assessing the availability, quality, and structure of enterprise data will determine the effort needed for preprocessing, cleaning, and integration. Technical considerations such as the type of models, the token size, and vector storage, along with other essential BTP services drive the cost and timeline. This is where SAP's Discovery Center plays a critical role and accelerates the entire process by providing the required components, especially for estimation.

CHAPTER 6   BUILDING CUSTOM AI APPLICATIONS USING SAP BUSINESS AI FOUNDATION

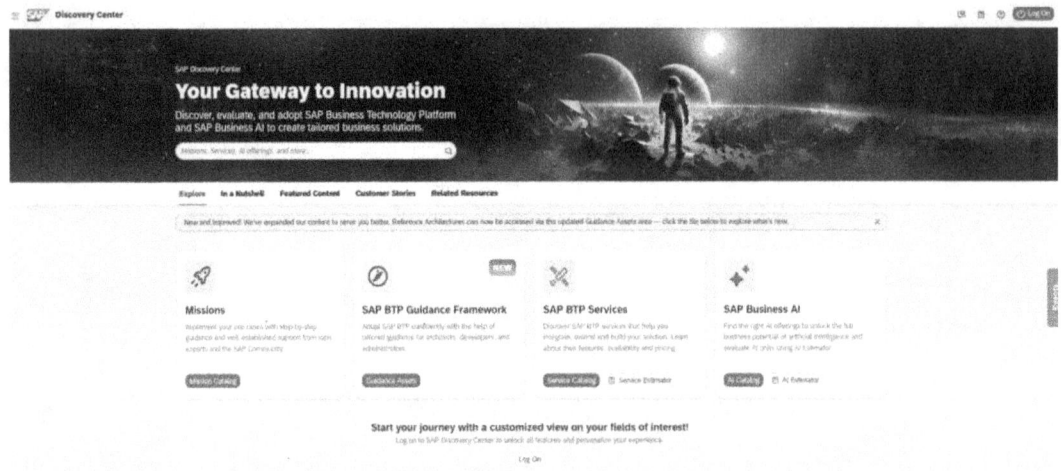

*Figure 6-21. The SAP Discovery Center*

The SAP Discovery Center, as shown in Figure 6-21, is designed to help enterprises accelerate their journey with the SAP Business Technology Platform by providing a guided, hands-on experience. One of its key features is the collection of prebuilt "missions" that offer step-by-step guidance, best practices, and reference architectures to quickly implement use cases. It also provides access to explore a wide range of services and tools within BTP, enabling teams to explore capabilities like integration, data management, analytics, and AI in a structured way. Another important feature is the cost estimator, which helps organizations forecast expenses and plan their cloud usage effectively. Using the SAP BTP Service Estimator, developers can prepare an estimation by adding the required models and services based on the scenario.

The BTP service tiles, as shown in Figure 6-22, show the complete set of services offered by the platform. You can create an estimation and add the potential services you need to build the solution.

CHAPTER 6   BUILDING CUSTOM AI APPLICATIONS USING SAP BUSINESS AI FOUNDATION

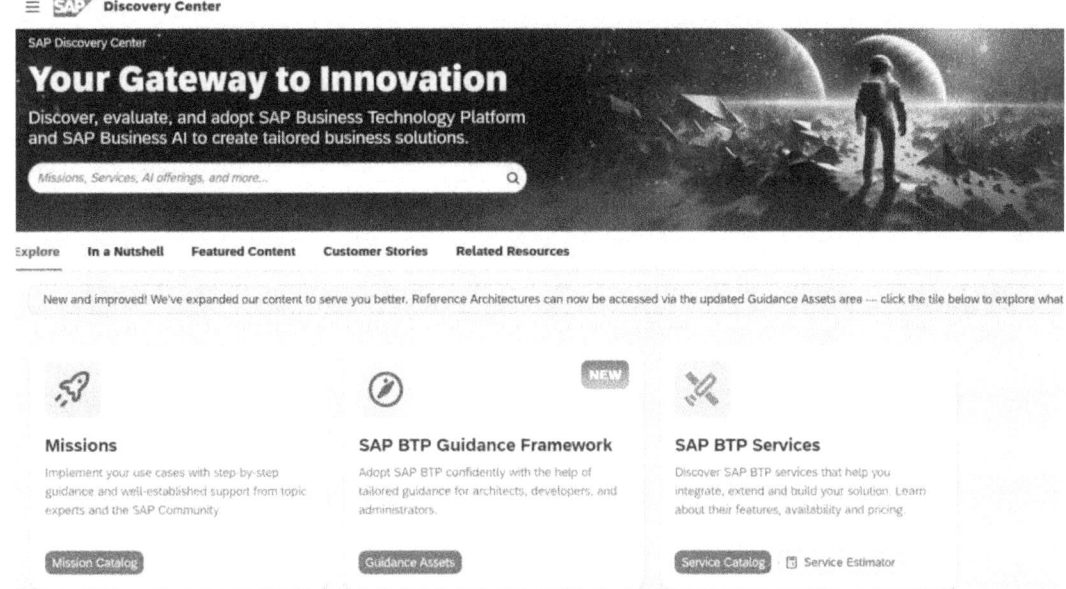

***Figure 6-22.*** *SAP BTP service tiles*

As shown in Figure 6-23, you can easily create an estimation by clicking the + icon at the bottom of the tile of each service.

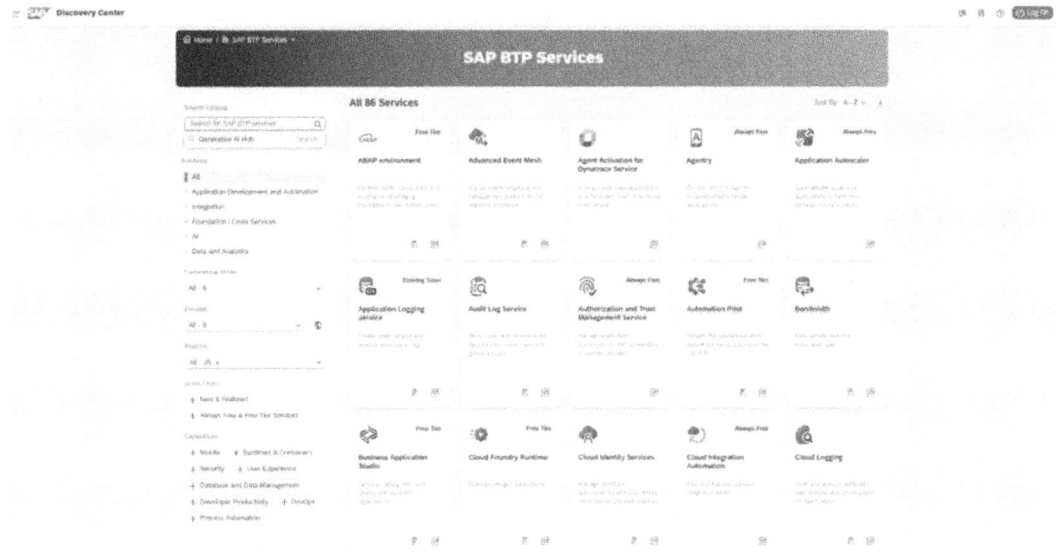

***Figure 6-23.*** *SAP BTP services*

# CHAPTER 6   BUILDING CUSTOM AI APPLICATIONS USING SAP BUSINESS AI FOUNDATION

While preparing the estimation, you can first select the region or provider relevant to your use case and use the Add Services button to add the required BTP services. Choosing the right cloud region is an important decision that can influence how well your system performs, how secure your data is, and how much you end up spending. When the region is closer to your users, applications run faster with lower latency. At the same time, many countries have strict data residency rules, so selecting a region within legal boundaries helps you stay compliant. Costs can also differ between regions, making it worth comparing options before deciding. So picking the right region ultimately ensures that your cloud setup is reliable, compliant, and cost-effective. See Figure 6-24.

*Figure 6-24.  Creating an estimation*

Clicking Add Services shows a popup with all listed services, as shown in Figure 6-25.

CHAPTER 6    BUILDING CUSTOM AI APPLICATIONS USING SAP BUSINESS AI FOUNDATION

*Figure 6-25.  Adding services from a collection*

Most of the services are pretty straight forward, but for some, you may need to calculate the capacity unit by using the SAP AI Core calculator.

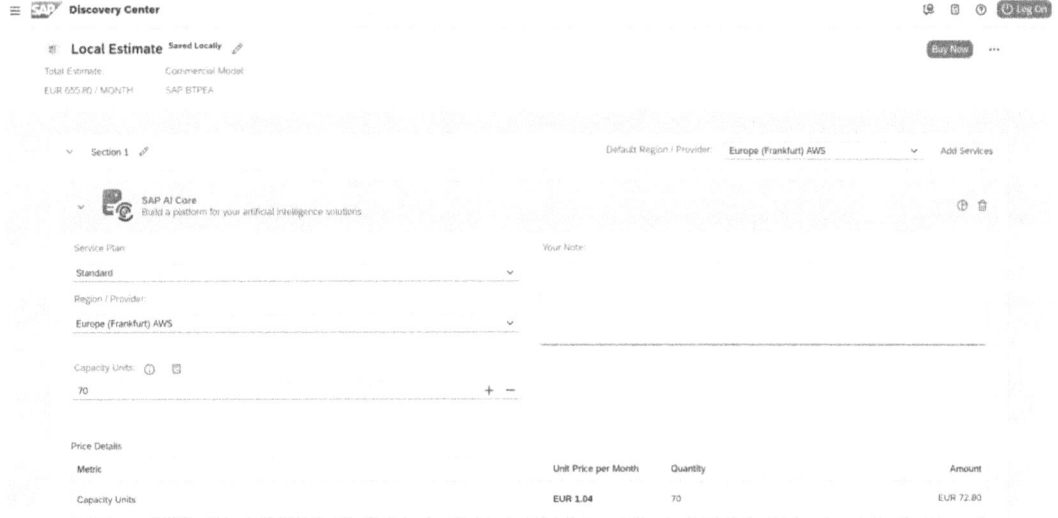

*Figure 6-26.  Calculating the capacity units*

To access the SAP AI Core capacity unit calculator, you need to click the calculation sign next to the Capacity Units input fields, as shown in Figure 6-26.

167

CHAPTER 6   BUILDING CUSTOM AI APPLICATIONS USING SAP BUSINESS AI FOUNDATION

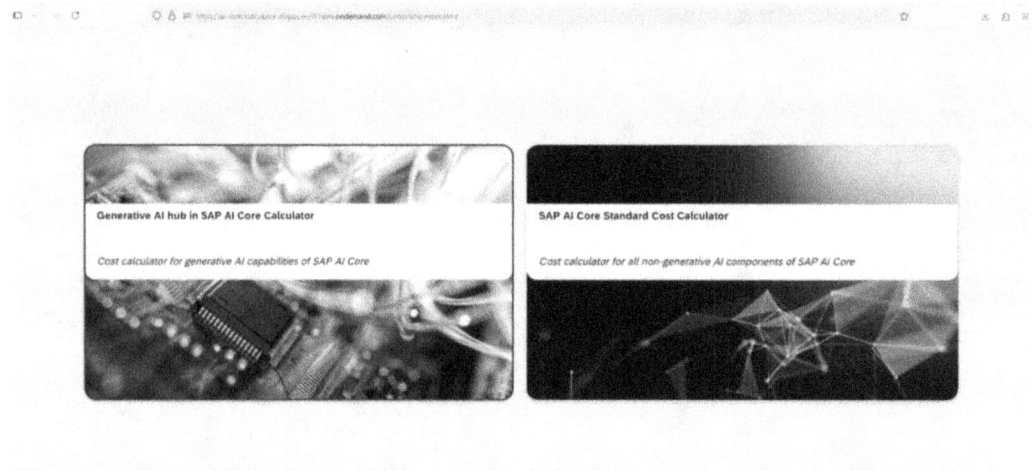

*Figure 6-27.  Select the calculator based on purpose*

As shown in Figure 6-27, SAP AI Core offers capacity unit calculator for both generative and non-Generative AI-based scenarios. As the focus here is on Generative AI, this section explains how the capacity unit calculation works when choosing a Generative AI model.

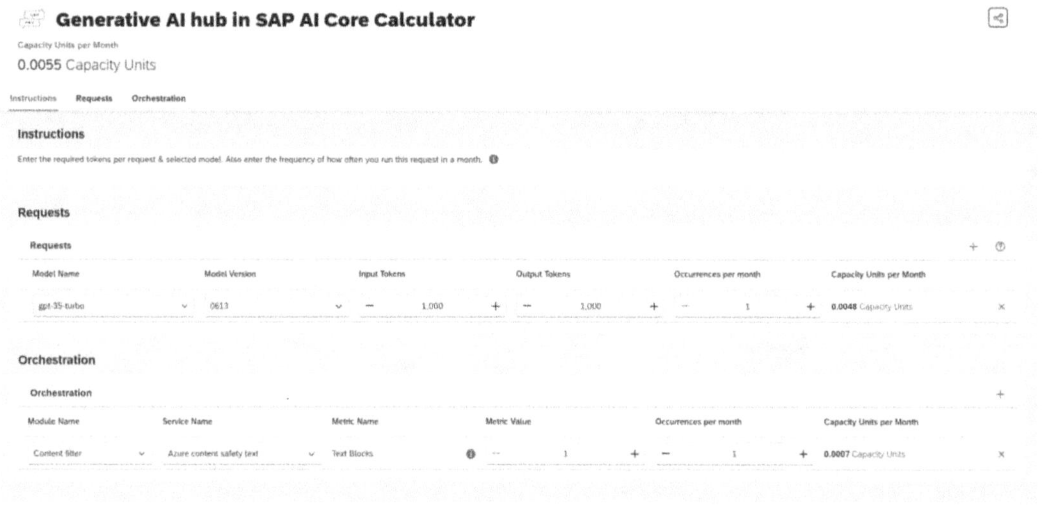

*Figure 6-28.  Capacity unit calculation*

CHAPTER 6    BUILDING CUSTOM AI APPLICATIONS USING SAP BUSINESS AI FOUNDATION

As shown in Figure 6-28, the token size is one of the most critical parameters and it is essential to determine the right token size required for your use case. In this context, the input token refers to the smallest unit of text that the model processes. Input from the users as prompts or instructions is broken down into small tokens, often words, sub-words, or even characters so that it can better understand the context and meaning. An output token is the generated text that the model delivers in response, constructed one token at a time until the full answer is formed. The ratio between the input and output tokens varies depending on the prompt and the use case. For example, in summarization tasks, the ratio of input to output tokens could be 3:1 or even 4:1. In contrast, tasks like generating explanations or drafting longer pieces of text could have an inverse ratio, with output tokens significantly outnumbering input tokens. Token consumption varies with the capabilities of the LLM being used, with more advanced models typically requiring and processing a higher number of tokens. Occurrences per Month refers to the number of times a specific type of request, interaction, or workflow happens in a month that would involve invoking the LLM, which is also critical for determining the capacity units.

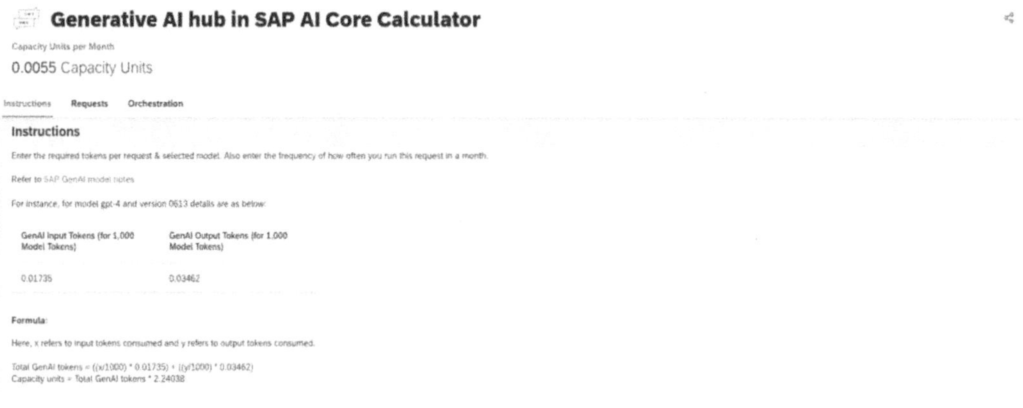

**Generative AI hub in SAP AI Core Calculator**

Capacity Units per Month
**0.0055** Capacity Units

Instructions | Requests | Orchestration

**Instructions**

Enter the required tokens per request & selected model. Also enter the frequency of how often you run this request in a month.

Refer to SAP GenAI model notes

For instance, for model gpt-4 and version 0613 details are as below:

GenAI Input Tokens (for 1,000 Model Tokens) | GenAI Output Tokens (for 1,000 Model Tokens)
0.01735 | 0.03462

**Formula:**
Here, x refers to input tokens consumed and y refers to output tokens consumed.
Total GenAI tokens = ((x/1000) * 0.01735) + ((y/1000) * 0.03462)
Capacity units = Total GenAI tokens * 2.24038

***Figure 6-29.*** *Capacity unit calculation instructions*

Figure 6-29 shows the Instructions tab with details about the formula being used to determine the capacity unit based on the input and output model tokens.

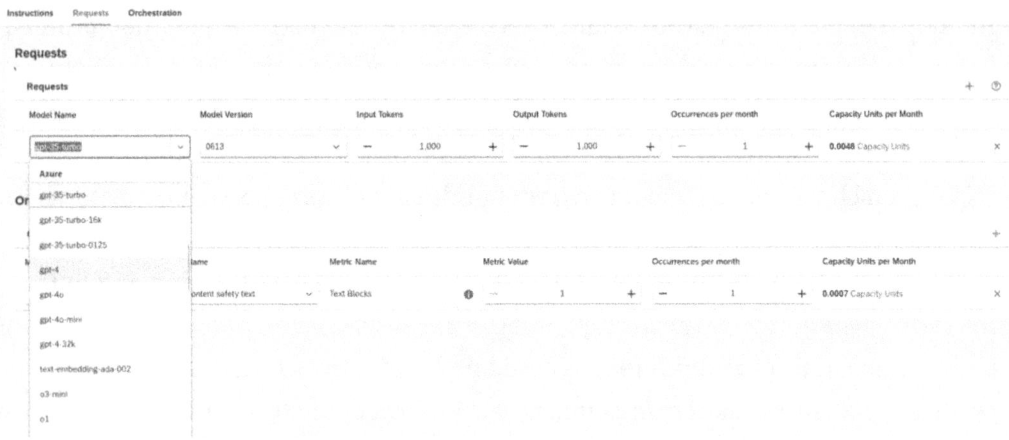

CHAPTER 6   BUILDING CUSTOM AI APPLICATIONS USING SAP BUSINESS AI FOUNDATION

*Figure 6-30.  List of available models from partners*

Figure 6-30 shows the various partner foundation models that you can pick from when calculating the capacity unit. If you choose the "latest" version of the model, you will automatically be moved to a new version when a version is deprecated.

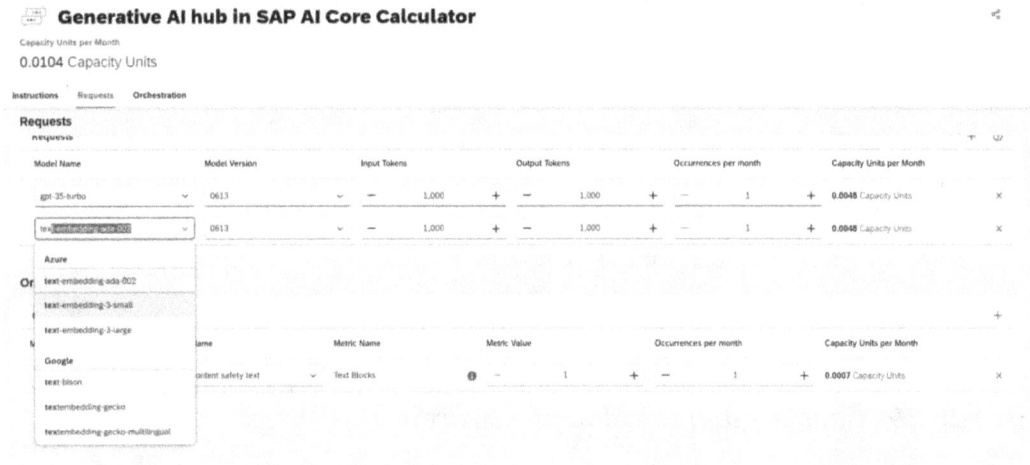

*Figure 6-31.  Embedding models*

In addition to the chat completion model, you can also pick an embedding model, as shown in Figure 6-31. This is especially helpful for RAG-based use cases, where you need to generate embedding from business documents.

170

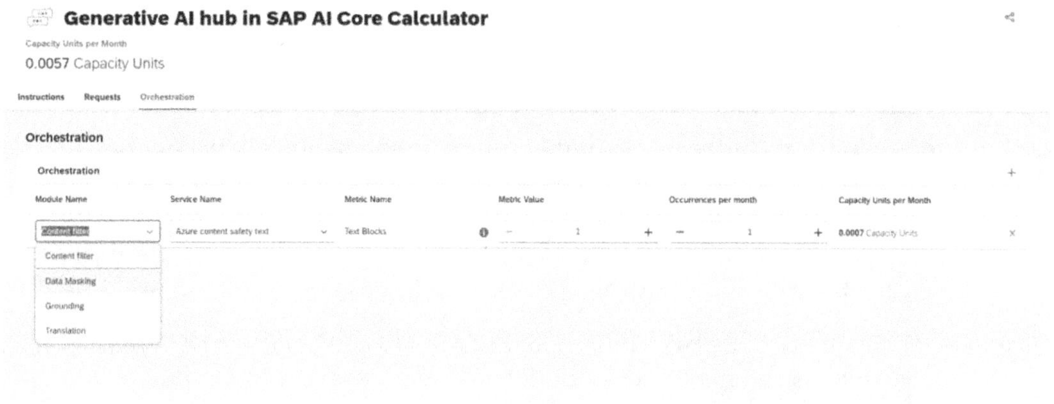

*Figure 6-32. Orchestration*

The next critical component that you need to consider for estimation is related to content safety. This is especially relevant for establishing the orchestration process for enterprise applications. As shown in Figure 6-32, SAP AI Core currently supports content safety through various modules like content filters, data masking, grounding, and translation. Content filters block harmful, unsafe, biased, or policy-violating information. Data masking hides or anonymizes sensitive data, grounding connects AI-generated outputs to a reliable source of truth, and translation converts text or speech from one language to another.

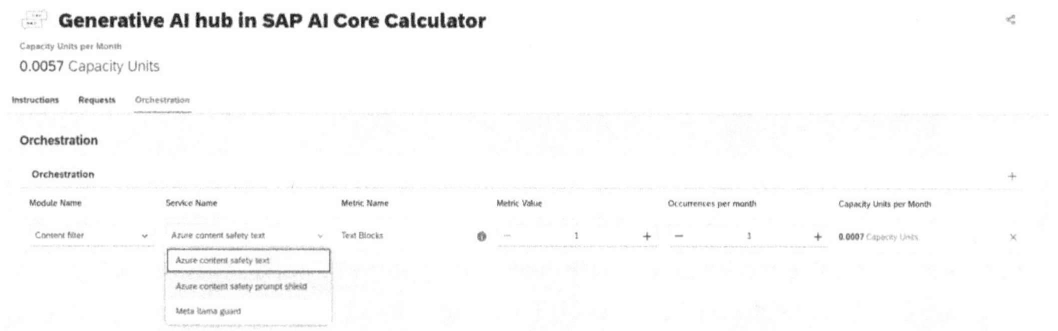

*Figure 6-33. Content safety related services*

As shown in Figure 6-33, SAP AI Core currently support various services, including:

- **Azure Content Safety:** Text is a Microsoft Azure service designed to detect and classify harmful or inappropriate content. It can identify categories such as hate speech, sexual content, violence, and self-harm, assigning severity scores that allow developers to decide whether to block, flag, or review the content. This makes it easier to moderate both user-generated input and AI-generated output, ensuring that applications remain safe, compliant, and aligned with community or regulatory guidelines.

- **Azure Content Safety Prompt Shield:** Prompt Shield focuses on protecting AI systems from malicious prompt-injection attacks. In Generative AI scenarios, attackers may craft prompts intended to override instructions, access hidden system prompts, or manipulate the AI into producing disallowed content. Prompt Shield analyzes incoming prompts before they reach the AI model, detecting jailbreak attempts or other harmful manipulations. This proactive filtering helps safeguard chatbots, copilots, and other LLM-based applications from security and safety risks.

- **Meta Llama Guard:** This an open-source safety classifier developed by Meta for filtering prompts and outputs of LLMs, including LLaMA. It can detect unsafe categories like violence, hate speech, and sexual content, and being open-source, it offers flexibility for customization according to specific business or compliance needs. Llama Guard can be deployed before or after AI model interactions, acting as a lightweight moderation layer that can run locally or in a controlled environment. This makes it ideal for organizations seeking transparent and adaptable AI safety solutions.

Once you choose a content safety module and an associated service, in the next step you need to decide on the number of text blocks. According to SAP, one text block is equivalent to 1,000 characters. Figure 6-34 shows a possible capacity unit required for developing an AI application using SAP BTP Business AI foundation. It includes models related to chat completion, embedding, and content safety, and this may vary on a case by case basis.

CHAPTER 6   BUILDING CUSTOM AI APPLICATIONS USING SAP BUSINESS AI FOUNDATION

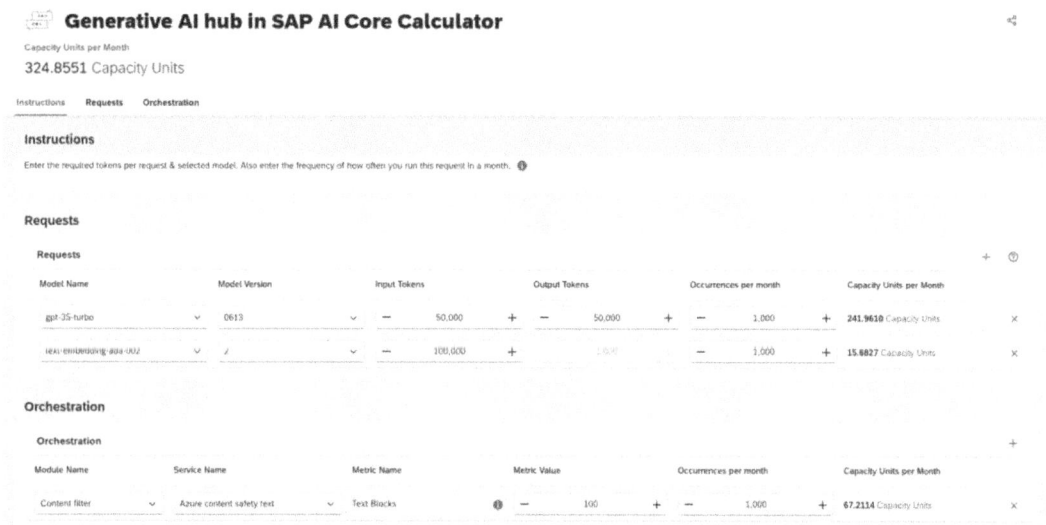

*Figure 6-34.* Total capacity unit: LLM model and content safety

In contrast, capacity unit calculations for non-generative use cases are driven by a completely different set of factors. Training and inference of AI models are the key driving aspects of this type of application. The capacity unit calculation in this context is driven by three key factors, as shown in Figure 6-35, which are instances, storage, and baseline resources. They basically form the core infrastructure layer that enables training and inference of the chosen AI model.

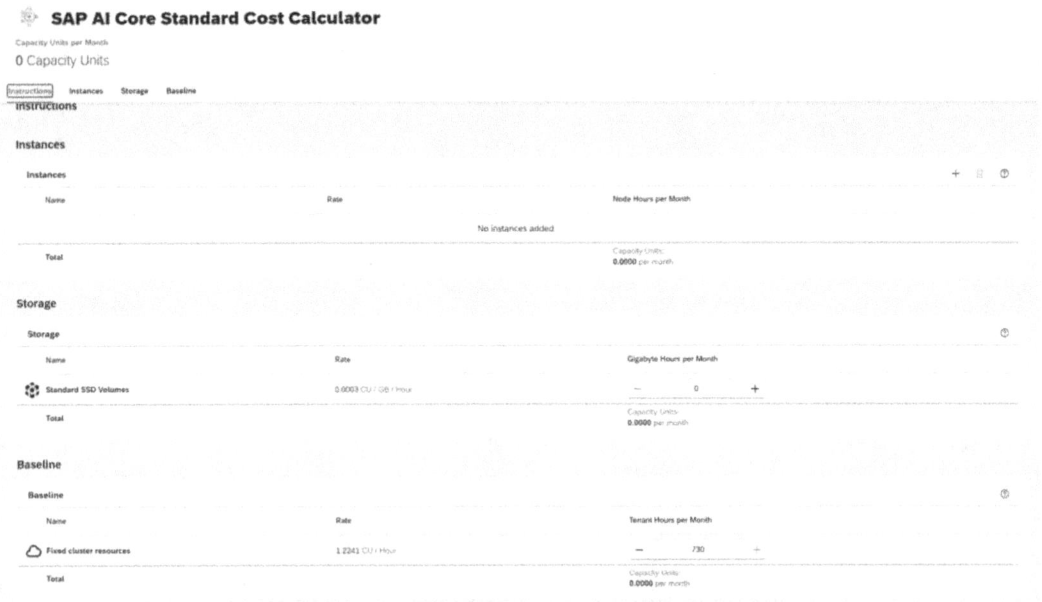

CHAPTER 6   BUILDING CUSTOM AI APPLICATIONS USING SAP BUSINESS AI FOUNDATION

*Figure 6-35. AI Core standard cost calculator*

As shown in Figure 6-36, the capacity calculation is initiated by selecting the required instance supporting the necessary computing power for model training and inference. SAP AI Core supports different instance types to fulfil the varying compute needs of AI workloads, ranging from lightweight development to high-performance training and inference. For example, smaller configurations like Starter and Basic instances provide minimal CPU and memory for simple tasks or experimentation, while Infer-S, M, and L are optimized for inference with balanced CPU, RAM, and GPU capabilities to handle real-time predictions at scale.

CHAPTER 6   BUILDING CUSTOM AI APPLICATIONS USING SAP BUSINESS AI FOUNDATION

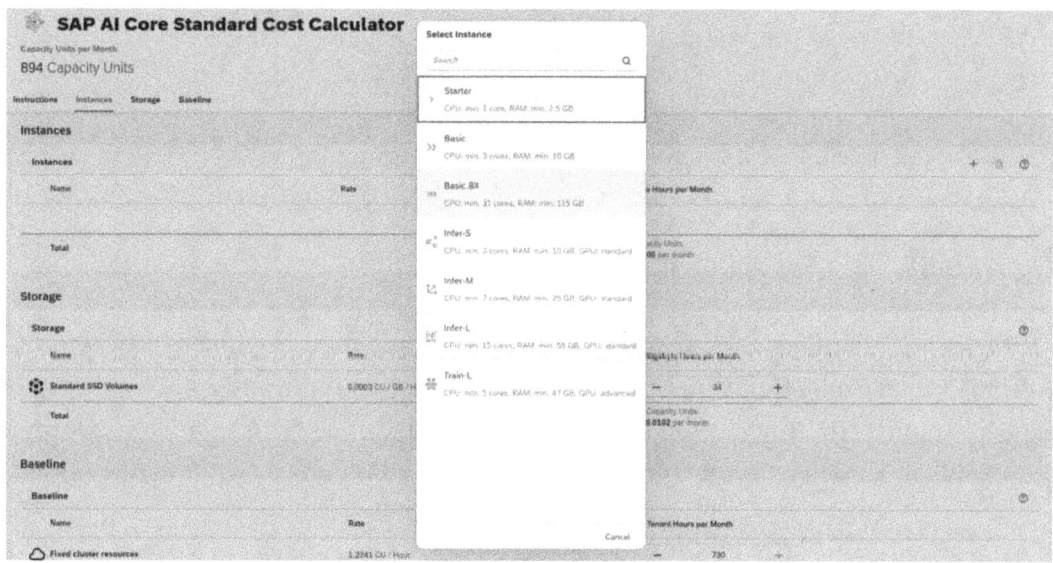

*Figure 6-36.* *Instance selection*

The next most significant component after instances is the storage that supports model training and inference. During training, the storage is used to handle large datasets, save model checkpoints, and store the resulting trained models. For inference, it ensures fast access to deployed model artifacts and any supporting data needed for generating predictions in real time. As shown in Figure 6-37, SAP AI Core supports standard SSD volumes, billed based on gigabyte hours per month, thus ensuring the speed and reliability required to manage data efficiently across the entire AI lifecycle.

*Figure 6-37.* *Storage configuration*

In the context of model training, baseline resources provide the core infrastructure for scheduling, orchestration, and resource management required to support large-scale computations. For model inference, they basically provide the foundation needed to serve models reliably, handle requests, and manage workloads consistently. As shown in Figure 6-38, inside SAP AI Core, baseline is charged at a defined rate per hour and multiplied by the total tenant hours in a month, typically 730.

175

## CHAPTER 6  BUILDING CUSTOM AI APPLICATIONS USING SAP BUSINESS AI FOUNDATION

*Figure 6-38.  Baseline configuration*

Figure 6-39 demonstrates a probable capacity unit estimation with 8 vCPUs, a GPU for scalable inference supported by 200 node hours/month, and a scale based on expected request traffic, followed by a baseline configuration of 730 tenant hours/month for reliability. This ensures that models can be served continuously without downtime.

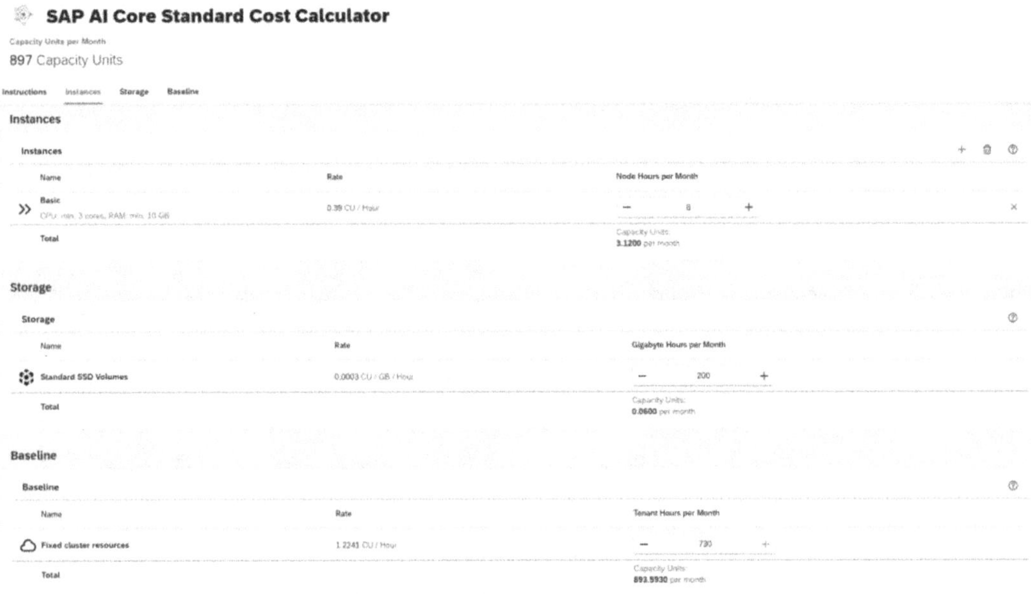

*Figure 6-39.  SAP AI Core standard cost*

SAP HANA Cloud is one of the most critical components for persistence in both generative and non-Generative AI-based applications. Being available in different sizes, it can also act as a vector engine, which is especially relevant in the context of RAG-based Generative AI applications. As shown in Figure 6-40, you can either pick from available preconfigured sizes like small, medium, or large or you can choose a custom configuration based on your hot, warm, and cold data sizes.

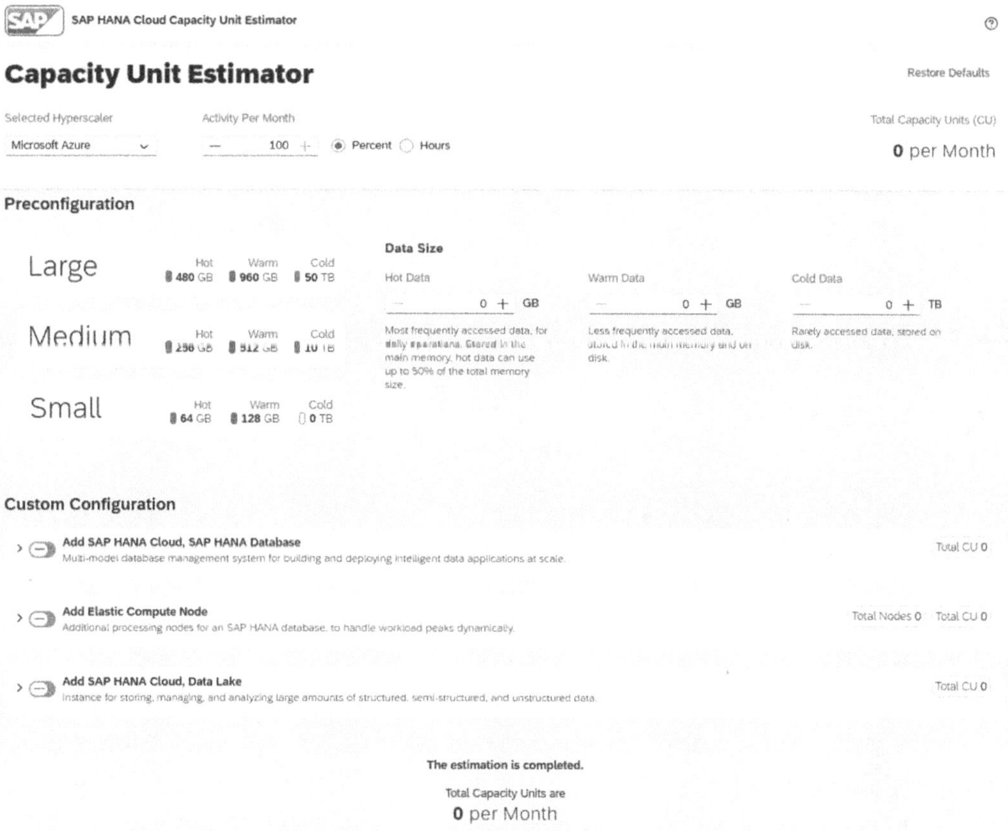

*Figure 6-40. SAP HANA pre-configurations*

If the recommended sizes are not suitable, you can choose custom sizing and configure your hot, warm and cold data size using the Custom Confirmation section.

CHAPTER 6   BUILDING CUSTOM AI APPLICATIONS USING SAP BUSINESS AI FOUNDATION

*Figure 6-41.  Total cost*

Figure 6-41 shows the final bill of materials for this demo use case. This is more of a development related estimation, so services related to DevOps, authorization, and so on, are not included here.

Now that you have seen the process of estimating a SAP BTP-based business AI application, the next section moves toward the original goal of building a business use case by using various components of the SAP BTP Generative AI Hub.

## Building the RAG-Based Solution

The use case in this chapter builds a RAG-based solution that can accelerate the maintenance execution process. Before you start building the solution, you need to set up some of prerequisites. One of them is the deployment of the required LLM and collating the deployment ID and end point for further integration .This step is essential, as LLM serves as the core reasoning engine that the RAG pipeline will rely on during retrieval and response generation.

To initiate the deployment, navigate to the ML Operations ➤ Deployment segment and choose Create, as shown in Figure 6-42.

CHAPTER 6   BUILDING CUSTOM AI APPLICATIONS USING SAP BUSINESS AI FOUNDATION

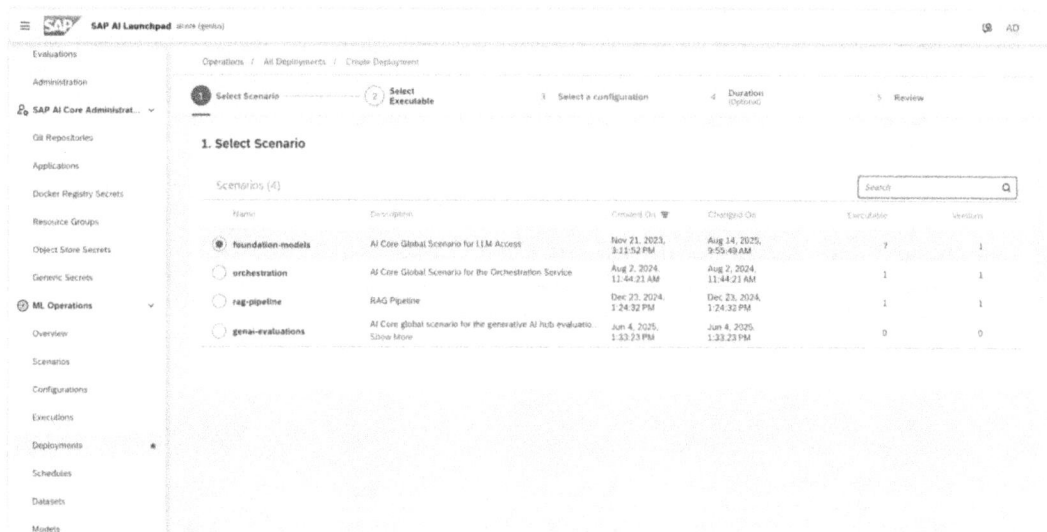

*Figure 6-42.* *Creating the deployment*

The Create Deployment wizard, as shown in Figure 6-43, starts with selecting from the pre-configured scenarios, followed by selecting an executable.

*Figure 6-43.* *Scenario selection*

In the Select Executable step of the wizard, as shown in Figure 6-44, you need to choose from the available service executable. A serving executable, as shown in Figure 6-44, is a program used to deploy an AI model for online predictions. It works like any other executable but includes placeholders for input artifacts (such as models), parameters (like hyperparameters), and sometimes output artifacts. These placeholders are filled in through a configuration, which together with the serving executable enables the deployment of the model for real-time inference.

179

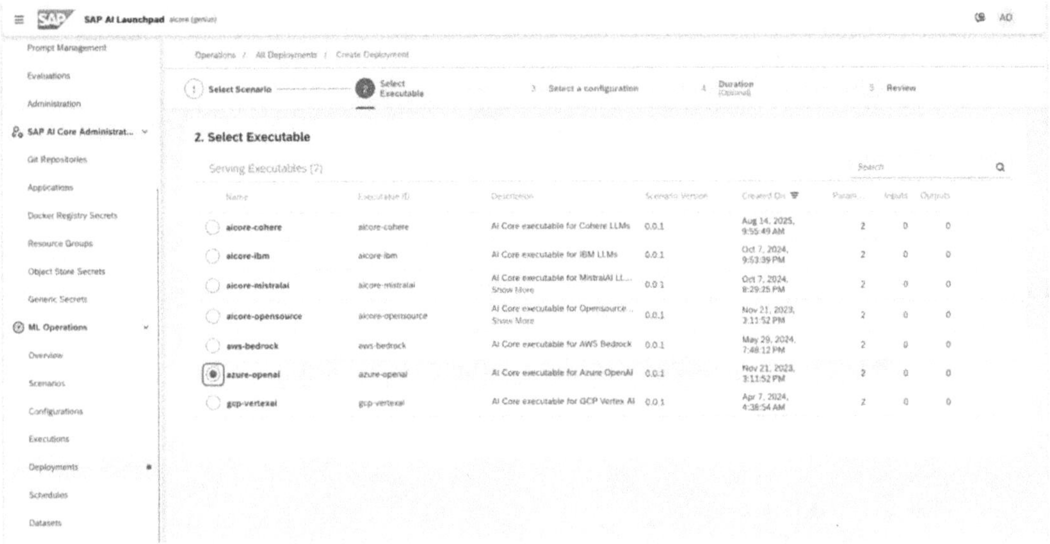

CHAPTER 6   BUILDING CUSTOM AI APPLICATIONS USING SAP BUSINESS AI FOUNDATION

*Figure 6-44.  Selecting an executable*

In the next step, you need to select the configuration. If the configuration is not in place, you can create one instantly using the Create Configuration option, as shown in Figure 6-45. Configuration helps define how an AI process, such as training or deployment, is carried out by combining executables with the required artifacts and parameters.

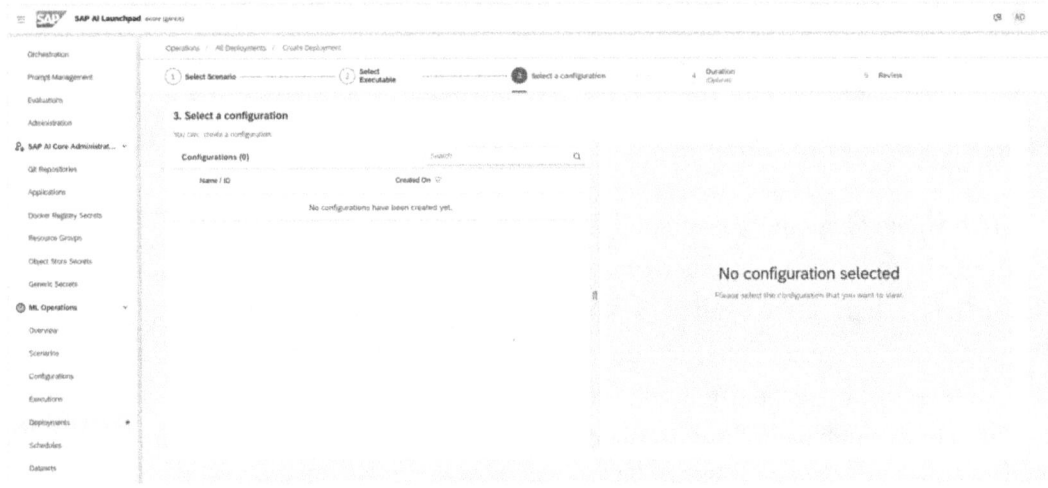

*Figure 6-45.  Choosing a configuration*

CHAPTER 6   BUILDING CUSTOM AI APPLICATIONS USING SAP BUSINESS AI FOUNDATION

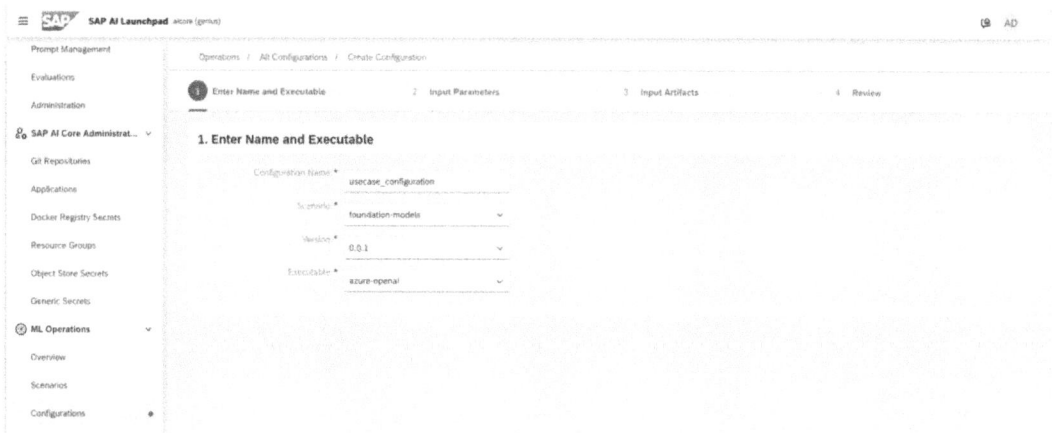

*Figure 6-46. Creating a configuration*

To define a new configuration, you simply supply a configuration name, followed by a scenario, related version, and executable, as shown in Figure 6-46.

*Figure 6-47. Configuration parameters*

As part of the Input Parameters tab, you need to specify the name of the model and model version, as shown in Figure 6-47.

CHAPTER 6   BUILDING CUSTOM AI APPLICATIONS USING SAP BUSINESS AI FOUNDATION

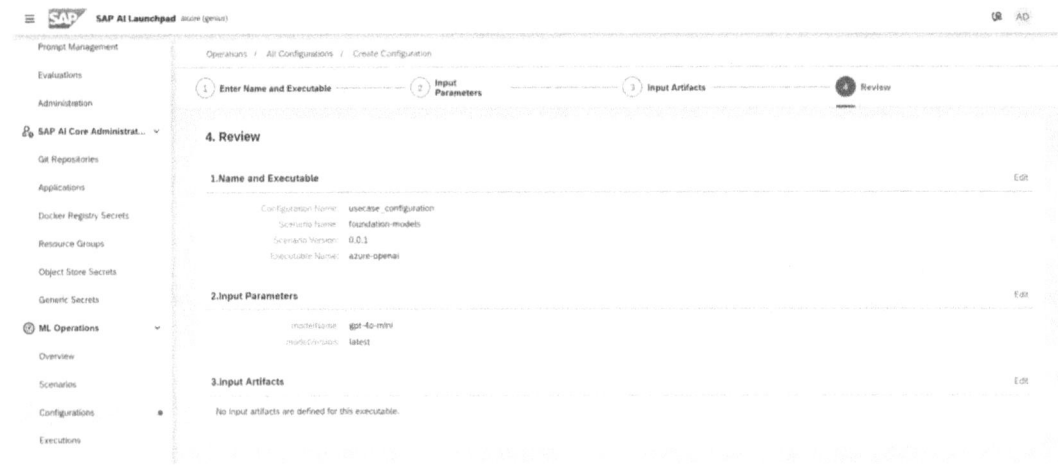

*Figure 6-48.*  *Reviewing the configuration*

After you review the configuration, as shown in Figure 6-48, create the configuration using the Create button at the bottom of the screen. Then you're ready to deploy the configuration, which you do using the Create Deployment button, as shown in Figure 6-49.

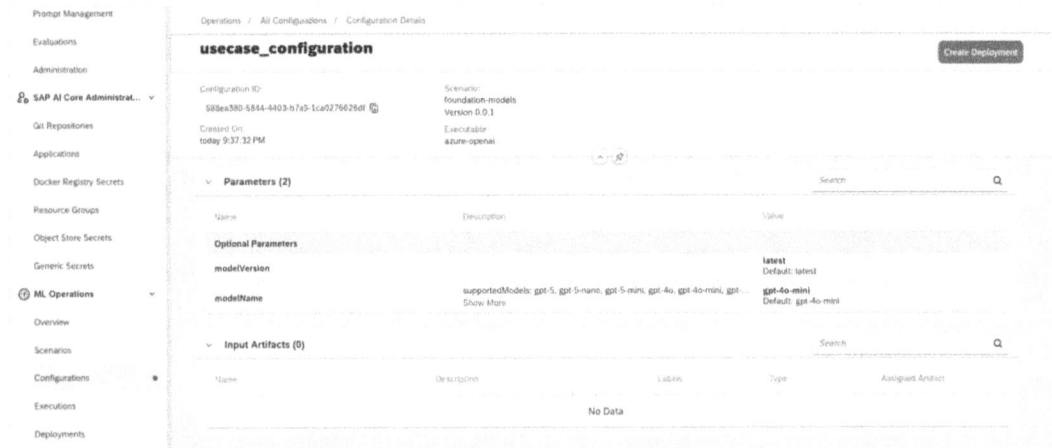

*Figure 6-49.*  *Clicking the Create Deployment button*

After you deploy the configuration, the most critical pieces of information to take note of are the deployment ID and the URL generated from the deployment process; these are shown in Figure 6-50.

182

CHAPTER 6   BUILDING CUSTOM AI APPLICATIONS USING SAP BUSINESS AI FOUNDATION

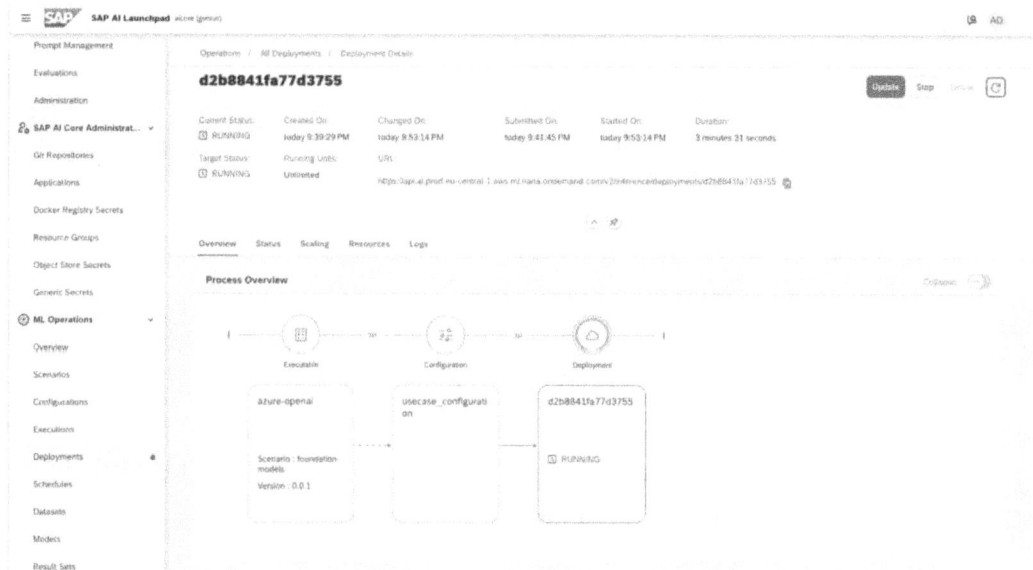

***Figure 6-50.*** *Deployment details*

Now, you are going to leverage the parameters like the deployment URL, the resource group (which is created at the initial stage of setting up SAP AI Core instance), the model name version, and so on, inside the package.json file to establish connectivity between the CAP application and AI Core. See the following code snippet:

```
"gen-ai-hub": {
  "gpt-4": {
    "destinationName": "LLMChatCompletionAPI",
    "deploymentUrl": "/v2/inference/deployments/d9e06d7e043a020a",
    "resourceGroup": "genius",
    "apiVersion": "2024-06-01",
    "modelName": "gpt-35-turbo"
  },
  "text-embedding-ada-002": {
    "destinationName": "LLMChatCompletionAPI",
    "deploymentUrl": "/v2/inference/deployments/dc9c1fec4d5de737",
    "resourceGroup": "genius",
    "apiVersion": "2024-06-01",
    "modelName": "text-embedding-ada-002"
  }
```

183

CHAPTER 6  BUILDING CUSTOM AI APPLICATIONS USING SAP BUSINESS AI FOUNDATION

```
    },
    "LLMChatCompletionAPI": {
      "kind": "rest",
      "credentials": {
        "destination": "LLMChatCompletionAPI",
        "requestTimeout": "300000"
      }
    },
```

You also need to create a destination using the name that you defined in `package.json` against the `destinationName` parameter, within the destination service instance in the BTP space. Navigate to the space in the BTP cockpit, and then click the destination service instance, as shown in Figure 6-51.

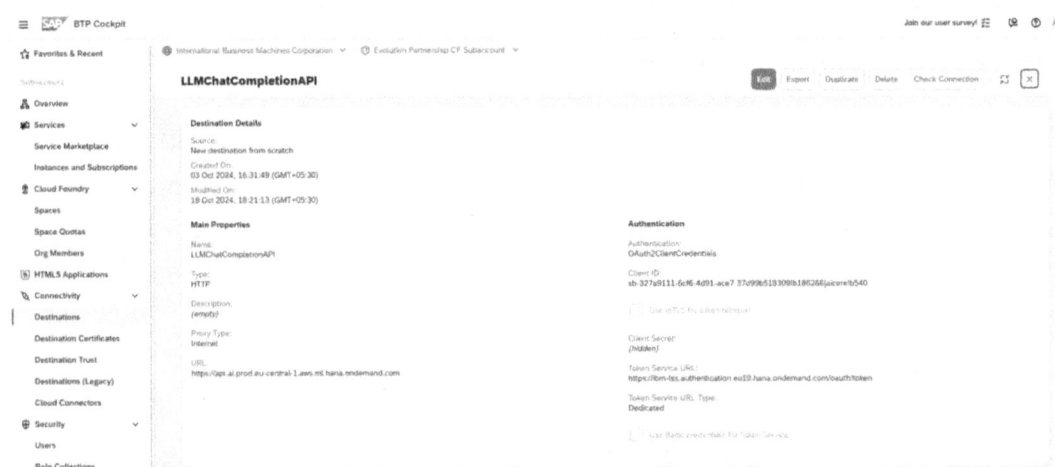

***Figure 6-51.*** *Destination configuration*

This use case is segregated into two applications. One application is designated to upload relevant files followed by generating embeddings and saving them into the SAP Hana Cloud Vector Engine. This is a CAP-based application that leverages the CAP-LLM plugin to the embedding LLM model via SAP AI Core and generates embeddings seamlessly. The CAP-LLM plugin provides an integrated solution to streamline the complete RAG workflow, from generating embedding values for user inputs and performing similarity searches, to appending relevant search results to prompts and finally invoking the LLM for a response.

In a typical setup, a developer building an application based on the RAG architecture configures both the embedding and chat models on the SAP Generative AI Hub, enabling seamless access to these models. The knowledgebase, generally made up of documents, is divided into smaller text segments, which are then converted into vector embeddings using embedding models. These embeddings are stored in SAP HANA Cloud according to a predefined CAP entity schema.

For the chat model to deliver accurate, context-aware responses without hallucinations, it must have access to the relevant text segments stored in the SAP HANA Cloud. This entire process involves generating vector embeddings, conducting similarity searches, and leveraging the chat-based LLM to produce precise and meaningful outputs. The uploaded documents are split into text chunks using the `getEmbeddingWithConfig()` method provided by the CAP LLM plugin, as shown here:

```
getEmbeddingWithConfig(config, input)
config (object): The configuration for the embedding model.
input (string): The input string to be embedded.
```

During the schema definition process for entities within CAP, the plugin empowers developers to seamlessly create entities with data elements of type vectors. These data types can be used to handle embeddings. Following deployment, these vector types are converted to the REAL_VECTOR data type. The incorporation of this vector type implementation will bolster support for RAG solutions.

This abstracts away most of the boilerplate code required to generate the embeddings, such as connecting to the embedding model via the SAP Generative AI Hub, passing in the necessary configurations for inferencing the model. The embeddings are then stored in the SAP HANA Cloud.

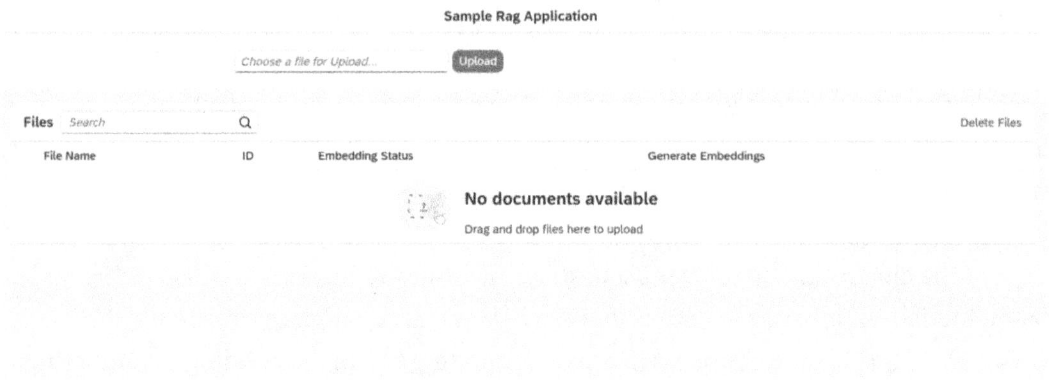

CHAPTER 6   BUILDING CUSTOM AI APPLICATIONS USING SAP BUSINESS AI FOUNDATION

*Figure 6-52.  RAG-based application for file upload*

As shown in Figure 6-52, the first BTP-based custom application uploads any PDF files using the Upload option.

*Figure 6-53.  Upload feature*

As demonstrated in Figure 6-53, after a file is uploaded, its metadata appears in tabular format, which includes a provision to generate embedding using the button inside the Generate Embedding column. In this case, we are uploading a sample worker safety handbook. We are using a small size document due to limitations in token size, but if you want, you can use any other relevant document based on your token size.

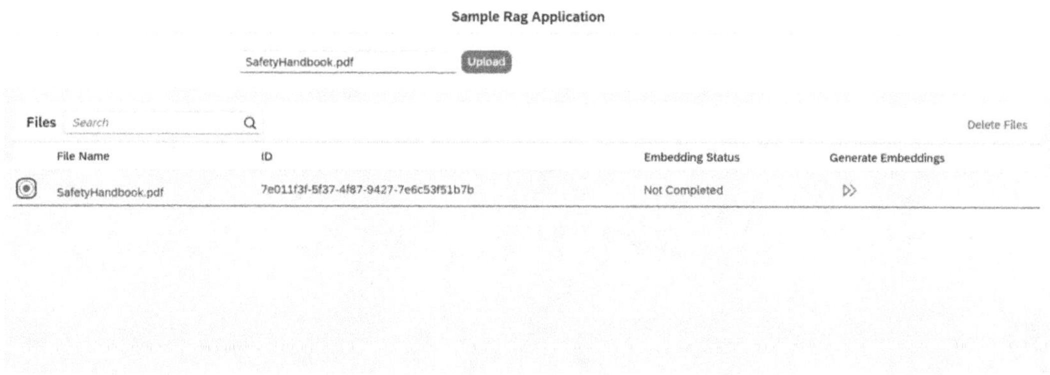

CHAPTER 6  BUILDING CUSTOM AI APPLICATIONS USING SAP BUSINESS AI FOUNDATION

***Figure 6-54.*** *Embedding status*

The Embedding Status column shown in Figure 6-54 tells you the embedding generation status. In this case, it is Not Completed.

***Figure 6-55.*** *Embedding generation successful*

As shown in Figure 6-55, clicking the Generate Embeddings button quickly generates the embedding, which is saved in the HANA Cloud Vector Engine. After it's generated, the application also shows a message at the bottom of the screen informing about the successful embedding.

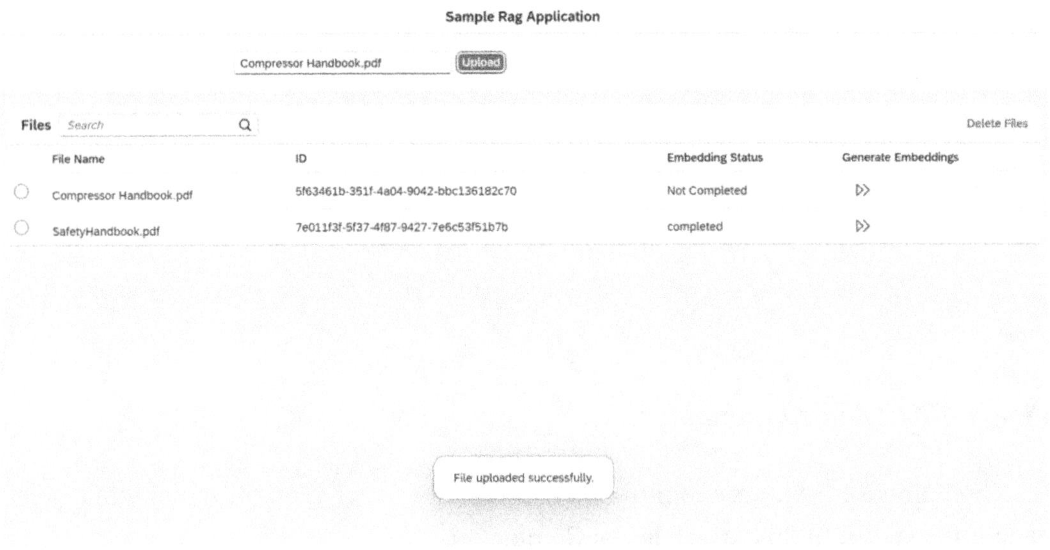

CHAPTER 6    BUILDING CUSTOM AI APPLICATIONS USING SAP BUSINESS AI FOUNDATION

*Figure 6-56.  File uploaded successfully*

In the next step, as shown in Figure 6-56, you upload the subsequent file, which in this case, is an equipment specification document for spare parts related to industrial compressors. This is also a very small PDF document; you can upload your document based on your own token size.

*Figure 6-57.  Generating embeddings*

Chapter 6  Building Custom AI Applications Using SAP Business AI Foundation

The embedding generation process remains the same, as shown in Figure 6-57. After the generation process, it shows a successful message, as shown in Figure 6-58.

*Figure 6-58. Embedding generation is successful*

As shown in Figure 6-59, we have uploaded and successfully generated the embeddings for the required files related to worker safety related norms and spare part specifications for compressors.

*Figure 6-59. Embedding status*

Now it's time to focus on the second application, which is basically a BTP-based chatbot application to interact with the maintenance related data that you vectorized and stored in the HANA Cloud Vector Engine using the first solution.

This is also a CAP-based application deployed on Cloud Foundry. It uses the CAP-LLM plugin to interact with the LLM and perform similarity searches based on the entity structure of the CAP model. Leveraging SAP HANA Cloud's robust similarity search feature, the plugin uses various methods like getRagResponseWithConfig, similaritySearch, and getRagResponse to efficiently retrieve relevant data, as shown in following code snippet. The plugin supports the COSINE_SIMILARITY and L2DISTANCE algorithms and will continue to support future available algorithms too. The following list explains the input parameters supported by getRagResponseWithConfig method:

```
async getRagResponseWithConfig(input, tableName, embeddingColumnName,
contentColumn, chatInstruction, context, [topK=3], [algoName='COSINE_
SIMILARITY'], [chatParams], embeddingConfig, chatConfig)
```

Here are the parameters:

- input (string): User input.
- tableName (string): The full name of the SAP HANA Cloud table that contains the vector embeddings.
- embeddingColumnName (string): The full name of the SAP HANA Cloud table column that contains the embeddings.
- contentColumn (string): The full name of the SAP HANA Cloud table column that contains the page content.
- chatInstruction (string): The custom prompt users can pass in. Important: Ensure that the prompt contains the message content, which is enclosed in triple quotes.
- embeddingConfig: The configuration for the embedding model.
- chatConfig: The configuration for the chat completion model.
- context (object, optional): The chat history.
- topK (number, optional): The number of the entries you want to return. The default value is 3.

- algoName (string, optional): The algorithm of the similarity search. Currently only COSINE_SIMILARITY and L2DISTANCE are accepted. The default is COSINE_SIMILARITY.

- chatParams (object, optional): The other chat model params.

Here are the returns:

- (object): Returns the RAG response from the LLM in the form of { "completion": Chat completion response from getChatCompletionWithConfig method, "additionalContents": Complete similarity search results from SAP HANA Cloud }

This section only highlights the significant pieces of code relevant to LLM integration into the CAP-based application on BTP. For the complete code, refer to the Git repository at https://github.com/creativeavijitdhar/buildintentwithbai and follow the instructions given in the Readme file to further build and deploy these applications.

Let's now walk through the features of the second application, which basically helps you interact with maintenance data in natural language and get the most relevant response. When you launch the CAP application, you will see the screen shown in Figure 6-60.

***Figure 6-60.*** *Initial screen*

CHAPTER 6    BUILDING CUSTOM AI APPLICATIONS USING SAP BUSINESS AI FOUNDATION

At the bottom of the screen, you can see a Digital Assistant button, which you can use to launch the chat window.

*Figure 6-61.* Chat Window

Besides a warm welcome, the chat window, as shown in Figure 6-61, has a text area with a Send button where you enter prompts and get responses.

*Figure 6-62.* Prompt input

As shown in Figure 6-62, the first prompt that we create as a maintenance operator is related to the manufacturing details for a relief valve.

*Figure 6-63.* *Bot response*

As shown in Figure 6-63, the bot responded accurately by performing a similarity search across the vectorized spare parts data that we uploaded earlier, using the first application of the use case.

Figure 6-64 shows a preview of the information from the spare parts PDF that the bot used to respond to the query.

CHAPTER 6   BUILDING CUSTOM AI APPLICATIONS USING SAP BUSINESS AI FOUNDATION

**FK-103**   Heavy Duty Side Outlet Relief Valve is manufactured from cast brass and features a brass inlet and stem. This heavy duty hard seated valve is designed for harsh environments requiring a durable valve with a side outlet that allows for closed system integration. Well suited as a pump unloader in pressurized liquid systems. The FK-103 is a liquid only relief valve. <u>Set pressure range 5 to 300 psi (5 psi increments only). Maximum temperature 250°F</u>

FK-103

**FK-103SS**   <u>Hard Seated Side Outlet Relief Valve</u> is manufactured from cast brass and features a brass inlet and stainless steel ball. This hard seated valve is designed for harsh environments requiring a durable valve with a side outlet that allows for closed system integration. Well suited as a pump unloader in pressurized liquid systems. The FK-103SS is primarily a liquid relief valve that can also be used in some non-code, air applications. <u>Set pressure range 5 to 500 psi (5 psi increments only). Maximum temperature 250°F</u>

FK-103D-2

**FK-103D-2**   High Pressure Side Outlet Relief Valve is manufactured from cast brass and features a stainless steel inlet and ball. This versatile hard seat valve is designed for high pressure environments with a side outlet that allows for closed system integration. Well suited as a pump unloader in pressurized liquid systems. Available only in 1/4 inch NPT, the FK-103D is primarily a liquid relief valve that can also be used in some non-code, air applications. <u>Set pressure range 10 to 1000 psi (5 psi increments only). Maximum temperature 250°F</u>

*Figure 6-64.   Information source*

The next prompt, as shown in Figure 6-65, queries about the environment required for the relief valve to operate.

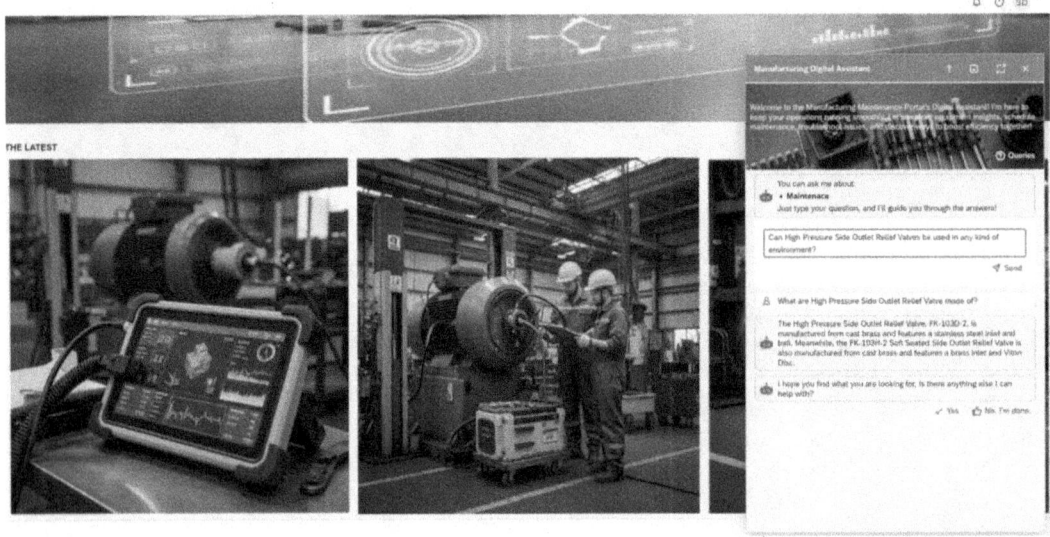

*Figure 6-65.   Prompt input*

CHAPTER 6  BUILDING CUSTOM AI APPLICATIONS USING SAP BUSINESS AI FOUNDATION

As shown in Figure 6-66, the bot accurately describes the kind of environment best suitable for a relief valve to operate.

***Figure 6-66.*** *Bot response*

These interactions clearly demonstrate how to integrate and interact with enterprise data, which in this context, is a spare part guide for an industrial compressor.

Let's now move on to the next set of interactions, for taking care of maintenance operators in hostile manufacturing environments. To operate in this kind of environment, the maintenance operator may need to know various details, and this is where the chatbot can help.

CHAPTER 6   BUILDING CUSTOM AI APPLICATIONS USING SAP BUSINESS AI FOUNDATION

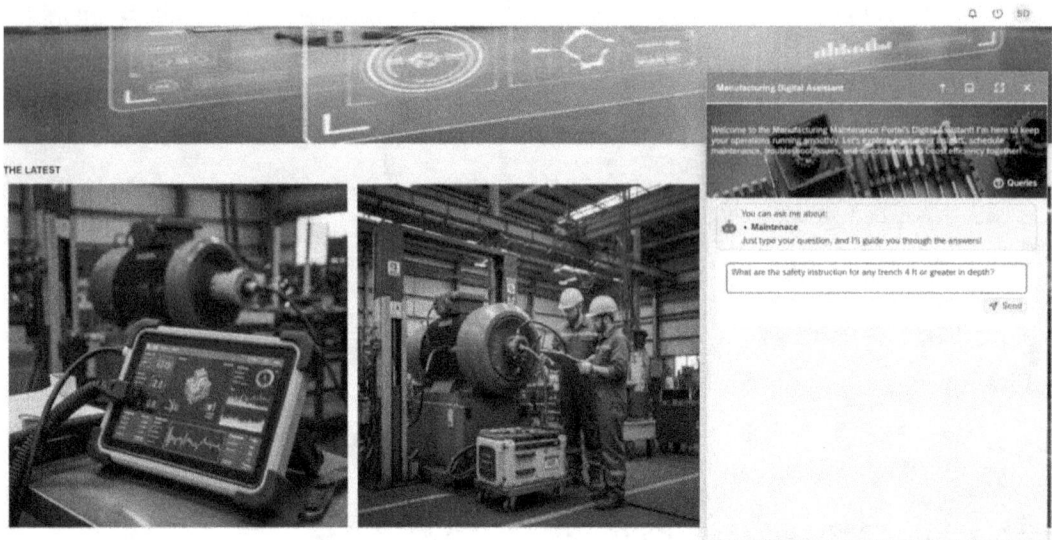

*Figure 6-67.* *Prompt input*

As shown in Figure 6-67, this prompt asks about safely operating in a trench of four or more feet in depth.

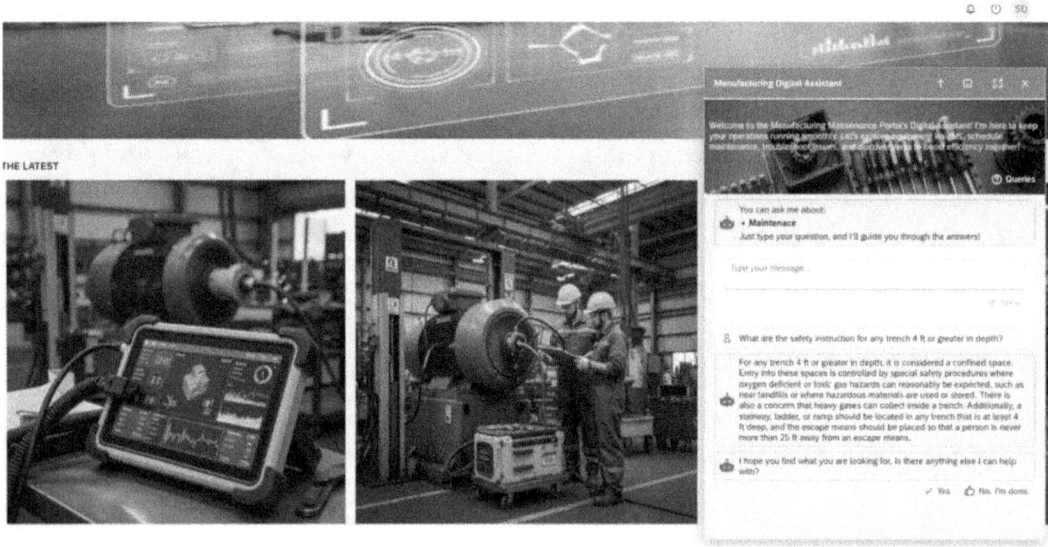

*Figure 6-68.* *Bot response*

Figure 6-68 shows how the bot finds the relevant information about safety measures to be taken when performing maintenance in a trench of four or more feet deep.

CHAPTER 6   BUILDING CUSTOM AI APPLICATIONS USING SAP BUSINESS AI FOUNDATION

Figure 6-69 shows a preview of the piece of information from the safety handbook PDF that the bot used to respond to the query.

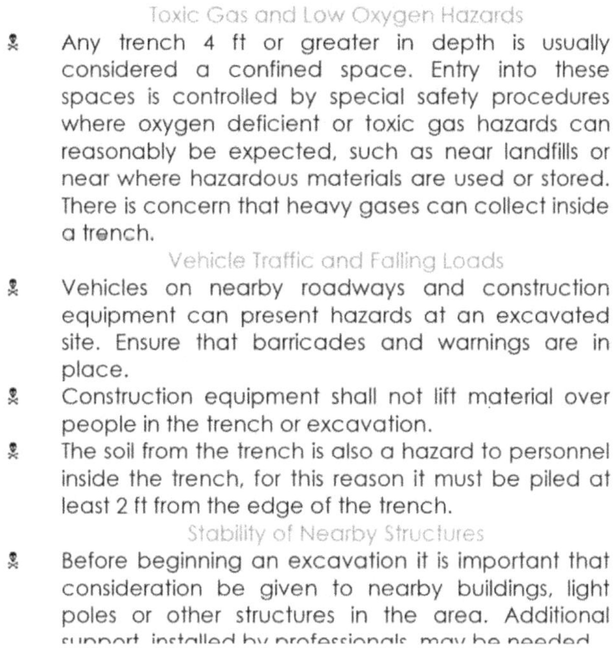

**Toxic Gas and Low Oxygen Hazards**
- Any trench 4 ft or greater in depth is usually considered a confined space. Entry into these spaces is controlled by special safety procedures where oxygen deficient or toxic gas hazards can reasonably be expected, such as near landfills or near where hazardous materials are used or stored. There is concern that heavy gases can collect inside a trench.

**Vehicle Traffic and Falling Loads**
- Vehicles on nearby roadways and construction equipment can present hazards at an excavated site. Ensure that barricades and warnings are in place.
- Construction equipment shall not lift material over people in the trench or excavation.
- The soil from the trench is also a hazard to personnel inside the trench, for this reason it must be piled at least 2 ft from the edge of the trench.

**Stability of Nearby Structures**
- Before beginning an excavation it is important that consideration be given to nearby buildings, light poles or other structures in the area. Additional support installed by professionals, may be needed

***Figure 6-69.*** *Information source*

The next prompt, shown in Figure 6-70, is related to the measures to take by area and location management when performing civil work. The bot returns a relevant response.

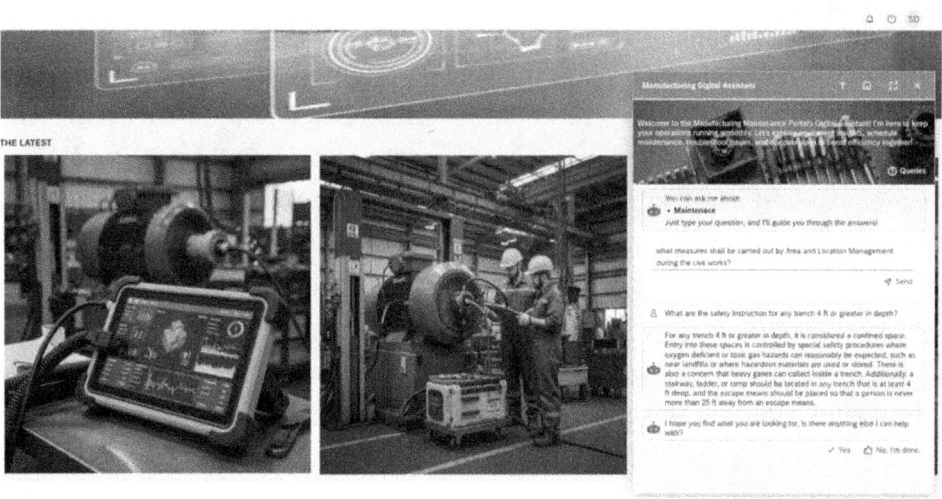

***Figure 6-70.*** *Prompt input*

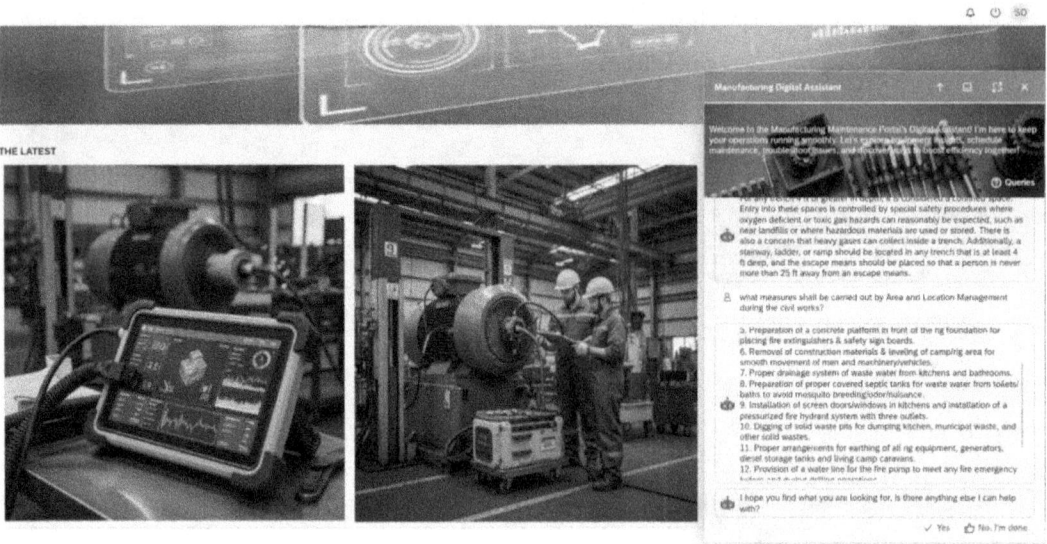

***Figure 6-71.** Bot response*

Figure 6-71 shows a preview of the measurements related to civil works from the safety handbook PDF.

The key purpose of this demonstration was not only to show the capabilities of SAP AI Core on custom business AI applications but also to elevate your ideas about adopting SAP AI Core services for addressing business challenges in your areas.

## Conclusion

This chapter started by introducing an enterprise-oriented use case addressing typical business challenges in the industrial equipment maintenance area. It also covered the key components and prerequisites that are essential for building this kind custom business AI solution. The chapter also covered the process of choosing the right language models for building an enterprise solution and how to take advantage of SAP BTP AI Launchpad to evaluate different partner foundation models and pick the right one. The chapter also explained how you can take advantage of SAP Discovery Center to prepare estimations for SAP BTP-based custom Business AI applications. It further went through the steps to set up the required prerequisites for use case development, including provisioning and deployment. It walked through the critical code snippets and application features. Overall, through a comprehensive demonstration from idea to implementation, this chapter proves that AI can be enterprise ready.

# CHAPTER 7

# Building AI Agents Using SAP Business AI Foundation

The previous chapter covered comprehensive details about the SAP AI and Generative AI Hub and further realized the concepts by going through a step-by-step process of building a Generative AI use case. This chapter explores a new dimension in the world of Generative AI and explains the concept of AI Agents or Agentic AI. Starting with a basic introduction, the chapter discusses some history, followed by Agentic AI's key features, components, use cases, and more. It finally goes through a step-by-step process of building a custom AI Agent using the SAP BTP Generative AI Hub.

## Introduction

The world of Generative AI is going through a transformation and its concepts are evolving every moment. It was only a few years ago that we were introduced to the generative dimension of AI and concepts like transformer architecture, LLMs, and RAG. At an unprecedented speed, we now need to get familiar with the world of Agentic AI and its associated concepts. In simple terms, we have moved from a stage where a LLM only tells you about your next holiday destination to the stage where it can even book a flight with the best possible deal and inform you with the detailed itinerary! Interesting, right? Before jumping into the technicalities around this, the first section takes a step back to explain what AI Agents are all about and how they are different from traditional AI, ML driven programs, or automations.

CHAPTER 7   BUILDING AI AGENTS USING SAP BUSINESS AI FOUNDATION

# What Are AI Agents?

An *AI Agent* is a software entity that performs NLP and activities. The journey of AI Agents begins with the theoretical foundation of AI in the 1950s and the development of early, rule-based systems like ELIZA (1966). The concept gained more prominence in the 1990s. Russell & Norvig called them "intelligent agents," which was goal-oriented software that perceived an environment.

In the enterprise world, we see how an end-to-end business process automation or workflow can execute sequential steps to achieve an end result, but this is driven by predefined rules or `if-else` conditions and business logic. To make these automations or workflows better, we can even combine them with AI and ML models. However, they are still limited to predefined rules and business logic. In contrast, AI Agents help us achieve the desired end result or mitigate business challenges when we know what the goal is but don't know how to achieve it. Today's highly autonomous, goal-directed systems powered by the advanced reasoning and planning abilities of modern LLMs are called *AI Agentic*. These agents are built to perform non-deterministic tasks autonomously by combining fuzzy logic with autonomy, adapting to changing environments and simulate human-like reasoning. Unlike traditional Generative AI models that simply reply to prompts, AI agents can independently manage complex, multi-step tasks from beginning to end. For example, in the case of an insurance claim, an agent can interpret the claim's text, images, and attached PDFs; pull relevant data from customer records; cross-check details against policy terms; and even interact with the customer to request missing information. What makes this more powerful is its ability to maintain context and continue the process seamlessly even if the customer's response arrives days later.

Some of the key capabilities that distinguish AI Agents from conversational system include:

- **Contextual understanding:** The key difference between a basic chatbot and an AI Agent is its capacity for memory and context. This ultimately helps maintain context across long, complex interactions, leading to recall preferences or referring back to earlier statements and handling multi-step requests seamlessly.

- **Tool integration:** AI Agents are not just language processing machines; they are powerful orchestrators. Their real utility comes from their ability to plug into the digital world by integrating with external tools like databases, company APIs, or various third-party services.

- **Autonomous task execution:** One of the most promising features of today's sophisticated AI Agents is their autonomy. Given a high-level goal, the agent is capable of planning, breaking down, and executing complex tasks without needing constant hand-holding or step-by-step human intervention.

- **Multi-agent collaboration:** For truly large and difficult problems, the system doesn't rely on a single entity. Multiple agents need to collaborate, share information, and work together to solve complex problems, leading to a more robust and complete solution than any single agent could achieve alone.

- **Human in the loop:** Despite their autonomy, the Human-in-the-Loop principle helps AI Agents incorporate human decision-making and feedback whenever human oversight, review, or approval is critical.

Now that you have preliminary understanding of AI Agents and their key features, the next section shifts the focus to understanding the underlying components.

# Key Components of AI Agents

To fully understand how AI Agents operate, it's essential to break down their internal architecture. Each core component plays a critical role in how the agent perceives, processes, and acts within its environment. As shown in Figure 7-1, these components form the foundational architecture of AI Agents.

CHAPTER 7  BUILDING AI AGENTS USING SAP BUSINESS AI FOUNDATION

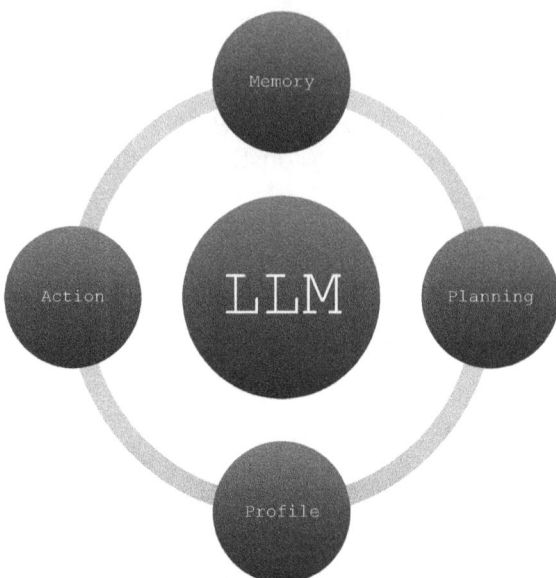

*Figure 7-1. Key components of AI Agents*

- **LLM:** For AI Agents, LLM acts as a brain or core intelligence that helps it understand language, process information, make sense of requests, formulate a coherent plan, and ultimately generate responses. For example, when you prompt "What's the weather like in Paris tomorrow, and can you also remind me to call Mom at 3 PM?", the LLM deciphers "weather in Paris," "tomorrow," "remind me," "call Mom," and "3 PM." It understands the intent behind each phrase and recognizes that these are two distinct tasks.

- **Actions:** The Action component refers to the agent's ability to do things in the real world by utilizing tools and functions. AI Agents basically perform various activities like searching the web, checking weather, sending emails, setting reminders in thew calendar, and interacting with enterprise data or even with other AI Agents via numerous tools and functions. This could be anything, including setting a calendar reminder, sending an email, searching the web, or controlling smart home devices.

- **Memory:** Memory is one of the most crucial components and allows AI Agent to recall past interactions, learn from experiences, and maintain context across numerous conversations. Without memory, every interaction would be starting from scratch. Memory can range from short-term (the current conversation) to long-term (user preferences, past behaviors). For example:
    - **Short-term:** Suppose you have prompted an AI Agent with a query like "What was the capital of France again?" The agent remembers from your previous query that you were asking about "Paris" and connects the dots.
    - **Long-term:** Over time, the agent might notice you frequently ask for Indian restaurant recommendations. The next time when prompt the agent with "I'm hungry, suggest something for dinner," its long-term memory about your preferences might lead it to suggest a nearby Indian restaurant without you even mentioning it.

- **Planning:** The Planning component of AI Agents are all about its ability to break down a complex request into smaller, manageable steps to better understand the most efficient and logical sequence of actions that it needs to follow to achieve the user's goal. This kind of planning process often leverages chain-of-thought (CoT) reasoning or task decomposition via LLM orchestration, allowing the agent to understand dependencies and optimize execution.

    For example, when you tell an AI Agent, "I need to book a flight to London for next month, find a hotel near the British Museum, and then add those details to my travel itinerary." The given task requires understanding of various dependencies and logical execution to achieve the end result, which includes:
    - **Step 1 (Book a flight).** Initiate a search for flights to London for the specified month. (Action: Flight Search API)
    - **Step 2 (Book a hotel).** After the flight is booked, search for hotels near the British Museum, within a certain price range or rating. (Action: Hotel Search API) .

- **Step 3 (Create an itinerary).** After the flight and hotel are confirmed, consolidate all the details and add them to your travel document or calendar. (Action: Itinerary Management API).

- **Profile:** Next in line is the Profile component, where the agent stores information about the user, including user preferences, habits, personal details, frequently used services, and even communication style. This is what makes the agent feel tailored and truly personal.

In totality all these components create a dynamic and capable AI Agent where the LLM processes your input, the Planning component figures out how to tackle it, the Action component takes care of executing the necessary tasks, and the Memory and Profile components ensure the interaction is personalized and efficient. Now that you understand the key components of AI Agents, the next section explains some use cases that are good candidates for an Agentic AI solution.

# Agentic AI Use Cases

Having tremendous potential, Agentic AI can bring value to countless business scenarios across the industry, accelerating many human-driven tasks and automations. Potential use cases include the following:

- **Customer service agents:** One of the most common use cases is replacing human agents that need to address queries from customers all day. AI Agents shine and support human agents with instant answers or even perform reasoning for complex queries ad guide users with relevant information. With integration to enterprise systems like CRM and others, the AI Agent can help customer service provide a more personalized experience based on rich context extracted from past history, substantially cutting response time to close a ticket and freeing up human staff for complex issues.

- **Supply chains:** In the fast-paced world, supply chains are one area where speed is everything. AI Agents capable of sensing, planning, and acting autonomously can bring value to many areas like inventory management, order fulfilment, route planning, and so on. For instance, in inventory management, agents can continuously monitor real-time demand signals, predict potential shortages, and automatically adjust orders with suppliers, eliminating the need for constant human supervision. They can also serve as logistics optimizers, evaluating thousands of parameters like shipping rates, weather delays, and traffic in milliseconds to reroute shipments and minimize costs or delays.

- **Finance:** The financial sector can benefit immensely by taking advantage of AI Agents. AI Agents can help prioritize various anonymous tasks like fraud prevention, compliance monitoring, cash forecasting, credit scoring, and many other sophisticated and high-volume tasks. In essence, AI Agents can help financial institutions shift from a reactive to a proactive and autonomous operating model, allowing human capital to be redirected to strategic analysis, complex problem-solving, and relationship management.

- **Healthcare:** Healthcare is another potential sector where AI Agent adoption can bring acceleration to multi-step clinical and administrative execution. AI Agents can immediately tackle the crippling problem of staff burnout by serving as virtual medical scribes, automatically generating comprehensive, structured clinical notes during patient-doctor conversations. Beyond administration, AI Agents can ensure patient safety and outcomes by acting as diagnostic and preventative assistants continuously monitoring real-time data from various medical equipment and wearables.

- **Manufacturing and IoT:** In manufacturing, AI is focused on preempting problems before they become costly breakdowns. Predictive maintenance bots are intelligent learning agents that constantly ingest data from sensors monitoring vibration, temperature, and pressure. By using real-time stream data, they can even help detect subtle anomalies that can lead to equipment failure. By learning from every past incident, these agents can trigger an alert just in time for scheduled maintenance, drastically reducing costly, unplanned downtime.

The use cases discussed in this section are just a glimpse of the enormous potential that AI Agents can bring to various industries and based on these use cases, developers can further ideate the adoption of similar agents in other industries.

So far, this chapter has laid the foundation for understanding AI Agents. The next section shifts the focus to building an AI Agent based on a real industry use case to further harden your understanding.

# Building AI Agents

The exponential trajectory of Agentic AI adoption is quite prominent across various industries. These overwhelming needs are getting fueled by a handful of Agentic AI platforms that give developers the necessary scaffolding to turn their agents into reality. Global giants like IBM, Microsoft, and SAP are the prominent frontrunners in this space, alongside various open-source platforms. The most prominent platforms in this space include the following:

- **LangChain:** LangChain, with its component LangGraph, offers a comprehensive development toolkit to build AI Agents from the ground up. It is a comprehensive toolkit supporting every component required to build every part of the agent's brain including memory, tool integration, and prompt management. While LangChain is designed for linear workflows using Directed Acyclic Graphs (DAGs), LangGraph takes things a step further by allowing cycles within workflows. This means LLM agents can revisit steps, loop through processes, and make decisions as conditions change. With this capability, developers can create agent systems that are not only more complex but also smarter, more flexible, and able to adapt dynamically. In the next section, we take a closer look at LangGraph and see how it can be used to build a custom agent on BTP.

- **IBM Watson Orchestrate:** IBM Watsonx Orchestrate is a powerful, enterprise-grade platform specifically designed to help organizations build, launch, and govern their AI assistants and agents for automating complex processes and everyday workflows. The core strength of the solution lies in its ability to act as a central hub, ensuring seamless integration across your entire technology stack. It doesn't force you to adopt new tools; instead, it effortlessly connects to all your existing business applications, any AI Agent or model you currently employ, and every automation tool already in

CHAPTER 7   BUILDING AI AGENTS USING SAP BUSINESS AI FOUNDATION

use. This unified approach not only simplifies the deployment and management of individual AI entities but also facilitates genuine collaboration between your various AI assistants and agents, all operating within a single, cohesive user experience.

- **Azure AI Foundry:** Azure AI Foundry is built to simplify and transform the way intelligent agents are developed. The platform brings together models, tools, frameworks, and governance within a single, unified platform. At the heart of this ecosystem is the Azure AI Foundry Agent Service, which powers agent operations across the entire lifecycle, starting from development to deployment and production, resulting a secure, scalable, and production-ready environment for agents. By handling infrastructure complexities and embedding trust and safety into its design, the AI Foundry Agent Service enables teams to seamlessly transition from experimentation to real-world deployment with confidence.

- **SAP Agent Builder:** SAP has been a pioneer in enterprise solutions for several decades. It introduced its AI copilot called SAP Joule across its SaaS solutions. Beyond its out-of-the-box capabilities, SAP Joule skills can be easily extended using Joule Studio, which is integral part of SAP Build. Joule studio on BTP is a comprehensive suite of low-code and pro-code solutions designed to accelerate application development and automation with the power of Generative AI. In addition to Joule skills, SAP Joule Studio can also be utilized to create autonomous AI Agents by defining expertise and instructions to optimize the agent's performance. AI Agents created using Joule studio uses tools like document grounding, calculator, A2A (one Joule Agent can invoke other Joule Agent) and skills for enterprise system integration. You can either integrate existing with Joule skills as tools or create new skills from ground up. In this context, a skill is part of an advanced AI model and can act on specific operations by leveraging the content of the conversation. Additionally SAP Joule studio for Agents also supports MCP (Model Context Protocol) through which can integrate or source various tools from other platforms in a unified manner.

To build our use case we are going to take more pro-code approach and will build our custom AI Agent from scratch using a combination of LangGraph, SAP AI Core, and SAP Business Application Studio on the SAP BTP Cloud Foundry environment.

Now that you have a basic understanding of some of the leading development platforms in the Agentic AI space, the next section puts this knowledge to use to build an AI Agent from scratch using LangGraph, SAP AI Core, and SAP BTP Business Application Studio based on a real-world enterprise use case.

# Supply Chain Industry Use Case

Enough of the theory! This section shifts the focus to creating an AI Agent on BTP using the LangGraph open-source toolkit, guided by a real-world use case. This real-world use case is from the supply chain industry and addresses one of the most recent and prominent challenges in the recent world. The trade rate is a critical and deciding factor for determining costs and profits when dealing with foreign countries. Due to recent changes in global economics, many companies are attempting to mitigate the challenges. To that end, you are going to build a custom AI Agent using SAP AI Core on SAP BTP by leveraging key components, including these:

- **LangGraph:** LangGraph provides a set of tools and libraries that enable users to create, run, and optimize LLMs in a scalable and efficient manner. At its core, LangGraph uses the power of graph-based architectures to model and manage the intricate relationships between various components of an AI Agent workflow. Key libraries include `langchain_core` and `langgraph`.

- **SAP Cloud SDK for AI (Python):** SAP Cloud SDK is a powerful toolkit that simplifies the integration of Generative AI capabilities into SAP applications. It connects seamlessly with SAP's Generative AI Hub and AI Core, giving developers access to leading LLMs from providers like OpenAI, Amazon, and Google.

    With built-in LangChain integration, it streamlines model initialization and orchestration, while also supporting advanced features such as templating, grounding, and data masking through the orchestration service.

CHAPTER 7   BUILDING AI AGENTS USING SAP BUSINESS AI FOUNDATION

For more details, refer to https://help.sap.com/doc/generative-ai-hub-sdk/CLOUD/en-US/_reference/README_sphynx.html.

- **Jupyter Notebook:** In addition to LangGraph tools and libraries, this example utilize Jupyter Notebook on SAP Business Application Studio to do the coding. Jupyter Notebook is an open-source web application that allows users to do live coding, clean data, and perform visualization for AI/ML based applications using languages like Python, R, and Julia. Jupyter Notebook is now supported on Business Application Studio. Before you run Jupyter Notebook in SAP Business Application Studio, you need to install the package installer `pip` for Python and some of the publicly available packages such as `langchain_core`, `langgraph`, and so on. The SAP Business Application Studio requires `pip` in order to install `ipykernel`, which is needed to run the notebook within the environment.

## Building Steps

To build this AI Agent, you use Jupyter Notebook inside SAP Business Application studio. Launch your SAP Business Application, as shown in Figure 7-2, with the relevant workspace and navigate to the extension segment.

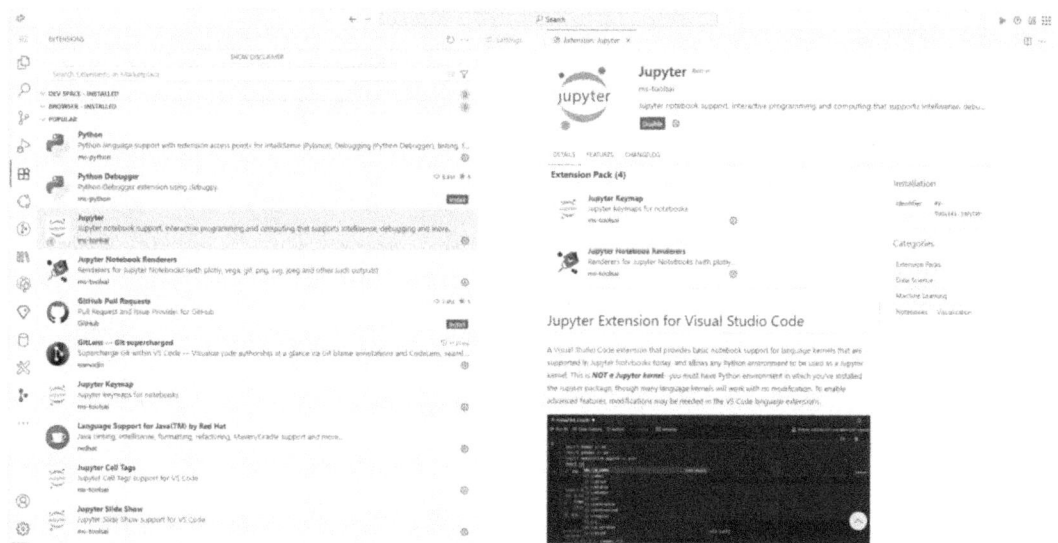

*Figure 7-2. Extensions inside SAP Business Application Studio*

209

CHAPTER 7   BUILDING AI AGENTS USING SAP BUSINESS AI FOUNDATION

As shown in Figure 7-2, you need to install the Jupyter and Python extension under the popular segment.

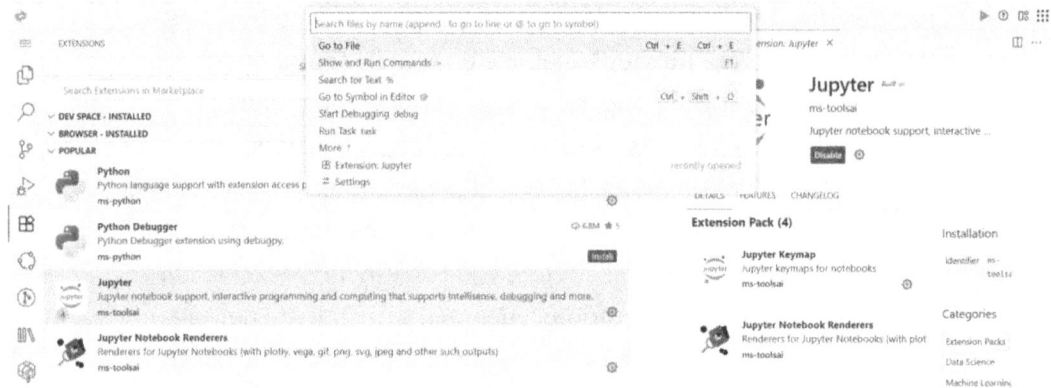

*Figure 7-3.* Open Search bar

After you install the Jupyter extension, create a notebook to run the AI Agent-related experiments. As shown in Figure 7-3, you need to navigate to the search bar at the top of the screen and type the required command to create the notebook.

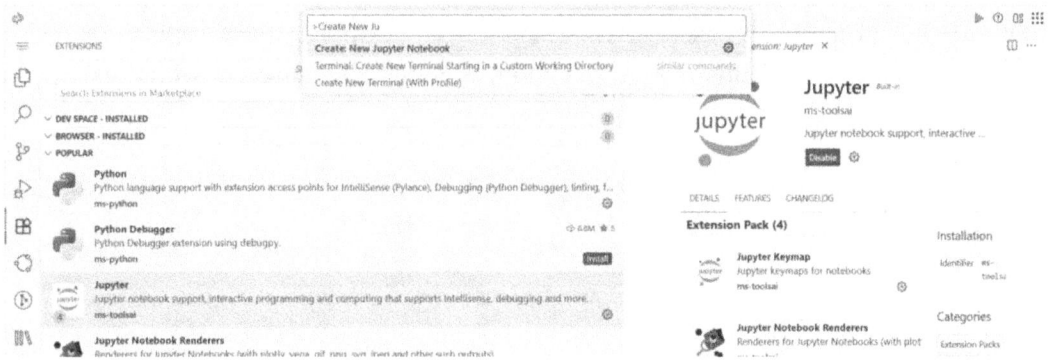

*Figure 7-4.* Enter the command

Type `Create New Jupyter Notebook` in the top search bar, as shown in Figure 7-4. You will see that an embedded new blank notebook. as shown in Figure 7-5, appears inside BAS, where you can script the agent using Python.

210

CHAPTER 7    BUILDING AI AGENTS USING SAP BUSINESS AI FOUNDATION

*Figure 7-5.*  *New Notebook*

Before you start scripting the agent, you need to install and import all the required modules using the `pip install` command, as shown in Figure 7-6. The key libraries include `langchain_core`, `langgraph`, and `generative-ai-hub-sdk`.

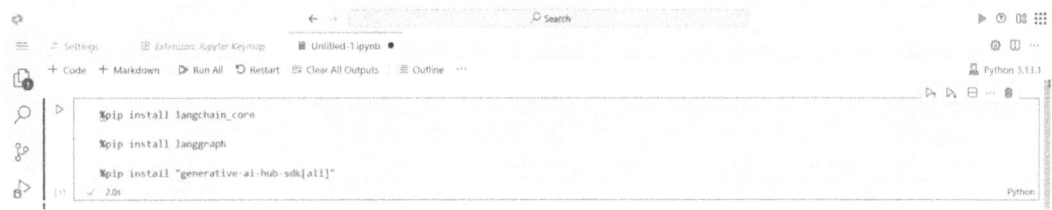

*Figure 7-6.*  *Install the required libraries*

After the installation, you are all set with the required foundation to start scripting the AI Agent. But wait! Is that all you need or will you need some more information?

Oh yes! Don't forget the required SAP AI core credentials that you will need to integrate the LLM into the AI Agent. You will need some key information from the service key attached to your SAP AI Core service instance. The service key on SAP BTP is essential for securely connecting to SAP AI Core, as it provides the authentication credentials and endpoint information such as client IDs, secrets, and service URLs, and so on, required for applications or agents to access AI Core resources.

211

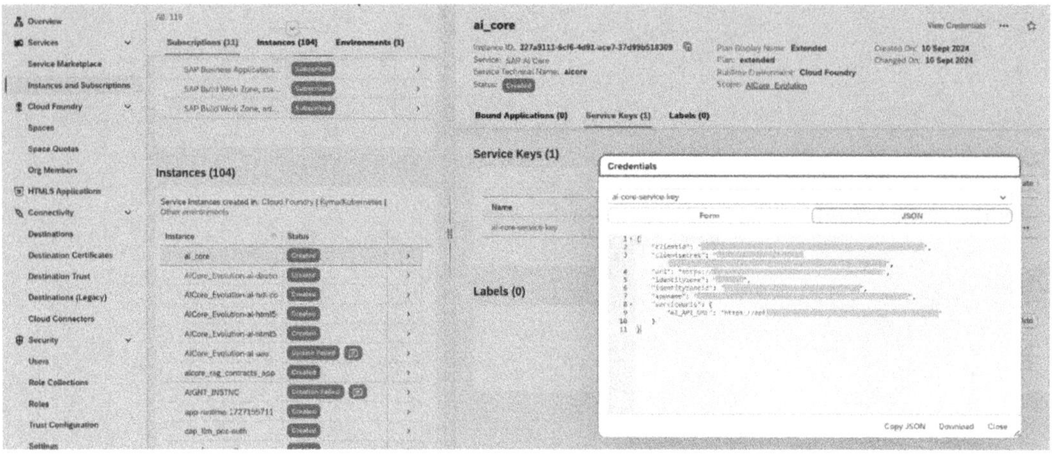

CHAPTER 7   BUILDING AI AGENTS USING SAP BUSINESS AI FOUNDATION

*Figure 7-7.   Service key credentials*

As shown in Figure 7-7, navigate to the Instances and Subscriptions segment inside your SAP BTP cockpit and open the service attached to your AI Core service instance. Write down the credentials shown in Figure 7-7.

Additionally, you need the name of the Resource Group that was configured as part of your SAP AI Core setup. You can get it inside SAP AI Launchpad, as shown in Figure 7-8.

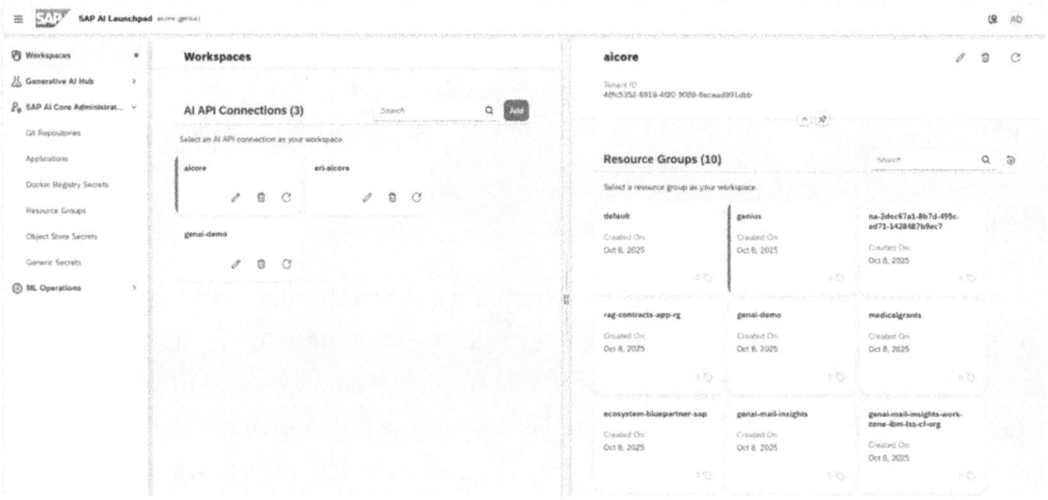

*Figure 7-8.   Resource Group*

CHAPTER 7   BUILDING AI AGENTS USING SAP BUSINESS AI FOUNDATION

```json
{
    "SAP_AI_CORE": {
        "AICORE_CLIENT_ID": "...",
        "AICORE_CLIENT_SECRET": "...",
        "AICORE_AUTH_URL": ".../oauth/token",
        "AICORE_RESOURCE_GROUP": "...",
        "AICORE_BASE_URL": ".../v2"
    }
}
```

*Figure 7-9. The credentials.json file*

Coming back to SAP Business Application Studio, create a JSON file called credentials.json, as shown in Figure 7-9, to maintain the AI Core credentials that you obtained in the previous step. Even though this is not a recommended approach, you save it here to simply the process.

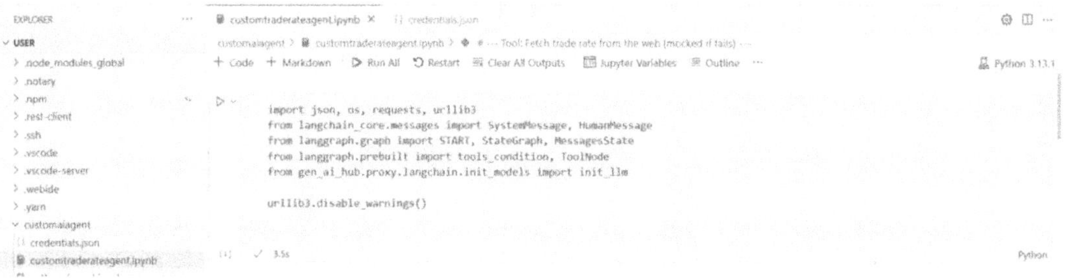

```python
import json, os, requests, urllib3
from langchain_core.messages import SystemMessage, HumanMessage
from langgraph.graph import START, StateGraph, MessagesState
from langgraph.prebuilt import tools_condition, ToolNode
from gen_ai_hub.proxy.langchain.init_models import init_llm

urllib3.disable_warnings()
```

*Figure 7-10. Add the import statements*

In the first code cell of the notebook, as shown in Figure 7-10, add the import statements required to include the necessary libraries.

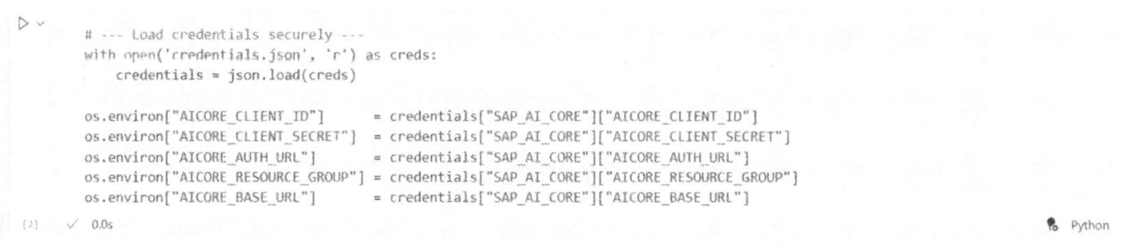

```python
# --- Load credentials securely ---
with open('credentials.json', 'r') as creds:
    credentials = json.load(creds)

os.environ["AICORE_CLIENT_ID"]       = credentials["SAP_AI_CORE"]["AICORE_CLIENT_ID"]
os.environ["AICORE_CLIENT_SECRET"]   = credentials["SAP_AI_CORE"]["AICORE_CLIENT_SECRET"]
os.environ["AICORE_AUTH_URL"]        = credentials["SAP_AI_CORE"]["AICORE_AUTH_URL"]
os.environ["AICORE_RESOURCE_GROUP"]  = credentials["SAP_AI_CORE"]["AICORE_RESOURCE_GROUP"]
os.environ["AICORE_BASE_URL"]        = credentials["SAP_AI_CORE"]["AICORE_BASE_URL"]
```

*Figure 7-11. Load the credentials*

As shown in Figure 7-11, load the credentials from the credentials.json file created in the previous step.

213

CHAPTER 7    BUILDING AI AGENTS USING SAP BUSINESS AI FOUNDATION

Recall that AI Agents take advantage of different tools to perform autonomous tasks. In this case, you are also going to define some tools that will help the AI Agent optimize the trade rate.

```python
# --- Tool: Fetch trade rate from the web (mocked if fails) ---
import requests

def get_trade_rate_from_web(country: str, product: str) -> float:
    """Fetch average export price or trade rate for a product from a public trade API."""
    try:
        url = "https://comtradeplus.un.org/api/get"
        params = {
            'type': 'C',
            'freq': 'A',
            'px': 'HS',
            'ps': '2023',
            'r': country,      # e.g., 'IND' or numeric like '699'
            'p': '0',
            'rg': '2',
            'cc': product,     # e.g., '1001' (wheat)
            'fmt': 'json',
            'max': '10000'
        }
        response = requests.get(url, params=params, timeout=10)
        response.raise_for_status()
        data = response.json()

        dataset = data.get('dataset', [])
        if dataset:
            value = dataset[0].get('TradeValue', 0)
            quantity = dataset[0].get('NetWeight', 1) or 1
            avg_price = value / quantity if quantity > 0 else 0
            return round(avg_price, 2)
        else:
            return round(1000 + hash(country + product) % 500, 2)
```

*Figure 7-12.  Getting the trade rate tool (part 1)*

As shown in Figures 7-12 and 7-13, I have created a tool called get_trade_rate_from_web, which basically obtains the trade rate for a given country and product using a public API.

```python
    except Exception as e:
        print(f"⚠ Mocking trade rate due to error fetching for {country}: {e}")
        mock_value = {
            "China": 950.0,
            "Germany": 1050.0,
            "India": 870.0,
            "Japan": 990.0
        }
        return mock_value.get(country, 1000.0)

# Example test
print(get_trade_rate_from_web("IND", "1001"))  # Wheat from India
```

*Figure 7-13.  Getting the trade rate tool (part 2)*

If the web API fails to respond, I kept some backup values as a fallback option.

```python
# --- Tool: Calculate landed cost ---
def calculate_landed_cost(rate: float, tariff: float = 5.0, freight: float = 10.0) -> float:
    """Calculate the landed cost including tariff and freight."""
    return round(rate + (rate * tariff / 100) + freight, 2)
```

```python
# --- Tool: Compare trade rates ---
def compare_trade_rates(product: str, destination: str, countries: list):
    """Compare trade rates by country and propose the best import source."""
    results = []
    for c in countries:
        rate = get_trade_rate_from_web(c, product)
        cost = calculate_landed_cost(rate)
        results.append({"country": c, "rate": rate, "landed_cost": cost})

    if not results:
        return "No data found."

    best = min(results, key=lambda x: x['landed_cost'])
    summary = f"✅ Best country to import {product} to {destination}: {best['country']} (${best['landed_cost']} per unit)\n"
    summary += " + Detailed comparison:\n"
    for r in results:
        summary += f"   - {r['country']}: Rate=${r['rate']}, Landed=${r['landed_cost']}\n"
    return summary
```

***Figure 7-14.*** *Defining the tools*

As shown in Figure 7-14, the `calculated_landed_cost` and `compare_trade_rates` tools calculate the landed costs and compare the trade rates based on product, destination, and country.

The `calculated_landed_cost` function basically calculates the landed cost by adding the base rate, the tariff, and the freight charge, and then rounds the result to two decimal places for precision. This ensures a clear representation.

On the other hand, `compare_trade_rates` retrieves the trade rate for each country using the `get_trade_rate_from_web` function and then calculates the total landed cost, which includes tariffs and freight, via the `calculate_landed_cost` function.

215

CHAPTER 7   BUILDING AI AGENTS USING SAP BUSINESS AI FOUNDATION

```python
# --- Register Tools ---
tools = [get_trade_rate_from_web, calculate_landed_cost, compare_trade_rates]
```

```python
# --- Initialize LLM ---
llm = init_llm('mistralai--mistral-large-instruct', max_tokens=300)
llm_with_tools = llm.bind_tools(tools)
```

```python
# --- System Instruction ---
sys_msg = SystemMessage(content="You are a helpful assistant tasked to compare trade rates and suggest the best import source.")

# --- Assistant Node ---
def assistant(state: MessagesState):
    """Main assistant logic node."""
    return {"messages": [llm_with_tools.invoke([sys_msg] + state["messages"])]}

# --- Build LangGraph ---
builder = StateGraph(MessagesState)
builder.add_node("assistant", assistant)
builder.add_node("tools", ToolNode(tools))
builder.add_edge(START, "assistant")
builder.add_conditional_edges("assistant", tools_condition)
builder.add_edge("tools", "assistant")
graph = builder.compile()
```

*Figure 7-15. Coding the agent*

As shown in Figure 7-15, in the code cells [6], [7], and [8] basically do the following things:

- Cell [6] registers the defined tools that so that in the subsequent Python scripts, you can easily reference and execute them.

- Code cell [7] takes care of initializing the LLMs. In this case, we are using `mistralai-mistral-large-instruct` model and binding the tools defined in the previous steps.

- Cell [8] takes care of defining an AI Agent with the required system prompt and the tools instantiated in cell [7]. The model decides whether to respond directly or use tools based on the tool conditions. If the model decides to use a tool, it goes to the `toolNode` and after the tool runs, it passes the result back to the `assistant` for a final summary.

CHAPTER 7   BUILDING AI AGENTS USING SAP BUSINESS AI FOUNDATION

```python
# --- Test Harness ---
if __name__ == "__main__":
    print("🚀 Running Trade Rate Comparison AI Agent...\n")

    # Simulate a user query
    user_query = HumanMessage(content="Compare the trade rates of product 721 for importing into India from China, Germany, and Japan.")
    result = graph.invoke({"messages": [user_query]})

    print("\n--- AI Agent Output ---")
    for msg in result["messages"]:
        if hasattr(msg, 'content'):
            print(msg.content)
```

*Figure 7-16.   Testing the agent*

Figure 7-16 shows the final script required to test the AI Agent with sample input. It prints the result.

Once it's ready, you can execute all the code cells at once to see how the agent responds when given a task to compare the trade rate for a particular product for different three different countries. As shown in Figure 7-17, the agents respond with the name of the best country to import.

```
🚀 Running Trade Rate Comparison AI Agent...

⚠ Mocking trade rate due to error fetching for China: Expecting value: line 1 column 1 (char 0)
⚠ Mocking trade rate due to error fetching for Germany: Expecting value: line 1 column 1 (char 0)
⚠ Mocking trade rate due to error fetching for Japan: Expecting value: line 1 column 1 (char 0)

--- AI Agent Output ---
Compare the trade rates of product 721 for importing into India from China, Germany, and Japan.

📊 Best country to import 721 to India: China ($1007.5 per unit)
 • Detailed comparison:
   - China: Rate=$950.0, Landed=$1007.5
   - Germany: Rate=$1050.0, Landed=$1112.5
   - Japan: Rate=$990.0, Landed=$1049.5

Here is the comparison of trade rates for importing product 721 into India from China, Germany, and Japan:

- China: Rate=$950.0, Landed=$1007.5
- Germany: Rate=$1050.0, Landed=$1112.5
- Japan: Rate=$990.0, Landed=$1049.5

The best country to import product 721 to India is China, with a landed cost of $1007.5 per unit.
```

*Figure 7-17.   Agent response*

So far, you have seen how to create a custom AI Agent on BTP using LangGraph and SAP AI Core. This sets the basic foundation of your journey toward creating enterprise agents addressing real-world enterprise use cases. The agent in this chapter can be further enhanced with an interaction UI and deployed on Cloud Foundry.

## Conclusion

You are now at the verge of closing your journey in this book. Before you finish, let's recap the key learnings from this chapter. The chapter started by introducing the concept of Agentic AI followed by a discussion about the key components and features of AI Agents. It also explored potential use cases from various lines of businesses that are ideal candidates for building AI Agents. The chapter also covered various Agentic AI platforms offered by key players, including IBM, Microsoft, and SAP, and provided step-by-step instructions for building an AI Agent using SAP BTP, AI Core, and LangGraph.

AI Agents are transforming the landscape of intelligent automation. With the right combination of strategy, technology, and data, they can empower enterprise businesses to achieve remarkable improvements in efficiency, scalability, and innovation. In the near future, enterprises that strategically adopt and scale AI Agents will not only streamline operations but also unlock new opportunities for competitive advantage and business transformation.

# Index

## A

Accuracy, 48
Action component, 202
Add & Norm layer, 68
Administration section, 133, 134
AI, *see* Artificial intelligence (AI)
AI-powered functionalities, 143
ALBERT, *see* A Lite BERT (ALBERT)
A Lite BERT (ALBERT), 72
Amazon, 37
ANN, *see* Approximate Nearest Neighbor (ANN)
ANNs, *see* Artificial neural networks (ANNs)
Approximate Nearest Neighbor (ANN), 94
Artificial Intelligence (AI)
    history, 2, 3
    processing, 1
    types, 3, 4
Artificial neural networks (ANNs), 81
Attention bias, 77
Attention mechanism, 64–66
Automation, 44, 106, 150
Autoregressive models, 40
Azure AI Foundry, 207
Azure Content Safety, 171
Azure Content Safety Prompt, 171

## B

Backpropagation process, 26, 76

BERT, *see* Bidirectional Encoder Representations from Transformers (BERT)
BERT2BERT, 75
Biased output, 48
Bidirectional and auto-regressive transformer, 74
Bidirectional Encoder Representations from Transformers (BERT), 72, 82
BTP Service Estimator, 163, 164
Business Accelerator hub, 107
Business Application Studio, 145
Business data, 134–137
Business Technology Platform (BTP), 103, 105

## C

CAP LLM plugin, 142
Chain-of-Thought (CoT), 89, 103, 203
ChatGPT, 28
Chat section, 125
Cloud Foundry Runtime, 147
CNN, *see* Convolutional neural networks (CNN)
Code cell, 216
Code generation, 158
Coding, 216
Configurations, 114, 115
Context management, 88
Convolutional neural networks (CNN), 17, 18, 52–58, 64

# INDEX

Cosine Similarity, 140
CoT, *see* Chain-of-Thought (CoT)
Customer service agents, 204

## D

DAGs, *see* Directed Acyclic Graphs (DAGs)
Data anonymization, 142
Data anonymization techniques, 143
Data drift, 37
Data freshness, 99
Data management tools, 105
Data masking, 131
Datasets, 117
Decision-makers, 43
Decoder, 70, 71, 86
Decoder-only transformer models, 73–75
Deepfakes, 47
Deep learning, 22, 24
    algorithms, 10
    discriminative models, 10, 11
    foundational technology, 9
    generative models (GI), 11, 12
    neural network, 12–15
Deployment, 116
Diffusion models, 41
Directed Acyclic Graphs (DAGs), 206
Discriminative models, 10, 11
Disparate performance, 48
DistilBERT, 72
Docker Registry Secrets, 112, 119, 120
Document grounding, 142
Domain-specific optimization, 151

## E

Efficiently Learning an Encoder that Classifies Token Replacements Accurately (ELECTRA), 72

ELECTRA, *see* Efficiently Learning an Encoder that Classifies Token Replacements Accurately (ELECTRA)
Embeddings, 59–61, 140, 184
    boilerplate code, 184
    bot response, 194
    CAP application, 190
    chatbot, 194
    chat window, 191
    column, 185
    generation, 186, 188
    generator, 146
    information source, 193
    input parameters, 189
    LLM model, 183
    maintenance, 195
    models, 169
    power search, 150
    prompt, 191, 195
    retrieval-augmented generation (RAG), 93, 94
    SAP business environment, 145
    status, 186, 189
    use case, 141
    vector, 143
Encoder, 69, 70, 84
Encoder-decoder transformer model, 74, 75
Encoder-only models, 71, 72
End-to-end enterprise, 139
Estimation, generative AI-based
    capacity unit, 168
    components, 177
    configurations, 173, 175
    costs, 165
    data readiness, 162
    foundation models, 169

## INDEX

generative and non-generative
AI-based, 167
instance selection, 174
non-generative use cases, 172
orchestration process, 170
SAP Discovery Center, 163
Executables, 111
Executions, 115

## F

Face-aging simulations, 42
Feed-forward network, 57
Feedforward neural networks (FNNs), 17, 67, 85
Financial sector, 205
Fine-tuned models, 91
Fine-tuning, 35, 88
Flexibility, 76
Flow models, 41
FNNs, *see* Feedforward neural networks (FNNs)

## G

GANs, *see* Generative adversarial networks (GANs)
GenAI, *see* Generative AI (GenAI)
Generative adversarial networks (GANs), 23, 39
Generative AI (GenAI), 101, 130, 133, 137
   accuracy, 48
   capability, 21
   components
      data, 29
      foundation model, 30
      large language models (LLMs), 31
      parameters, 31
      probability distribution, 29
      prompt engineering, 31
   computer hardware, 33
   contextual patterns, 21
   deepfakes, 47
   diffusion models, 41
   evolution of, 23, 24
   foundation models, 33
   framework, 34
   hallucinations, 46
   integration of, 43
   labelling, 36
   legal risk, 46
   marketers and developers, 45
   marketing strategies, 44
   misusing, 47
   model safety, 37
   model supervision/AI observability, 37
   pre-labelled data, 45
   prompt injection, 48
   roles of, 25–28
   synthetic data, 36
   transformer models, 42
   types
      flow models, 41
      GANs, 39
      user-facing apps, 32
Generative AI Hub, 124, 129
Generative pre-training (GPT) model, 54
Generative Question-Answering (GQA), 34
Generic secrets, 122
GitOps, 119
Git repositories, 119
GNMT, *see* Google Neural Machine Translation (GNMT)
Google Neural Machine Translation (GNMT), 74, 82

221

INDEX

GPT, *see* Generative pre-training (GPT) model
GPUs, *see* Graphics processing units (GPUs)
GQA, *see* Generative Question-Answering (GQA)
Graphics processing units (GPUs), 33
Grounding, 130

# H

Hallucinations, 46
Healthcare, 205
Hyperscaler storage system, 118

# I

IBM Watson Orchestrate, 206
In-context learning, 89
Inference, 39
Inferencing, 111
Input embedding, 84
Input filtering, 132
Interpretability, 77
Interpretable representations, 77

# J

Jupyter extension, 210
Jupyter Notebook, 209

# K

Knowledge graph, 135, 136

# L

Labelling, 36

LangChain, 206
LangGraph, 208, 217
Large language models (LLMs), 23, 31, 79, 141, 143, 202
  add & norm layer, 68
  architecture, 83–87
  attention mechanism, 64–66
  decoder, 70, 71
  democratization, 52
  development process, 87
  encoder, 69, 70
  enterprise-oriented prompting, 156
  enterprises, 150
  evolution, 81–83
  foundation models, 148
  generative AI hub, 148–150
  image input prompt, 154
  innovations, 52
  language tasks, 79
  material description, 156, 157
  metadata, 159
  model configuration, 158
  model library, 151
  multi-attention, 65
  natural language processing, 80
  near-human levels, 79
  neural networks, 53
  positional encoding, 61–63
  pre-trained models, 80
  RNN *vs.* CNN, 54–58
  rule-based systems, 81
  SAP BTP Generative Hub, 162
  searchability, 159
  taxonomy, 51
  templates, 161
  text input prompt, 153
  transformer architecture, 51–54
  transformers, 52

translation, 155
variable definitions, 155
Layers, 14
L2 Distance, 140
Lifecycle management, 105
Linear layers, 86
LLMs, *see* Large language models (LLMs)
Long Short-Term Memory (LSTM), 82
Long-term, 203
LSTM, *see* Long Short-Term
    Memory (LSTM)

# M

Machine learning (ML), 1, 21, 81
    algorithms, 4, 22
    analysis and prediction, 24
    program, 4
    supervised learning, 5
    techniques, 9
Machine learning operations
    (MLOps), 38, 113
Masked multi-head attention, 66, 67
Memory, 3, 203
Message Block section, 153
Metaflow Library, 121
Mistral 7B mirrors, 73
ML, *see* Machine learning (ML)
MLOps, *see* Machine learning
    operations (MLOps)
Model Library section, 124
Model serving, 111
Models section, 118
Multi-attention mechanism, 65
Multi-head attention, 66, 70, 85
Multi-head self-attention mechanism, 73
Multi-head self-attention module, 74
Multi-modal models, 30

# N

Natural language processing (NLP), 1, 6,
    29–33, 71
Neural networks, 12–15, 23
    description, 25
    driving force, 27
    generative AI, 25
    history, 16
    input layer, 26
    patterns, 27
    probability theory and statistics, 26
Neural networks function, 15
    hidden layers, 15
    output layer, 15
Neural network simulation, 2
Neurons, 13
New Jupyter Notebook, 210
NLP, *see* Natural language
    processing (NLP)
Node.js, 145
Normalization, 86

# O

Object Store Secrets, 119, 121
OpenAI, 82
Orchestration process, 170
Orchestration section, 129–132
Output embeddings, 86

# P

Parallelization, 75
Parameters, 31, 89
Perceptron, 16
Personalized recommendation service, 108
Planning, 203
Positional encoding, 61–63, 84

# INDEX

Pre-trained models, 76
Pre-training, 87
Probability distribution, 29
Profile, 204
Prompt Editor, 133
    option, 161
    section, 127–129, 152
Prompt engineering, 88
Prompts, 160
Python scripts, 216

## Q

Query processing, 98

## R

RAG, see Retrieval-augmented generation (RAG)
Reactive AI, 3
Readme file, 190
Rectified linear unit (ReLU), 13
Recurrent neural networks (RNNs), 18, 40, 52–58, 75, 82
Reinforcement learning, 8, 9
Reinforcement learning with human feedback (RLHF), 90
Resource group, 121
Response generation, 98
ReLU, see Rectified linear unit (ReLU)
ReLU activation, 69
Retrieval-augmented generation (RAG), 90, 143
    backend AI engine, 145
    chat model, 184
    code snippet, 182, 183
    configuration, 179, 181

    destination, 183
    Digital Assistant button, 191
    embedding, 93, 94, 186
    industrial compressors, 187
    large language models (LLMs), 96–99
    parameters, 180
    pipeline, 177
    placeholders, 178
    pre-configured scenarios, 178
    SAP Hana Cloud Vector, 183
    SAPUI5 app, 145
    schema definition process, 184
    services, 141
    similarity searches, 95, 96
    upload option, 185
    vector databases, 94, 95
RLHF, see Reinforcement learning with human feedback (RLHF)
RNNs, see Recurrent neural networks (RNNs)
RoBERT, see Robustly Optimized BERT Pretraining Approach (RoBERT)
Robustly Optimized BERT Pretraining Approach (RoBERT), 72

## S

SAP Agent Builder, 207
SAP AI Core, 108–111, 211
SAP AI Core calculator, 166
SAP AI Launchpad, 111–118, 140
SAP BTP Destination service, 146
SAP Business AI
    administration, 118–122
    agentic AI use cases, 204–206
    application, 120
    architecture, 199

autonomous task execution, 201
collaborations, 102
configurations, 114, 115
contextual understanding, 200
conversational system, 200
datasets, 117
deployment, 116
Docker Registry Secret, 120
document, 107
embedded intelligence, 102
enterprise, 200
enterprise businesses, 104
executions, 115
human-in-the-loop, 201
key components, 201–204
models section, 118
multiple agents, 201
Object Store Secrets, 121
personalized recommendation service, 108
resource group, 121
result set, 118
SAP AI Launchpad, 111–118
scenarios, 113
schedules, 116
services, 106–108
tool integration, 200
SAP Business Application Studio, 209–217
SAP Cloud SDK, 144
SAP Cloud SDK (Java, JavaScript), 144
SAP Cloud SDK for AI (Python), 208
SAP Document AI, 108
SAP HANA Cloud, 110, 133, 135, 136, 175
SAP HANA Cloud Vector Engine, 141
SAP Joule AI, 103, 104
SAPUI5, 145
Scalability, 76

Schedules, 116
Self-attention, 85
Self-attention mechanism, 76
Self-Aware AI, 3
Semi-supervised learning, 6, 7
Short-term, 203
Similarity searches, 95, 96
Softmax, 86
Stakeholders, 139
State-of-the-art performance, 77
Supervised learning, 5, 6
Supervised learning algorithms, 22
Supply chains, 204, 208, 209
Synoptic connections, 25
Synthetic data, 36

# T

Templating, 130
Tenant-wide secret rotation, 122
Tensor Processing Units (TPUs), 33
Text-to-Text Transfer Transformer (T5), 73
T5, *see* Text-to-Text Transfer Transformer (T5)
Theory of mind, 3
Tokenization, 59, 84
    embeddings, 59–61
Tools, 215
TPUs, *see* Tensor Processing Units (TPUs)
Transformer-based models, 51
Transformers, 63
    architecture, 51–54, 56, 58
    benefits, 75–77
    components, 58
    decoder-only, 73–75
    encoder-only models, 71, 72
    limitations, 77, 78

225

INDEX

Transformers (*cont.*)
    long-range dependencies, 57
    mechanism, 57
    models, 42
    sequence transduction, 54
Translation, 130
Trial and error learning, 8

## U

Unsupervised learning, 7, 8, 22
Use case identification
    AI-driven business, 140
    features and functionalities, 139
    RAG-based enterprise application, 140
    RAG technique, 141

## V

VAEs, *see* Variational autoencoders (VAEs)
Variational autoencoders (VAEs), 23, 39
DB retrieval, 98
Vector databases (DB), 35, 94, 95
Vector engines, 105, 134
Virtual efficiency, 44

## W, X, Y

Weights, 14
Word-by-word sequence, 51

## Z

Zero-shot prompting, 88

GPSR Compliance

The European Union's (EU) General Product Safety Regulation (GPSR) is a set of rules that requires consumer products to be safe and our obligations to ensure this.

If you have any concerns about our products, you can contact us on

ProductSafety@springernature.com

In case Publisher is established outside the EU, the EU authorized representative is:

Springer Nature Customer Service Center GmbH
Europaplatz 3
69115 Heidelberg, Germany

www.ingramcontent.com/pod-product-compliance
Lightning Source LLC
LaVergne TN
LVHW081450060526
838201LV00050BA/1752